FEMINISM,
Nation and Myth
La Malinche

FEMINISM,
Nation and Myth
La Malinche

Rolando Romero and
Amanda Nolacea Harris, Editors

Arte Público Press
Houston, Texas

This volume is funded by grants from the City of Houston through The Cultural Arts Council of Houston/Harris County.

Recovering the past, creating the future

Arte Público Press
University of Houston
452 Cullen Performance Hall
Houston, Texas 77204-2004

Jacket design by James Brisson
Cover art "La Malinche, 1993" courtesy of Alfredo Arreguín

Feminism, nation and myth: La Malinche / edited by Rolando Romero and
Amanda Nolacea Harris.
   p.   cm.
  ISBN-10: 1-55885-440-1 (alk. paper)
  ISBN-13: 978-1-55885-440-6 (alk. paper)
  1. Marina, ca. 1505-ca. 1530—Influence—Congresses. 2. Marina, ca.
1505-ca. 1530—In literature—Congresses. 3. Feminism—America—
Congresses. 4. Sex role—America—Congresses. 5. Ethnicity—America—
Congresses. 6. Racism—America—Congresses. 7. Mexican American
women—Social conditions—Congresses. 8. Mexican American women—
Intellectual life—Congresses. 9. Mexican Americans—Social conditions—
Congresses. 10. Mexican Americans—Intellectual life—Congresses.
I. Romero, Rolando.   II. Harris, Amanda Nolacea.
  F1230.M373F46 2005
  972.02′092—dc22   2004062284
                                                        CIP

5 6 7 8 9 0 1 2 3 4   10 9 8 7 6 5 4 3 2 1

Contents

Acknowledgments

Dan Banda's *Indigenous Always: The Legend of La Malinche and the Conquest of Mexico,* triggered this project. In order to film the documentary, the Latina/Latino Studies Program at the University of Illinois, Urbana Champaign, in conjunction with the College of Letters and Sciences and the Illinois Program for Research in the Humanities, held a conference designed to bring experts on La Malinche together in one setting. The documentary aired nationally on PBS. Dan Banda's documentary won Best Documentary and Best Videography in the 2001 National Communicator Awards. The documentary received five Emmy nominations for artistic achievement from the National Academy of Television Arts and Sciences, Midwest Chapter.

The original conference owes much to Amanda Nolacea Harris, who traveled with the production crew in Mexico, and to Victoria González at the Latina/Latino Studies Program at Illinois who handled all the logistics of the conference. And of course, we also owe our debt of gratitude to Ron Sousa, who as head of the Spanish, Italian, and Portuguese Department supported the project. Guisela Latorre also worked in the logistics of the conference.

We also want to thank all the participants of the conference. Sandra M. Cypess has been enthusiastic and supportive of the project as well.

Critical Introduction
La Malinche and Post-Movement Feminism
Amanda Nolacea Harris

Feminism, Nation and Myth: La Malinche examines the literary and cultural debates La Malinche has generated in critical circles by addressing the state and direction of Malinche scholarship. This contribution joins voices from the humanities and the social sciences to interrogate the development of feminism, queer studies, Chicano studies, Chicana studies, Latina/o studies, and the interaction particular to our post-Civil-Rights-Movement field. La Malinche has forced us to critically analyze the interaction and interdependence of race, class, and gender. She demands that we decolonize all facets of her legacy, and disassemble and reconstruct concepts of nation, community, agency, subjectivity, and social activism. The fact that she is the "paradigmatic figure of Chicana feminism," as Norma Alarcón has stated, speaks to the errors of culture. Her ironic silence demands attention. Alarcón has stated, concerning La Malinche and the direction of Chicana/o history that, "to let go of figures that offer both a paradigmatic example of experience and a syntagmatic one is for women to work against themselves."[1] Alarcón urges us to stop isolating epistemologies of oppression, and to heed those figures whose wholeness provides a model for whole decolonization. This volume takes us beyond the isolation of the agendas within Latina/o studies, proposing that we cease to look at feminism, Marxism, and race as antithetical critical perspectives. The participants in the conference and the authors of these essays recognize the responsibility of the decolonial desire that Emma Pérez describes in her *Decolonial Imaginary.* Latina/o studies, not fitting into post-colonial or colonial studies, seeks to rescue neglected subjectivities, revise simple binaries, treat internal issues with parity, and provide history. These daughters and sons speak with the speech and silence of our foremother, taking the necessary steps towards meeting her demands of holistic decolonization.

This volume originates in the 1999 "U.S. Latina/Latino Perspectives on La Malinche" conference that brought together Malinchistas (to make the term our own) from across the nation. Filmmaker Dan Banda interviewed many of the presenters for his documentary, *Indigenous Always: The Legend of La Malinche and the Conquest of Mexico.* Generations of scholars, poets, and artists from the beginnings of Latina/o studies to the present engaged in the future of the field through discussions on La Malinche, the most appropriate figure for such discussions as she necessitates the simultaneity of often exclusive perspectives and the integration of critical spheres that arise separately in the discourses of revolution. The examination of La Malinche allows us to deconstruct the separation of spheres. Studying figures that force us to address sexism and racism simultaneously makes us look beyond denouncing dominant culture and look critically at the way that we have constructed ourselves. Though it is necessary to look outwards at exclusion and negative characterizations, it is also necessary that we look inwards. If we neglect this responsibility we effectively diminish the potential to create the circumstances for equality within our communities, academic and otherwise.

Movement Discourse and Malinchismo

Alicia Gaspar De Alba's contribution to this volume deconstructs the Chicano Movement's approach to women's participation in social struggle and exposes the isolation of feminism (and women) from ethnic nationalism. She writes:

> Indeed, in the early chauvinist years of "el" Movimiento, Chicanas were granted one of two patriarchally defined identities. They were either "Adelitas," depicted in the popular Mexican revolutionary song as loyal supporters and followers of their men, or they were "Malinches," Eve-like traitors of la Causa, perniciously pursuing their own individual interests. (48)

Gaspar De Alba's statement about Armando Rendón's "Chicano Manifesto" and the rhetoric of the Chicano Movement echoes similar observations and criticism made by Chicana writers from the late 1960s to the present postmovement era. Volumes of collected works—including Alma García's *Chicana Feminist Thought,* Adela de la Torre and Beatriz Pesquera's *Building with our Hands,* Carla Trujillo's *Chicana Lesbians,* and Teresa Córdova's *Chicana Voices*—dedicated to the compound concerns of Chicanas as ethnic minority activists and feminists, attest to the pervasiveness of the polemic of chauvinism present in Chicano nationalism. The Movement assigned limited roles to women; the Chicana as faithful follower and sexual partner or nurturing mother figure to the Chicano revolutionary—or "the 'three f's," as Cherríe Moraga articulates it in "Queer Aztlán": "feeding, fighting, and fucking" (Moraga *Last*

Generation 157). According to Gaspar de Alba, the assignation results from a heterosexual and patriarchal imaginary that determines the value of the Chicana's contributions to ethnic and class activism through conformity to male authority. Angie Chabrám-Dernersesian (along with Rosalinda Fregoso, Beatrice Pesquera, and Adela de la Torre) explains that cultural nationalism describes and prescribes culture through the male subject position. Chabrám-Dernersesian writes, cultural nationalists "subsume the Chicana into a universal ethnic subject that speaks [along] with the masculine instead of the feminine, and embodies itself in the Chicano male" (qtd. in Fregoso 38). We can recognize the overwhelming use of patriarchal definitions for Chicana womanhood in the classic literature of the Chicano Movement. Generally the literature of the Movement portrays Chicanas as wives and mothers, but in many instances the women fill similar roles of sexual partner and nurturer without direct family ties. Either way, the heterosexual and heterosocial relationships between the men and women of the classic Movement literature confirm the male as the authority or the developing leader in a family(-like) nucleus.

As "Adelitas," or soldadera figures borrowed from the Mexican revolutionary lore, Chicana activists contribute to the ethnic struggle as silent, unquestioning support systems. In the literature and in the general historical testaments, conformity to patriarchal authority through obedience, sexual control, food preparation, behind-the-scenes organizing, and child-rearing earned Chicanas a secure place in the ethnic community. Conversely, sexual independence (choosing if and with whom to be sexually active or chosing non-procreative sexuality), bringing feminist concerns to the table, public leadership, and refusal to have (Chicano) children, earned Chicanas epithets that imply the mutual exclusivity of Chicano activism and feminism—"agringada," "Malinchista," and "vendida"—under the assumption that feminism is a negative foreign influence as opposed to an authentic concern within Chicana/o communities.

Oscar Zeta Acosta's *Revolt of the Cockroach People* (1973) and Rudolfo Anaya's *Bless Me, Última* (1971), two novels that embody the Movement's goals of Chicano self-determination and student activism as outlined in El Plan de Santa Bárbara, illustrate classic Chicano literature's prescription for women's participation. Like in *Zoot Suit, . . . y no se lo tragó la tierra,* and other classic novels, the women in these texts serve the male activists and nurture the men's authority as the leader of the household, and by extension, the community. Anaya's bildungsroman, *Bless Me, Última,* shows the importance of Chicana mother figures in the formation of the future revolutionaries. The protagonist's mother hands the reigns of the household to her ten-year old son, and Última, his mentor and reservoir of cultural heritage, prepares him for his leadership role by nurturing his leadership skills and teaching him Chicano cultural history and regional heritage. Gaspar de Alba writes of the Movement, "Mujeres were seen, in fact, as the carriers of the culture, and their own revo-

lutionary role was circumscribed by their procreative function" (48). The two
mother figures in Rudolfo Anaya's *Bless Me, Última* fulfill either the procreative function or that of the nurturing of the developing Chicano leader.
The novel, which details the spiritual and social development of a rural
Chicano boy during World War II in New Mexico, culminates in the achievement of the child's authority as protector of the family and graduated recipient
of cultural heritage. Última, the benevolent old *curandera* who comes to live
with the family, recognizes the narrator's giftedness and immediately sanctions
his disobedience to his mother. The pattern of male-child-preference (a pattern
that becomes a major tenet of Chicana feminist criticism, particularly in Cherríe Moraga and Ana Castillo) continues, and Última's—albeit ironic—role as
preserver and perpetuator of patriarchal authority becomes clear. Both women
play an important part in paving Antonio's road to patriarchy—his mother sub-
mits to the superiority implicit in his maleness, and Última urges him to
become a man, all the while asserting his right to contradict his mother. The two
women cook and clean for the men of the family as well. As the novel concludes, Última dies at the hands of evil forces and the protagonist-narrator
Antonio, becomes the head of the household despite the presence of his mother and older sisters. He orders his mother to take his older sisters to their room:
"It was the first time I had ever spoken to my mother as a man; she nodded and
obeyed" (Anaya 246). Although not the biological mother, Última is the midwife for the region as well as the nurturer of Antonio's manhood. She does not
take on the role of mother in the physical sense, and as a *curandera* and warrior for the forces of good in the novel, she carries the potential for a counter-
patriarchal role for women. She serves, however, as the key nurturer of the Chicano male subject, and the guardian of male authority, thus conforming to the
Movement's prescriptions for female participation in community struggle.
Gaspar de Alba finds that "To be an 'Adelita' (or a Loyalist, as was the popular term) a Chicana had to commit herself in body and spirit to the race-and-
class agenda of the macho leadership" (51). Zeta Acosta's *Revolt of the Cockroach People* demonstrates how the Adelita figures serve as props to the male
activist by complimenting his authority and virility through contented servitude
in the male-centered cause. The novel follows the life of Oscar Zeta Acosta,
Brown Buffalo, a Chicano lawyer during the explosive years of the Movement.
The novel presents a blunt perspective on the student blowouts, police violence,
Movement violence and frustration, court cases in defense of activists, the self-
doubts of a developing leader, drug abuse, and the role of women in the social
Movement. The Brown Buffalo, the narrator-protagonist, solidifies his authority as the patriarch and head-of-the-household in choosing for his companion-
ship three adolescent female cousins, all of whom are legal minors and several
years younger than he. He declares himself the "Big Uncle" of the "Zeta Girls,"
teenagers from one family who join the Movement and move in with the Chi-

cano lawyer under the condition that they cook, clean, and engage in sexual play with him (Zeta Acosta 87-88). To their compliance to such participation in the social revolution he states, "Isn't that how the women did it when Zapata and Villa took to the hills? Isn't that what young girls are supposed to do?" (86). Zeta Acosta celebrates the ethnic appropriateness of the gender roles, exclaiming, "Jesus, but this can't be. This can't be happening. I reach for a breast. It is small. Wonderfully small and firm. It fits into my palm. A brown pear in my hand. God Almighty! *This* is the revolution" (87). What is *this* that defines true revolution but the coming together of a man and wom*e*n in a manner that confirms the female role as sexual, supportive, and faceless while confirming the man's role as the deserving harvester of female servitude?

Although the role of the Adelita breaks from the traditional (catholic), virginal ideal of Chicana womanhood, the Adelita does not threaten male authority. In Zeta Acosta, the Adelitas confirm male authority. As Gaspar de Alba puts it, the Adelita of the Movement, though sexually promiscuous, was considered "the good whore, who offers her body to the machos of la Causa" (106).

Some women during the Movement looked to the Adelita role as a model for participation but found themselves at odds with the sexual stigma and the limitations that it imposed on female intellectual and political participation. An anonymous Orange County Brown Beret included in Alma García's anthology of Movement feminism, wrote "The Adelitas Role in El Movimiento" (1971), denouncing the sexual assault, exclusion, and defamation of the "girl" Berets at the hands of their male counterparts. Her article appears anonymously in fitting parallel with the nameless (selfless) Adelitas who take on the struggles of the men that they follow. In her efforts to find an ethnically affirming role model for women in the movement, she states, "The Chicanas in the Berets and outside the Berets are the Adelitas [. . .] of this Revolution. And in order to have a successful Revolution you must have full involvement from both the Chicanos and the Chicanas." She goes on to enumerate the injustices done to the Chicanas and lists the negative, "sexist stereotypes" that she would like to abolish from the Movement. The stereotypes include:

1. "A woman is only good for making love to."
2. "All women should do is stay at home, wash dishes, cook, and clean the house."
3. "Women don't rap as good as men; they aren't as heavy regarding the movement, and they don't command the respect of their peers."
4. "Women shouldn't be allowed to do community work; the work should be done by men." (119)

She then states that such beliefs are "by-products of deep-macho hang-ups." She does not blame the Chicanos, because "the Chicano family structure teaches the men to be the leaders while women are taught how to do household chores and to think in terms of the day they will be married" (119). This Beret is willing to accept limited roles as long as she can participate in the movement and not fall prey to insults and groping. But despite the fact that her demands do not upset Chicano male-authority by suggesting women take leadership roles in the Movement, she demonstrates the anxiety of malinchismo by carefully dissociating herself from feminism:

> And we're not talking about women's liberation because, like that's not ours—that's a white thing—we're talking about our Raza's Liberation and in order to get our Raza liberated, we all have to work together within our Raza. VIVA LA REVOLUCIÓN (119)

Such an internalization of the Movement's pointed separation of class and ethnic issues from feminist concerns lead many Chicanas to reject allying themselves with feminism, or "women's liberation." On one hand, Euro-American feminism does not address the compound concerns that race and class variables demand in the context of a patriarchal ethnic community within the larger patriarchal United States. The traditional (race, class, and ethnicity) blind spots of mainstream feminism would logically lead Chicanas' rejection of the discourse. On the other hand, however, the rejection also stems from the Movement's strategic separation of the ethnic cause from women's causes—a separation that urged many Chicana feminists to underscore the community rationale behind valuing female contributions and to demand recognition of female contributions along the lines dictated by the patriarchal imaginary. While the anonymous Brown Beret denounces exclusion of women, she does not ask for parity, instead she asks that women be valued in the struggle as Adelitas, the anonymous romantic women who followed their men on the battlefields of Mexico half a century earlier.

Armando Rendón's *Chicano Manifesto* chastises Chicanas who voice feminist concerns and brands them as Malinches or traitors: ". . . In the service of the gringo, malinches attack their own brothers, betray our dignity and manhood, cause jealousies and misunderstandings among us, and actually seek to retard the advance of the Chicanos, if it benefits themselves—while the gringo watches" (97).

Gaspar de Alba explains that in the classic period of the Chicano Movement, "feministas—that is, women who believed they should have more of a role in la Causa than making the beans and rice for the meetings, or having the future Emilianos and Panchitos of the Movement" often found themselves labeled "traitors, infiltrators, wannabe gabachas, and reactionaries against the true goals of Chicano liberation" (48). The labeling always implied the belief that feminism lies outside the limits of Chicana/o culture. "Rather than working toward cultural nationalism and the empowerment of the Raza brotherhood," she continues,

> . . . they were said to be dividing the Movement from within and splitting up
> the Chicano Holy (not to mention heterosexual) Familia. "Within this con-
> stricted familia structure," Cherríe Moraga writes, "Chicano políticos ensured
> that the patriarchal father figure remained in charge of both their private and
> political lives." (48)

This trend is particularly observable in Zeta Acosta's three cousins under the
roof of one big uncle. Were such characterizations and limitations no longer an
issue in the twenty-first century, Gaspar de Alba and the authors in this volume
would be beating a dead horse. However, in the age of nationally institutionalized Chicano/Latino Studies programs and publishing venues that seek to
reconstruct Chicano/Latino literary and social histories, the argument for critical feminist perspectives on the Movement and its literature remains relevant
and pressing. Although Chicana feminism and Chicana lesbian theory has
occupied the front lines of institutional debates, literary criticism, and literary
production since the 1980s, Chicano-centered reconstructions of the Movement continue to affirm the domestic image of Chicana participation. Gaspar
de Alba criticizes the rhetoric of the Movement itself, but her criticism can be
applied to contemporary reconstructions of the Movement that continue to perpetuate chauvinism in the face of post-movement feminist revisions.

Contemporary Reconstructions and the Enduring Concept of Malinchismo

Arturo Rosales' 425-page *Testimonio: A Documentary History of the Mexican-American Struggle for Civil Rights* (2000) collects primary texts from the
years surrounding the Movement and documents, as the title promises, the Mexican-American (and Chicano) struggle for Civil Rights. Rosales provides a wealth
of useful documentation that brings together otherwise scattered or anecdotal
information. Chicana anxieties of Malinchismo and the perpetual separation of
systems of oppression, however, lurk in the shadows of this recent reconstruction.
The prescribed limits of female participation in the struggle for civil rights persist
in the election and framing of Chicana feminism. Although the year of the book's
production indicates the potential retrospective exposure to decades of Chicana
feminist scholarship that has widened the gender scope of the Chicano Movement, *Testimonio* occupies itself with documenting newspaper articles, speeches,
manifestos, and interviews of the *classic* figures of the Movement.

Three of the five women documented in the book speak of following
men's causes in ethnic struggle: Patsy Tijerina, Dolores Huerta, and Emma
Tenayuca. The other two, Martha Cotera and Enriqueta Longauex y Vásquez
appear at the tail end of the book and present Chicana feminism as a minor,
unpopular thread with which very few women wished to concern themselves.

Patsy Tijerina's burning of U.S. Forest Service signs appears as the act of
"López Tijerina's young, wife Patsy, [which] demonstrated great courage"
(Rosales 327), rather than as an act drawing attention to land-rights. The inclu-

sion of an interview with Dolores Huerta quotes her praising of her husband, César Chávez's, accomplishments and summarizes her participation as the pension approval for former Bracero workers (211). Her contributions to women's causes and family causes do not figure in to the *Testimonios*. The *corrido* praising Luisa Moreno also confirms the role of woman as helper (258). And the inclusion of a *Time* magazine article about Emma Tenayuca's role as "Labor Crusader" (247) cites her saying "I love my husband and am a good cook" (qtd. in Rosales 247).

The two remaining women quoted at the end of the book underscore a supposed general Chicana desire to conform and to be subsumed into the male-defined ethnic cause. Both express their frustration with the sexism in the Movement, but concern themselves more with Chicana apathy and conformity. The first and only document under the content heading "Chicana feminism" is a piece by Enriqueta Longeaux y Vásquez. Rosales includes her statements about the deliberations of the Chicana's at the women's panel of the 1969 Chicano Youth Conference in Denver:

> When the time came for the women to make their presentation to the full conference, the only thing that the workshop representative said was this "It was the consensus of the group that the Chicana woman does not want to be liberated. [...] I understood why the statement had been made, and I realized that going along with the feelings of the men at the convention was perhaps the best thing to do at the time. (qtd. in Rosales 372)

Rosales prefaces the short segment on Chicana feminism thus,

> Many Chicana activists at the time saw a need for a separate critique of the Chicano movement. Enriqueta Longauex y Vásquez, a pioneer activist who attended the Chicano Youth Conference in Denver [1969], lamented the chauvinism that she encountered at that meeting from her fellow delegates. (372)

Given that this statement introduces the first appearance of Chicana feminist concerns in the book, one might expect a piece that details Chicana contributions to the Movement or a piece that highlights Chicanas' protest against the gender limitations imposed in the name of struggle for civil rights. Instead, however, Rosales engages in three strategies that further negate Chicana feminism. First, his preface brackets the chauvinism to "that meeting" in particular. Second, he suggests that Chicana feminists seek a "separate critique," ignoring the Movement's responsibility for separating feminism from ethnic concerns. Last, he negates his own statement that "*Many* Chicana activists at the time saw a need for a separate critique . . ." [my emphasis] by choosing an article that highlights many Chicana's *un*willingness to engage in critiquing the sexism in the Movement. The framing of the piece combined with its content effectively cancels out the importance and the demand for Chicana feminism. The preface might have better introduced Longauex y Vásquez's article as symptomatic of the fear of being stigmatized as a *malinchista* by the community.

The second and last piece on Chicana feminism from a separate section of the book quotes a 1976 speech by Martha Cotera. This piece also focuses on Chicanas' unwillingness to seek public visibility. Although Cotera does underscore women's behind-the-scene organizing, she generally expresses her frustration at the majority of Chicanas' reluctance to participate outside of their roles as supporters:

> I think what happens is that very often the women are very willing to do the work and they don't mind having a secondary role; they don't mind not having elected and appointed positions. Bringing the women in Crystal City itself was not something we had to do against the wishes of the men; it was something we had to do, in a way, against the wishes of the women. In other words, they didn't mind working, and they didn't mind being the ones left to do a lot of the organizing and picketing and later being supportive. (qtd. in Rosales 391)

Again, Rosales' decontextualized choice of document confirms women's willingness to conform to Chicano authority and demonstrates an example of men's implied accommodation of women's activism. Cotera's points exemplify, from a post-movement perspective, the female anxiety over upsetting gender roles and being labeled a traitor to the community (and to their husbands). Rosales presents them, however, as the norm, thus using feminism's battle for *concientización* as the proof that no such desire for recognition exists for the majority of Chicanas. Additionally, the concerns that the women finally do voice in Cotera's narrative of a 1970 Chicano conference express family and domestic issues like motherhood and food. The reluctant female voices that do finally speak conform to the family institution where the women deal with domestic issues and the man does not. The women she describes as unwilling to take on leadership roles fit neatly into the Movement's Adelita-Mother role.

Cotera closes her speech stating, "that for women to participate to this [public-leadership] level was to be *agringadas*" (393). Her assessment speaks to the fear that community rejection would often result from transgressing the Adelita and Mother roles. Rosales includes no other feminist documents that expand on the very real concern that Cotera presents. Rather, his choice of documents depicts Chicana feminism as an anomaly—even among Chicana women—and suggests that most women of the Movement wanted to remain within patriarchal confines. Rosales' year-2000 construction of the Chicano Movement builds the history with blinders on. The debates surrounding Malinchismo (from the patriarchal side and the feminist side) obviously had begun to achieve public attention during the period that he seeks to represent, not to mention the decades of debate ever since.

Alma García's 1997 compilation, *Chicana Feminist Thought: The Basic*

Historical Writings, includes more than two hundred pages of Chicana writings published in the 1960s and 1970s, including essays by Cotera and Longauex y Vásquez that do not conform to culturally reinforced rejection of feminism. The exclusion of Chicanas from leadership roles, the exclusion of Chicana feminism from the tenets of the Movement, and demands for the integration of women's issues into the greater demands of the Movement dominate the essays thematically. In a 1971 example, Ana NietoGómez writes "Empieza la revolución verdadera," a poem that demands the parity of Chicana concerns in the Chicano Movement. She agrees that internal gender struggles divide and weaken the "race with the 'man,'" but she blames the "Rigid boundaries of roles" that limit women's participation. She proposes that feminism not take a back seat to ethnic concerns (unlike the resignation that Cotera demonstrates in Rosales' compilation), stating:

> First,
> Humanity and freedom between men and women
> Only then
> Empieza la revolución verdadera. (73)

Similarly Lorna Dee Cervantes writes "Para un Revolucionario" in 1975, demonstrating that women are also part of the Chicana/o community. From behind the clatter of dishes, the screaming kids, and the boiling pot of beans, Cervantes's Chicana mother overhears the conversations her husband has in the living room with his "brothers" in arms. In view of her exclusion from the brotherhood and her relegation to the kitchen, she reminds her husband, "I too am raza" (74). Clearly Chicanas of the classic period of the Movement recognized that their feminism often resulted in their banishment and their classification as "malinchistas." So much so that La Malinche becomes a major object of study and revision as well as a template for the assertion of female agency, subjectivity, and parity. Adelaida del Castillo and Ana NietoGómez proposed in 1974 and 1973 respectively the systematic revision of La Malinche as a means of Chicana liberation. While Del Castillo insists on clearing Malinche's name in "Malintzin Tenepal: A Preliminary Look in to a New Perspective," NietoGómez goes so far as to add feminist issues to the debates in education reforms (i.e. El Plan de Santa Bárbara), demanding in a list of reforms that "B. *The History of the Chicana* would identify the heroines and the social roles of the past. Marina (Malinche) may be given a new interpretation as a positive symbol for the mestizo" (130).

New Malinchistas

Many of the authors in García's collection demand parity and inclusion. Others, like "The Adelita's Role in El Movimiento" and "Para un Revolucionario," demand the Movement's recognition of motherhood and female support as necessary and under-appreciated contributions without which the Movement could not survive. The heterosexual feminism, however, tends either to value or protest the roles assigned to women, but does not explore alternative roles for non-patriarchal selfhood. Much post-Movement same-sex criticism rejects motherhood as the only viable image of female contribution because of its limitations to biology, heterosexuality, and institutionalized patriarchy, exploring possibilities for female contributions to literary and social activism that go beyond the biological and institutional limits of the heterosexual family. Such authors ask that we look beyond service roles and contemplate leadership roles that do away with the accepted male-authority implicit in Movement discourse.

Cherríe Moraga's "Long line of Vendidas" in *Loving in the War Years* explores the confines of the family and the concept of Malinchismo. In the section entitled "We Fight Back With our Families," Moraga discusses the tie between the protection of the family structure and Malinchismo, stating that

> Because heterosexism—the Chicana's sexual commitment to the Chicano male—is proof of her fidelity to her people, the Chicana feminist attempting to critique the sexism in the Chicano community is certainly between a personal rock and a political hard place. (*Loving* 105)

Consequently, Moraga explains, for a Chicana feminist to remain within the community, "She must fight racism alongside her man, but challenge sexism single-handedly, all the while retaining her 'femininity' so as not to offend or threaten her man. This is what being a Chicana feminist means" (*Loving* 107). Her observation describes the anxieties present in Rosales decontextualized choices of representative Chicana feminism. It also describes the concept that Zeta Acosta exalts when he says, "*This* is the revolution." Moraga goes on to explain the family politics that protect male authority by subscribing to the belief that family unity protects Chicanos in the face of Anglo threats of genocide (*Loving* 108–111). She furthers the cultural critique by pointing to the "social and legal control of our [women's] reproductive function [...] and the social institutionalization of our roles as sexual and domestic servant to men," ultimately suggesting that in the absence of heterosexism, "Chicanas might very freely 'choose' to do otherwise" (*Loving* 111). Logically, lesbianism in its challenge to male familial authority, becomes stigmatized as anti-community, anti-Chicano, and thus malinchista—both in the sense that Chicanas borrow it from white feminism, and in the sense that women who engage in it put their own desires before those of the community. Like Malinche, Chicanas who don't conform to the "national" patriarchal family have preferred foreign concepts to authentic ones and spoken independently of their maternal-community role. Norma Alarcón explains that throughout history, a mother's role requires putting motherhood and self-sacrifice before personal achievement (in contrast to a father's role). She explains that "[…] a woman who speaks as a sexual being independently of the maternal role, as Malinche did, is viewed as a sign of catastrophe. The mother is meant to articulate not her own needs as desires but only those of her children" (*Loving* 281). Alarcón's assessment of Mexico's popular perception of Malinche as a cultural transgressor by virtue of sexual independence easily lends itself to application in the criticism of the Movement. The ultimate assertion of women's sexual and social independence, lesbianism and same-sex theory of the post-Movement, then personifies malinchismo. Moraga makes the connection directly in the section entitled "Malinchista":

> The woman who defies her role as subservient to her husband, father, brother, or son by taking control of her own sexual destiny, is purported to be a 'traitor to her race' by contributing to the 'genocide' of her people—whether or not she has children. In short, even if the defiant woman is not a lesbian, she is purported to be one; for, like the lesbian in the Chicano imagination, she is una *Malinchista*. Like the Malinche of Mexican history, she is corrupted by foreign influence which threaten to destroy her people. (*Loving* 113)

Moraga, like many Chicana feminists, identifies with Malinche. Her identification goes beyond the historical revisions proposed by Del Castillo and NietoGómez. Moraga proposes non-reproductive sexuality and female use of public discourse based in feminist activism that doesn't consider malinchismo and expulsion from the community a threat. Malinchismo, an inescapable cultural reality, becomes a positive space for theorizing female agency and subjective formation in a same-sex (not heterosocial) context. Her poem, "Foreign Tongue" in *The Last Generation* takes on the "traitor"-based identity and speaks to the feminists of the Movement as reluctant Malinches whom same-sex criticism can liberate. Read as a sexual allegory, the poem demonstrates the layered relationship between post-Movement feminism and the Movement's women:

> "Foreign Tongue"
>
> She withholds
> the language
> not the words
> but the abandon
> they evoke.
>
> She refuses
> bites her lip
> to repel
> el deseo
> que quiere
> estallar
> por la boca.

Traidora
que soy
to discover
la fuerza
de la lengua
por los labios
of another

not hers. (*Last Generation* 43)

In the first stanza "she," the Movement Chicana, possesses language but fears using it because its use "evokes" abandon from the community. In the second stanza the Movement Chicana continues to resist her desire to speak, but here the desire is not specified to language-use as in the first stanza. Here the desire that threatens to burst forth from her mouth could be sexual as well. The third stanza shifts to the poetic voice speaking to the first person. The speaker is the traitor for several reasons. First, she discovers her own potential through female identification (not hetero-social identification). She also discovers her potential to satisfy another women sexually, thus rejecting her patriarchal community. Additionally, she discovers the power to speak and use language through the example of the lips of another woman—through the lips of La Malinche as a role model, and through the reluctant closed lips of the Movement feminists who feared using their voices. The "lips of another" are the vaginal lips of Movement feminists, the silenced mouths of the Movement feminists depicted in the first two stanzas, and the speaking lips of La Malinche—the historical role model who by example helps the poetic voice to discover the power of "la lengua."

Moraga states of Chicano activism and cultural production, "What was missing was a portrait of sexuality for men and women independent of motherhood and machismo: images of the male body as violador *and* vulnerable, and of the female body as the site of woman-centered desire" (*Last Generation* 71). Her entire book explores that missing possibility for female roles outside of patriarchal constraints that still allow for direct participation in the community. As her title implies, she will spawn no more generations of chauvinist Chicano activism steeped in colonial and patriarchal cultural conceptualizations. From a perspective not tied to procreation, Moraga comes up with the role of Chicana lesbian as preserver of memory. In her poem "I was not supposed to remember," she simply states:

I am a woman, childless
and I teach my stories to other
childless women and somehow
the generations will propagate and prosper
and remember prememory. (*Last Generation* 99)

The "prememory" that she provides throughout the book agilely moves between pre-Columbian womanhood, the Conquest of Mexico, the Chicano Movement, and contemporary family politics of Chicana/o communities in the context of Anglo-American oppression. Her examples of the hate embedded in the hybridity that the Malinche-Cortés paradigm represents, beg for the termination of such cycles and patterns of gender and ethnic hegemony. Unlike Anaya's Última, Moraga's vision of a non-reproductive woman as the preserver of cultural memory challenges patriarchy by preserving the memory of the collusion of exclusion within the community instead of perpetuating that exclusion under the guise of cultural heritage. Moraga's post-Movement perspective on the Movement and its legacy challenges the patriarchally determined roles of women in movement literature and in the Movement, and challenges feminism that perpetuates male-centered concepts of Chicana/o culture. Moraga's book also speaks to the need for a multi-ethnic or pan-Latina/o approach to social revolution, thus deconstructing Chicano nationalism from several angles.

It is from such a post-Movement discursive position that the writers of this volume speak. Although Movement rhetoric continues to alienate feminism from class, race, and ethnic debates, contemporary Malinche scholarship demands the decolonization of Latina/o culture on all of these levels. Norma Alarcón and Luis Leal framed the "U.S. Latina/Latino Perspectives on La Malinche" conference with their opening and closing addresses respectively, and Alfred Arteaga, Dan Banda, Juan Bruce-Novoa, Antonia I. Castañeda, Debra A. Castillo, Sandra Messinger Cypess, Alicia Gaspar de Alba, Deena J. González, Ramón Gutiérrez, Max Harris, María Herrera Sobek, Guisela Latorre, Franco Mondini Ruiz, Johnny Presbítero, Tey Diana Rebolledo, Sylvia Rodríguez, Rolando J. Romero, Terezita Romo, and Margaret Villanueva and this author all participated, offering our knowledge, expertise, and unique perspectives to the discussions. This volume would not exist if not for the participants' valuable contributions to the forum.

In the section, "Malinche Triangulated," José Emilio Pacheco and Deena J. González consider history's selection of the Malinche-Cortés paradigm from the complex exchanges between the major communicators at the center of the conquest, namely La Malinche, Cortés, Jerónimo de Aguilar, and Gonzalo Guerrero. José Emilio Pacheco provides a new, annotated version of his canonical poem describing the origins of mestizaje and the parties involved in the process. Deena J. González discusses the concept of historical accuracy in the construction of Native women's history, proposing rhetorical questions around her performance that provoke a reconsideration of history. González looks at the accommodation of the Spanish and of La Malinche in the Malinche-Cortés-Moctezuma triangle, and theorizes historical selectivity and narrative.

Sandra Messinger Cypess and Alicia Gaspar de Alba consider the masculinist ideologies behind La Malinche's symbolic status as the abject mother of

Mexican and Chicana/o culture in the section entitled "Malinche and Gendered Histories." Cypess provides a wealth of Malinche resources as she examines the choice of La Malinche as the symbolic Mother of Mexicans and Chicanos, thus skillfully engaging in the now 50-year-old debate between Octavio Paz, Mexican feminism, and U.S. Latina/o feminism. In her critical summary of La Malinche as the foundational myth of Mexican identity, Cypess goes beyond the "victim or agent" and "harlot or heroine" binaries to propose ways to break the patriarchal and Eurocentric molds that imposed these categories. Rolando J. Romero contextualizes the Malinche/Guadalupe binary in Contemporary Mexican and Chicana/Chicano cultures, comparing and contrasting each tradition's genealogical construction through analyses of visual arts and literature. Romero contends that La Malinche's appearance as a Mexican symbol for globalization and Chicana/o culture perpetuates the tradition of scapegoating along the patriarchal and religious lines of chastity. He explains that while contemporary Chicana/o culture has sought to demystify the Virgin of Guadalupe and de-vilify La Malinche, Mexican culture has engaged in the opposite trend. Drawing upon the scholarship of Norma Alarcón, Romero concludes that both cultures' attempts to reunite the split mother figures result in drastically different ideologically charged constructions. Alicia Gaspar de Alba gives us the much needed essay that critically describes the relationship between La Malinche and the Movement. Her thorough discussion of what she calls the "Chicano colonial imaginary" explains the gendered racial stigma present in the machismo of the Chicano Movement, providing examples from manifestos, artwork, slogans, and popular writing of the time. Parallel to her discussion of the dominant gender dynamics in the Movement, she examines Chicana feminist artists', historians', and writers' criticism of the "Chicano colonial imaginary," presenting finally a "Chicana feminist lesbian revision of our infamous foremother" as a means to overcome 500 years of internalized racism and misogyny.

"Malinche: Cuerpo de Mujer" examines the symbolic proportions of La Malinche's body as it signifies the desired land or the place of allegorical violence—both inflicted and perpetrated. Alfred Arteaga exposes the sexuality behind Cortés's gaze in his poetic narrative of the connection between Cortés' arrival to the Mexican shore and our arrival at contemporary Aztlán. He also considers the driving masculinist force within the Conquest of Mexico and the selection of historical narratives. His discussion of race, sexuality and reproduction—both textual and sexual—questions our predisposition to create history according to aesthetic preference, thus challenging the difference between history and fiction. Through the lens of the female body, Debra Castillo examines the Malinche of Gaspar de Alba's poetry and short stories. Castillo employs the critical perspective of Kristeva's theories of the Mother as the "nurturing horror" and reads Gaspar de Alba's characters as feminocentric disruptors of the white male sexual expectations in both the Conquest and in contemporary sexual dynamics between "gringos" and Chicanas. In exposing the use of visceral metaphors for catharsis, abjection, forgetting, and resistance as forms of non-dominant memory creation, Castillo highlights Chicana feminism's unique ability to "unhinge" clichés of racial, ethnic, linguistic, and sexual otherness.

The following section, "Malinche et al.," explores related mythic and historical figures that have been used to prescribe roles for females in Chicano culture and racial attitudes among Chicana women. Antonia I. Castañeda addresses the ways in which the gendering of the "New World" as female has translated into a "history of Indian-woman-hating." Castañeda ties La Malinche into a line of mythical and historical Native American female figures that have been sexualized in the imperial (Christian) imaginary, informing us of a predecessor to La Malinche in California, and an eighteenth-century female Indian warrior. Castañeda explores how native and mestiza women of eighteenth and nineteenth century California articulated their identities despite the limits and contradictions of Spanish, Mexican, and US domination. Her essay emphasizes the distortion and destruction of narratives that address "native women's historical autonomy" and the contemporary scholarly production and cultural awakening that enables Chicanas to positively identify with their Indian heritage. Guisela Latorre analyses the relationship between La Malinche and the Adelita icon of the Mexican revolution. From the perspective of art history and Latina feminism, Latorre discusses the Chicana muralists' and easel painters' texts that upset the "helper" role designated to women in the Movement and the assertion of female subjectivity through layered revisions of women of color and participation in social movements.

"Malinche Myth and Metaphor," deals primarily with the construction of the Malinche myth. María Herrera Sobek provides examples of the visual representations of La Malinche from the sixteenth century to the present, incorporating colonial Tlaxcalan, Nahuatl, and Spanish drawings and paintings as well as Mexican, and Chicana art. In analyzing the iconography and the composition of the imagery, Herrera Sobek draws conclusions about La Malinche's prominence in the Conquest according to Native versions, early twentieth-century Mexico's perception of her, and Chicana revisions of traditional Malinche narratives. Luis Leal addresses the overlap between La Malinche and La Llorona, asserting the separate origins of these often-conflated figures of the Mexican oral tradition. Drawing on the mission testimonies of the early colonial period, and Mexican and Chicano historical writings and stories, Luis Leal contends the necessary pre-Columbian origins of La Llorona, concluding that the conflation of La Llorona and La Malinche has allowed the vilification of La Malinche. Tere Romo highlights the various representational roles that Malinche fills in the visual arts. Romo organizes the visual depictions from the sixteenth century to the present according to the major metaphoric construction in the works, constructions like "La Malinche as Mestizaje," "La Malinche as Indianness," and "La Malinche as Chicana," "La Malinche as Seductress," and "La Malinche as Lengua."

The last section, "Malinche, c'est moi," includes two creative pieces that present La Malinche as voice itself, as a liberating figure that allows for the recognition of colonial patterns and the discovery and assertion of identities that do not fit into easy categories. Franco Mondini Ruiz relates La Malinche to the sexual and ethnic coming of age of a gay Latino. My poem speaks to the familial recurrences of colonial patterns of womanhood and ethnicity from the perspective of Malinche's daughter.

Notes

[1]Alarcón's keynote speech at the 1999 "U.S. Latina/Latino Perspectives on La Malinche" conference organized by the Latina/Latino Studies Program at the University of Illinois, Urbana-Champaign.

Works Cited

Alarcón, Norma. "Traddutora, Traditora." *Dangerous Liasons.* Eds. Anne McClintock et al. Minnesota: U of Minnesota P, 1997. 278–297

Anaya, Rudolfo A. *Bless Me, Última.* 1972. Berkeley, CA: TQS Publications, 1991.

Anonymous. "The Adelitas' Role in El Movimiento." García 118–119.

Cervantes, Lorna Dee. "Para un revolucionario. New York: Routledge, 1997." García 74–75.

Del Castillo, Adelaida. "Malintzin Tenepal: A Preliminary Look into a New Perspective." García 122–126.

Fregoso, Rosalinda. *The Bronze Screen.* Minneapolis: U of Minnesota P, 1993.

García, Alma, ed. *Chicana Feminist Thought. The Basic Historical Writings.* New York: Routledge, 1997.

Gaspar de Alba, Alicia. "Malinche's Revenge." *Feminism, Nation and Myth: La Malinche.* Ed. Rolando Romero and Amanda Harris Fonseca. Houston: Arte Público Press, 2005.

Moraga, Cherríe. *The Last Generation.* Boston: South End Press, 1993.

———. *Loving in the War Years: Lo que nunca pasó por sus labios.* Boston: South End Press, 2000.

NietoGómez, Ana. "Empieza la revolución verdadera." García 74–75.

———. "The Chicana—Perspectives for Education." García 130–131.

Rendón, Armando. *The Chicano Manifesto.* New York: Collier Books, 1971.

Romero, Rolando J. "Texts, Pretexts, Con-texts: Gonzalo Guerrero in the Chronicles of the Indies." *Revista de Estudios Hispánicos* 26 (1992): 345–367.

Rosales, Arturo, ed. *Testimonio: A Documentary History of the Mexican American Struggle for Civil Rights.* Houston: Arte Público Press, 2000.

Zeta Acosta, Oscar. *The Revolt of the Cockroach People.* New York: Vintage Books, 1989.

Malinche Triangulated

Post Scriptum and Self-Critique
José Emilio Pacheco

I wrote "Traduttore, traditori" in 1974 and published it in the "Antigüedades mexicanas" section of *Islas a la deriva* (Siglo XXI, 1976). I wrote it with confidence in the then dominant, and now defeated, idea that the country "México" existed before the Spanish Conquest. Under such a criteria, Doña Marina commited "high treason" by uniting with Hernán Cortés and helping him conquer Moctezuma.

The books that brought me out of my error, especially Sandra Messinger Cypess's *La Malinche in Mexican Literature: From History to Myth,* had not yet been written. Now we know that Malinche did not betray anyone: national consciousness did not exist, and loyalty, therefore, could not be demanded of a victim of tyrants who sold her as a slave.

In 2000, the Fondo de Cultura Económica published *Tarde o temprano,* my *collected poems.* I revised "Traduttore, traditori" and I made some changes that, I believe, clarify the text. I supressed the violence of the title, but I did not adapt the poem to current ideas. I leave it as it is, yet another example that poetry is not as we used to believe, atemporal and eternal, but rather historical, and therefore ephimeral.

Doña Marina*
José Emilio Pacheco

Jerónimo de Aguilar and Gonzalo Guerrero, shipwrecked
made their lives among the tribe
and learned the Mayan tongue. Gonzalo
took a wife, engendered children. Aguilar
exorcized all contact, and prayed the rosary
to chase off temptations.

Cortés arrived and learned of the castaways. Gonzalo
renounced Spain
and battled as a Mayan among Mayans. Jerónimo
joined the invaders. He knew the language,
he could communicate with Malinche, who also spoke
Mayan and Mexican too.

To these translators
we owe largely
the conquest, the colony, and
our mestizaje,
this tangle called Mexico, and the strife
between hispanismo and indigenismo.

---

*Translated by Amanda Nolacea Harris

Malinchista, A Myth Revised*

Alicia Gaspar de Alba

(It is a traditional Mexican belief that La Malinche—Aztec interpreter and mistress of Cortés—betrayed her own people in exchange for a new life. It is said that La Malinche bore a son by Cortés, the first mestizo of Aztec and Spanish blood, whom she later sacrificed when Cortés threatened to take the boy to Spain. Some say that the spirit of La Malinche is La Llorona.)

1

The high priest of the pyramids feared La Malinche's
power of language—how she could form strange syllables
in her mouth and Speak to the gods without offering
the red fruit of her heart. He had visions of a white
man who would change her ways with an obsidian knife.

2

La Malinche hated the way Cortés rubbed his cactus-
beard over her face and belly. The way his tongue
pressed against her teeth. She was used to smooth
brown lovers who dipped beneath her, who crouched
on the ground and rocked her in the musky space
between their chests and thighs.

3

When the child was born, his eyes opened Aztec black,
his skin shone café-con-leche. His mother wet his
fine curls with her saliva to make them straight.
His father cursed the native seed in that
first mixed son.

4

They slept under the black silk of a Tenocha sky,
the hammock molded around the two bodies: a woman's
buttocks heavy after childbirth, an infant weighted by
the shadows in his skull. A coyote lurking near
the river could smell their blood.

*Originally published in *Beggar on the Córdoba Bridge. Three Times a Woman: Chicana Poetry.* Tempe: Bilingual Press, 1989. 16–17. Reprinted with permission.

5

The woman shrieking along the littered bank of the
Rio Grande is not sorry. She is looking for revenge.
Centuries she has been blamed for the murder of her
child, the loss of her people, as if Tenochtitlan
would not have fallen without her sin. History
does not sing of the conquistador who prayed
to a white god as he pulled two ripe hearts
out of the land.

Malinche Triangulated, Historically Speaking

Deena J. González

Malinche has not escaped the mythification that besets our studies of Native peoples in the Americas, of the sort Richard Drinnon wrote about long ago, but applied to the Indians Euro-Americans encountered and supposedly conquered.[1] Drinnon reminded us that physical attributes (Montezuma's long, white hair), color, and skin type, but also cultural artifacts, artistic production, beadwork, basketry, and so on were recorded so continuously that by the nineteenth-century Euro-Americans had become hell-bent on eradicating the producers of the very cultural artifacts, assets, attributes that they would ascribe to Native peoples; these ascriptions stretched far beyond the attitudinal, that is the attitudes towards Natives carried their own capital, as it were, because through them, whites also ascribed "value;" price, dollars and the assignment of a value implied that the goods were the remains of "vanished peoples." One thing reinforced the other, as we historians who work with stereotypes assert constantly.[2]

Malinche deserves better study, to be sure, and requires assessments stretching far beyond those "values" that were heaped on her. It is hard for historians to resist decades and centuries of ascription, whether those attributes assigned to her were "organic" or culturally specific, or foisted by outside observers. The powerful images created by Diego Rivera that etch our memories, and others by scholars portraying her standing defiantly between the Spanish conquerors, the Tlaxcalans, the Aztecs, and everyone in between, suggest her prominence or centrality, and depict an imaginary full of rich pronouncement. Moctezuma II, with his white beard, an elderly man, Cortés with his trusty allies and smelly companions—the Spaniards, the Aztecs' documents of the Conquest report, did not bathe while the Aztecs bathed daily—provide the most exquisite sort of detail needed to make films and to effect "accuracy," but as we have seen, the very same relegate the woman, her life, her values, her ideas, her person to second-class status. In the U.S. popular imagination, she shares this status with Pocahontas, most recently depicted in the popular "made-for-children" movie (was it?), or in the perpetual indulgences of amateur historians and buffs alike in the Sacajawea character. Like her colleagues, Malinche is all image, imagined, unreal.

Although increasingly more realistic these days in the profession of history, we argue still in our minds if not on paper about this value we have come to assign to the word "accuracy" in the matter of women's lives especially. Many of us suspect the task of "uncovering" or "recovering" as largely illusive, and well we should, given the fact that so few dedicated professional researchers receive the sponsorship or dollars needed to begin a "true" recovery, to train the student and professional researchers we need to scour hundreds of archives for literally hundreds of thousands of documents that would reveal or depict the lives of women. What do we mean in the case of Malinche? First, the Archivos General de la Nación in Mexico City, the Archivos de las Indias in Sevilla, and thousands of regional repositories containing letters, journals, and official reports that would help us know more about indigenous women of her period or era.

In the popular and feminist imaginary, and as professors and teachers, we would also like to join ranks with the artists and poets to say that "our" Malinche is as real as those Rivera images we find on posters for conferences, on murals all over México.[3] Her performance in the colonial period, her actions, are viewed less and less as enactment, but in the minds of post-structuralists and even before, in the hands of the linguist, Tzvetan Todorov, her every move, we conclude, was but a simulation. Todorov, like Bernal Díaz del Castillo five centuries ago, describes her on just two pages of a volume dedicated to "unraveling" what he considers "the greatest event in human history."[4]

Women's absence, invisibility, or annihilation in history's pages, then, forces us to ask: What if there is no "she" there? What if after uncovering the "known" details, our historical composite is so sketchy or fragmentary, that we can hardly trace Malintzin's parentage or her marriage to Juan Jaramillo, Cortés' lieutenant and conqueror later of Guatemala and other areas of the Americas?

It remains our critical task to situate Malinche both historically and anthropologically, to view her from many angles, to read and imagine meaning into the conquest of these lands by the Europeans, or, if we are so committed equally, to unravel the mysteries of encounter, and work toward their de-mystification while simultaneously exploring what at the moment of the Columbus Quincentinerary madness, Kirkpatrick Sales, in *The Conquest of Paradise,* labelled "mythification."[5]

While today we are less enamored with labelling one event superior to another, one conquest more interesting than another (given the breadth of choice in the matter), and clearly not in the ways presented during the Columbus jamborees of the early 1990s, I want to focus here on what it might mean to view the conquest through Malinche's eyes, to ascertain her position, predicament, and avoid at the same time iconographing her as symbol for our age. A symbol for whom? This would be the social historian's question, but also lament.

What did Malinche see? What could she have known? For decades now, Chicana scholars and poets and writers have belabored this question. Some determined that the answer lies in her maternity, and not so much on Cortés' paternity (of the son they produced); her maternity or maternal-ness is also read and extended in the direction of Cortés—she mothered him until he "grew up," that is returned to Spain to claim his "true" wife, a Spaniard/penisular and abandoned her, but also, their son.[6] Cortés, the first deadbeat dad of the Americas!

Carlos Fuentes, México's favored son, whom some consider its greatest living essayist, struck another responsive chord when he termed Malinche the forerunner to the Virgen de Guadalupe, that is, the illegitimate mother of the nation displaced in 1531, not that long after Malinche's own appearance in the records of the period, by the virgin, Guadalupe. "In one fabulous stroke, the Spanish authorities transformed the Indian people from children of violated women to children of the pure Virgin." For Fuentes, the Virgen becomes the legitimator of Mexicanness and of the nation, a task to which poor Malintzin Tenepal, as its first betrayer—in such constructions—could not rise. The Virgen appears above, to the Indian, Juan Diego (always constructed in those terms, "Indian"—rarely distinguished by his ethnicity—and clearly a convert to Catholicism, known by his Spanish name).[7]

Once, I called Malinche a lesbian; I did not mean that I had found evidence of her attraction to or for other women, or her sexuality, or her romantic interests, if she had any. Like the purpose of her diplomacy, her sexuality is still to be presumed. She is called, repeatedly, the mistress of Cortés, rendered artistically, as "his woman," to be passed on when the conqueror tires of his concubine. I wanted to present Malintzin, or Doña Marina—woman of multiple names and by extension, talents—as a person of independent judgment, of intense and dramatic qualities, and of superior intellect (so, why couldn't she be a lesbian, I ask?), a person of such enormous self confidence and introspection (how could she not have had those, serving as a diplomat?) that she had to be a lesbian? A woman of unparalleled confidence, visibility, and achievement, in a certain sense, are the sorts of assumptions I brought to my article and posed both for their rhetorical value and their historical evidentiary base.[8]

The questions we ask of Malinche have much to say about the state and status of Chicana historiography, historians Emma Pérez, Antonia Castañeda, and Elizabeth Salas have posed, as have Chicana cultural critics.[9] If we inquire about how much decision-making power she had (or see her as slave or mistress), we are really asking about her relationship to and around men. If we marvel at her ability to learn Spanish in six weeks, and believe Bernal Diaz del Castillo's rendition (remember, his book appears many decades after the event, upon his return to Spain) of her value and assistance, she becomes a diplomat; we restore more of her, it seems to me, through her public persona than we do through her role as mother of that "first mestizo child of the Americas," which is of course, pure drama and not factual. If we lend Malinche "sexuality," inevitably we also mean to lend her choice, not dependency but independence, and erroneously also conclude that she is significant primarily and entirely "in relations," sexual or physical ones, and of course, again to the Spaniards. Her image, in other words, might simultaneously need to be reconstructed both relationally and independently of her relations, social, sexual, physical. The same case can be made for any of the prominent female figures of the Americas.

If the matter of Malinche is significant in a sort of post-Oedipal historical moment, of the sort the historian, Emma Perez traces out for us in *The Decolonial Imaginary: Writing Chicanas into History,* Malinche is the third point on the triangle, with her companions, Cortés and Moctezuma, and is her own person outside of that triangle—that is, actress, diplomat, mother, lover, or mistress. Malinche is the mother of Chicanos/Chicanas, if configured in this way, for she symbolizes the uneasy accommodation of the Spaniard, and yet she remains indigenous and largely, unaccommodated. She provides a happy resolution to the matter of "how Spanish are we really, or do we want to be?" Her life and history provides an interesting reversal—in its retrievals—in some rather atypical ways that shed light historiographically as well as culturally.

For Chicanos, especially those writing as a generation of the 1960s/70s, and mostly to establish tenure in the academic settings that provided wages, it would seem that maternity was more at stake than paternity. Their investment remained in the category of "passing the torch," their own, I would say. The father was and remains Spain, except among a small core of indigenists; the mother, on the other hand, is more problematic as betrayer or as a violated woman, in other words, used goods, tainted, and all of the other imagery Catholicism foists on non-virgins. She is known, that is, she is Malinche *or* Doña Marina, but rarely Malintzin Tenepal. A related set of questions students ask—"exactly who was she? Did she become Spanish? Did she sell out?"—remain unanswerable until more researchers dedicate their time to primary recovery.

The questions for Chicano/as, as we grapple consistently on an intellectual and philosophical level, return us to ideas crucial to the formation of Chicano/a Studies to begin, and outline as well our place in the "world's order," in the academy and society: Why are we not Indians, not Spanish, but rather, mestizos, the focus on the "not this, not that?" The declarative, "both," thus brings forward the condition of borderlands, of vexing terrain, of illegitimacy, despite the efforts of Fuentes and others to meld the two. In another article, I attempted to lay out why this is significant, historically, for Chicanas, and to develop the notion that identity is given and assumed. Identity questions are posed just as often as "what one is," as much as "what one is not." The prevailing assumptions surrounding "not" Indian are what such Native/Chicana theorists as Inés Hernández have asked at our Chicano/a Studies gatherings for the past two decades, and we have provided some poor answers in response.[10]

We need to examine in greater detail the idea of maternity/paternity because the denial of the mother is equally strong in *Chicanismo,* save for a suffering mother, the sacrificing mother. In such a traditional rendition, Malintzin fits because she is the woman who gave in to the man, the whore, Malinche. Again, she fits the pattern of possibility, which is so much embedded in the search for paternity. It would seem then that the more traditional, Western European question (the law of the father or the identity of the father), which in turn spawns laws, codes, and nation states lies fallow in the Spanish-speaking and mostly Catholic Americas; in México, doubly so. While paternity must of course be rigidly and rigorously protected and defended—so fragile is the concept—maternity, it would seem, that is, is almost taken for granted, because "all human beings know who the mother is," for "we came from her," as witnesses at births so often attest.

In the case of Malinche, though, the thought sets up for mestizos, for mixed-race people of the Americas, an interesting conundrum—how to embrace the indigenous? For Chicanas, the puzzle is layered dynamically, for it also means embracing the conqueror, bedding down with him as Malinche did, and ultimately rejecting him as well. Chicana feminists have an even tougher time with this one; the difficulty resides not at all in the notion of choosing one conqueror or one patriarchy over another, but in determining what is the significance of Malinche's choices—do as she did, and get reassigned by either courts or families, as "belonging" to a different patriarch? Or, don't do as she did and risk lower, poorer status, no fame, presumably no mobility through the children or only by self-promotion. The sociological data on this latter choice reflect the reasons so many do not view the possibility as a "choice," in legitimate terms. Indeed, legitimacy underscores here the decisions, historically and contemporarily.

We really don't know that Malintzin was a self-promoter; we know she was capable, adept, present and visible, highly visible. We know she embodied status. We know subsequent generations would ignore Cortés—by virtue of no streets, statues, or buildings named after him today in México—and condem the woman. We know that an entire culture with great panache rejected the mother that Chicanas today reclaim as a foremother: the one who got screwed over and who screwed everyone else as a result. The mother of the lost land. The mother who cared, but not enough. The foremother of an illegitimate status, Chican*O*, in a highly stratified, race-conscious society.

Malinche's historical triangulation began at the moment when she was introduced to Cortés, or joined his party. Her strangulation, in historical memory, can also be situated at the same juncture. In many ways, she was too smart, too much a woman of her time, linguistic (learning Spanish in six weeks, speaker of Mayan and Nahuatl, the widespread, diplomatic language of the Americas), clearly physically fit and able to cross treacherous terrain, and full of the awareness that propelled her toward the Aztecs as much as it did Cortés.

Triangles are not happy places or meeting grounds, psychologists tell us; one person is always available to vote or act against another. It seems that one person also always loses while the other two march happily away. In the case of the dynamic unleashed in the meetings between Cortés and Moctezuma, we know that one died or was murdered shortly thereafter, and the other returned to his homeland after a series of long battles and discredits to his name. He found a partner, a wife, and married her. Malinche moved on, with Jaramillo, it appears. Her son found his place, "first mestizo child of the Americas" and claimed his proper paternity to gain *criollo* status, in the popular constructions of his time.

Who won in this historical rendition? Not Cortés, it would appear. Not Malinche, but perhaps the child of their intercourse? That's the place Chicano/as would like to reside, it would seem, asserting the racial configurations (but note, denying class which was very much at stake); his mixed heritage would be legitimated via erasure, he was labelled a *criollo*, American born and recognized as such, but of "pure" Spanish descent—even if we see the contradiction and "know" him not as pure but as mixed, racially. His status, rendered by the partriarchy, thus denies as well any debate about Malintzin's role and erases her, not just pyschologically, but historically. In the son, Chicano nationalists would find their father. Their mother, however, remains in the background, distant, unnamed, troubled or troubling.

Malinche, to Chicano/a nationalists, is a tragic figure, a woman duped by the great white man. One of their problems clearly resides in how feminist the same nationalists have to become to restore her to history, a move that seems impossible or improbable because so much of Chicano nationalism, in the 1960s and 70s, as today, requires mothers to remain on pedestals, honored but silent. To view Malintzin's time with Cortés, or even her interests in Cortés, is not so much a question of "was she a whore?" a *mujer ordinaria,* but rather requires a leap of faith that perhaps she knew what she was doing, perhaps she was using Cortés, perhaps women simply, plainly, as we say in lesbian-feminist discourse, are appropriating semen, agency of the worst kind. Were that to be found to be the case, a very big secret would be out, childbearers report today, and what little power accrues by virtue of producing offspring suddenly is unmasked.

Malinche was by every measure as great a figure as Cortés and Moctezuma. She occupies an almost unparalleled status—to be ranked in the pantheon with the Virgen de Guadalupe, perhaps La Llorona, and recently, Selena. Her image as traitor is seared in the popular imagination, but one has to ask the question about why she is sacrificed at that altar only? I would suggest that she is there because the matter of paternity and maternity are in this case equally elusive and yet essential to our understandings of identity, status, and historical placement. For and to whom is she a mother figure? Was Cortés really the father of that so-called "first" child of the Americas? How would we know? Did she have other lovers? More children?

What did she do/say in those translations where only she was in command of both languages, only she understood intimately or fully what was being said? Malinche had a tongue and used it, had space and occupied it, had knowledge and applied it. Hence, I offer my call that she be labelled or recast as not just first feminist of the Americas, but first lesbian of the Americas, too.

Notes

[1]See Richard Drinnon, *Facing West: The Metaphysics of Indian-Hating and Empire-Building.* (Minneapolis: U of Minnesota P, 1980).

[2]For a detailed explanation of both attitudes and their impact on ethnic minority peoples in the U.S. who were reserved, enslaved, or colonized, begin with Ronald T. Takaki, *Iron Cages: Race and Culture in 19th-Century America* (Reprint, New York: Oxford UP, 1990).

[3]See the work of Diego Rivera, Palacio Nacional, Mexico City and renditions as well in Carlos Fuentes, *The Buried Mirror: Reflections on Spain and the New World* (Boston: Houghton Mifflin Company, 1992) 112, 115, 145.

[4]See Tzvetan Todorov, *The Conquest of America: The Question of the Other* (reprint, New York: Harper Perennial, 1992) chap. 2; for her description in Bernal Díaz del Castillo, see *The Conquest of New Spain* (reprint, New York: Penguin, 1973) chap. entitled "Doña Marina."

[5]See Kirkpatrick Sales, *The Conquest of Paradise* (New York: Harcourt, 1991).

[6]See especially, Emma M. Pérez, *The Decolonial Imaginary: Writing Chicanas into History* (Bloomington & Indiannapolis: Indiana UP, 1999) 23–27.

[7]Fuentes 146; Juan Diego was Cuahtlatoatzin (1474–1548).

[8]See both "Malinche as Lesbian," *California Sociologist* 14 Winter/Summer (1991) and "Encountering Columbus," *Chicano Studies: Critical Connections Between Research and Community* ed. Teresa Córdova (National Association of Chicano Studies, 1992).

[9]See the work in this volume of Norma Alarcón, Debra Castillo about Chicana writers and poets, and of Sandra Cypess. Newer work can be found in the dissertations of recent Ph.D.s, including Dionne Espinoza, Margarita Barceló, and Rita Alcalá.

[10]See Inés Hernández, plenary address before the National Association of Chicano/a Studies, 1992; and at the MALCS Conferences of the 1980s: Davis, CA, Santa Rosa, CA, and Los Angeles.

Malinche and Gendered Histories

"Mother" Malinche and Allegories of Gender, Ethnicity and National Identity in Mexico

Sandra Messinger Cypess

In the 1970s, when I began to focus my research on women and women writers in Latin American culture, I viewed them primarily as inner exiles in a patriarchal culture. Indeed, women from diverse cultures and across time periods have been conceptualized as "the other," as noted in such dissimilar discourses as the anthropological studies of Michelle Rosaldo ("Women, Culture and Society: A Theoretical Overview") or the famously provocative essay on Mexican national identity—Octavio Paz's *El laberinto de la soledad,* in which Paz does not include "her" in the category of thinking human beings: "¿piensa acaso? ¿siente de veras? ¿es igual a nosotros?" ("Does she think? Does she really feel? Is she the same as us?" [Paz 60]). Mexican women seem to be exiles in their own country if we are to accept Paz's discourse. The image of the displaced woman, exiled or disconnected from her own community and nation, led me to think of La Malinche, and I have not stopped thinking about her since. She is a central figure in the Conquest, an emblem of Mexican national identity and also a symbol of all Latin American women.

In *La Malinche in Mexican Literature, from History to Myth* I studied the various ways she was "resymbolized" during key historical periods in Mexico. Clearly, her sign took on different meanings depending on the ideology of the people who were "reading" her. From the Spanish chronicles to the post-independence texts to twentieth century Mexican and Chicano/a works, she has been portrayed more often as the Mexican Eve, a traitorous woman who sold out to the conquerors; only a few writers, notably Rosario Castellanos, Sabina Berman, Adelaida del Castillo, and Lorna D. Cervantes, have deconstructed what Norma Alarcón has called the "masculine denigration of Malintzin" (Alarcón, "Traduttora" 72).[1] In this present overview, I offer a summary of the "ideas fijas" that continue to adhere to the Malinche construct and will then explore the consequences of the choice of La Malinche as the Mother in Mexico's foundational myth. Finally, I want to go beyond the "poetically alliterative" discussions of whether she was "victimizer or victim," "harlot or heroine" to consider other ways to move beyond the Eurocentrist, patriarchal perspective that engendered these categories.[2]

There are many challenging questions relating to her mythic configurations. For example, given that the historical figure was a multi-dimensional individual who performed in a variety of capacities, why is La Malinche so often only known (and criticized) for her sexual role? What are the repercussions for gender and ethnicity issues when La Malinche and Cortés are the designated couple around which Mexican national identity is centered? Isn't it time to examine the socio-cultural impact of the various maternal configurations given to La Malinche, primarily as the Mexican Eve or the Mexican Medea? Shouldn't we explore the consequences of the use of this foundational couple as a synecdoche for gender and racial relations and consider other ways to move beyond the Eurocentrist, patriarchal perspective.

Before I begin my commentary, I would like to clarify that my interest in Mexican culture does not stem from personal genealogy but from an academic affiliation, "una gran afición" that has been nurtured for many years. I learned to speak Spanish in Mexico, and more importantly, my serious investigation of Mexican literature developed at the University of Illinois when I was privileged to study with the distinguished scholar, don Luis Leal.

Three main points frame my discussion. First, research indicates that in Mexico, more than in any other country, women in their specialized role as mother figures have dominated the myths of nationality and cultural identity. (In the United States, for example, we speak about the "Father of our Country"—with no apparent need to call upon any mothers!) Roger Bartra says clearly in *La jaula de la melancolía,* that there exists in México "un fanático amor a la madre" ("a fanatic love of the Mother" [205]) so that an analysis of the configuration of the archetype of the mother is key toward an understanding of the "psique mexicana" ("Mexican psyche"). Second, of all the narratives of the American conquest, only Mexico has chosen to report its development as a mestizo nation by using the Biblical narrative of a founding couple. What other country has identified so specifically an Adam and Eve—that is, Cortés and La Malinche—with the product of their liaison, Martín Cortés selected as the first mestizo? The relationship between the mother and father, their characteristics not only in terms of gender, but also of class and ethnicity, serve as the synecdoche for the relations of power that influence male-female interactions, as well as those among the races and class structures. Third, in the development of the Mexican narratives of national origin, Amerindian myths and legends blended with those of the Western European tradition. Archetypal images from the European tradition—Eve, Mary, and Medea—combine with the mother figures from the Mexican-Aztec world—Tonantzin and Cihuacóatl—to stimulate the formation of syncretic figures that are La Malinche, the Virgin of Guadalupe, and La Llorona.

Although I use the term "archetype" I do not call upon its Jungian sense in which social reality is always derived from the psychic, that is, archetypal reality. Rather, I agree with such scholars as Naomi Goldenberg who remind us that the archetypal reality is culturally based and that we should examine the socially constructed nature of the archetype as it affects behavior. This is an important distinction for the whole enterprise we are engaged in. We tend to acknowledge that images, metaphors, myths—the whole of symbolic activity—reflect a particular reality, but also, images and myths structure experience, that is, motivate practices and behavior. Thus, the selection of a certain kind of "archetypal" founding Mother is not based on an unchangeable psyche so much as it is a reflection of a patriarchal ideology in the case of Mexico. Because the presence of a mother figure is significant and unique, the characteristics attributed to this mother and its impact on Mexican culture must be analyzed, discussed, and understood.

It is well known that the maternal model provided in the image of the "Virgen de Guadalupe" is considered a positive archetype of Mexican national identity. She is all-suffering, noble, selfless, and dedicated to her children—"los mexicanos."[3] In her iconography, La Virgen is a solitary mother, that is, peerless and pairless, and represents much that is positive as well as some conflictive associations for women today, associations such as those that Ana Castillo and Sandra Cisneros make in their contributions to *Goddess of the Americas / La diosa de las Américas*. As Luis Leal and Roger Bartra, among others have shown, she is always placed in opposition to La Malinche, the flawed mother, the impure, the traitor, the opportunist. Do these character traits derive from her historical activities? Relevant questions that need to be asked, and are often brushed aside, should entail, "what do we know of her actions, and how did we learn of them?"

In studying the Conquest and, in particular, the historical facts regarding La Malinche I find it troubling that facts are rarely taken into consideration in the formation of national imagery; significant gaps exist in our knowledge of the facts; when sources are available, the validity of their data is problematic. Most scholars of the conquest period conclude that it is not easy to determine the truthfulness of the chroniclers, nor is it always possible to know what events occurred, or even when they took place. Do we know the exact date of La Malinche's birth, or her birthplace? What was her family background, her relationship to her mother and the other tribes with whom she lived? What about the origin of her name? Or the details of her death? I have even found discrepancies regarding the details of the birth of her son Martín Cortés. In reference to the presence of factual errors in the historical records at our disposal, I suggest we recall the renowned polemics brought out by Bernal Díaz del Castillo, who quarrels with the history of the conquest as presented by Gómara.[4] Bernal Díaz is not the only one who has problems with what the official record would want us to believe—and he also may have embellished his narrative. Instead of pursuing elusive historical facts, we need to analyze which elements have been selected for incorporation into the national narrative, and to parse out the metaphorical ramifications of the story and its changes through time.

I cannot answer definitively WHY the metaphor of a national couple was selected in Mexico. Yet I can suggest that since it was necessary to refashion the various Amerindian national groups into good colonials, some aspects of the pre-colonial culture had to be included in the definition of national identity. La Malinche represented the Amerindian elements that were selected by the hegemonic powers. It is not just that she is designated the Mother, but that she is called the Mexican EVE, and in that sense, is made to share all the negative characteristics accrued by Eve as part of Christian symbology. I have previously documented this development of La Malinche as the Mexican Eve, the "vendepatrias," traitor, because of her dealings with Cortés and her interactions with the other indigenous peoples. I have also shown how this image does not completely reflect the historical record, especially if we consider the absence of a patria for La Malinche in that time period. But beyond that point, and it is an important point, let us review what it means to have the Amerindian woman as the Eve figure.

The placement of La Malinche in the Eve paradigm not only identifies her as the primary instigator of the fall from Paradise, but she also becomes linked to the punishments of Eve, including her inferior status within the patriarchy. Thus, she is perforce derived from the rib, a second-class citizen, commanded to obey her husband and not raise her voice, or even use her voice according to St. Paul's dictates. Yet in history, first and foremost, La Malinche was "la lengua" for Cortés. She transcended all gender constraints of both Aztec and European societies when she functioned in the role of intermediary and translator. For in Aztec society, too, "Women had no right to speak on high public occasions" as Inga Clendinnen reminds us in her book *Aztecs*. The Aztec leader, whom we have called "emperor" or "king" in European terms, was called "Tlatoani," meaning "He Who Speaks." "Hence the perturbation at the physical prominence and verbal dominance of Doña Marina" (Clendinnen 157). Thus, La Malinche disrupted the general Amerindian curb on "women's tongues in public places" as well as the Christian restrictions against women as speakers in public. In her anthropological study of Chamula society (in the Mexican state of Chiapas), Brenda Rosenbaum comments on the "existence of a profound ambivalence towards women" (66). I would suggest that her study reveals that women in non-Aztec Mexico (Chamula or Maya) were also not typically offered the position of speaker in social settings. For many feminist critics today, the use of voice by La Malinche, her role as a spokesperson, marks one of her most striking—and positive—disruptions of the patriarchy on both the indigenous and the European sides.

La Malinche's role as communicator and spokesperson had to be covered over, or controlled, in subsequent reformulations of the Conquest story, since her role was so disruptive of traditional acceptable female behavior. She descended from "la lengua" to become "la matriz," the "womb"–and in exercising that traditional female function, she was relegated to the position of a negotiable property, used for political alliances and sexual exploits. The historical record, as faulty as it is, nowhere indicates that she was sexually promiscuous, yet in subsequent myths and legends she became associated with conflictive motherhood and extreme sexual proclivity, as a whore as in Paz's synthesis of her image in *El laberinto de la soledad* and his association of her with La Chingada. My point in referring to her negative sexual reputation is not to restrain La Malinche within any naïve—or false—moral code that did not apply to her, but to suggest that those who condemn her as a whore do so on the basis of an erroneous sense of moral conduct that does not apply to her socio-historical context.

The invasion of Mesoamerica by the Europeans and their violent rape of virgin land have been related by metonymy to the "deflowering" of La Malinche by Cortés. La Malinche has become the woman who was not only raped and forced into motherhood, but who also betrayed her country and lost her children in the process. From the novel *Jicotencatl* (1826) through Paz's essay in 1950, to Fuentes's *El naranjo* (1993) and to sites on the Web in 2000 —all these *tlatoani* have been repeating that La Malinche is not only "la Traidora" but also La Chingada and La Llorona. This development reflects a mythic gesture repeated in other cases of women in history, as Elizabeth Janeway shows in her study *Man's World, Woman's Place* whereby "myth opposes belief [desire] to facts in order to change the facts or obscure them" (26). It has been far easier to blame La Malinche for any problems relating to the periods of the Conquest, Colonial, and post-Colonial periods, than to face the realities of difficult situations with regard to problems of gender, race and ethnicity, and class.

The Malinche-Cortés union must be viewed as more than a mere historical fact; it serves as a root paradigm that influences, on the personal level, female-male behavior in Mexico and in the public arena, it marks racial and ethnic interactions. Think of the painting by Orozco, in which he clearly depicted the two as Adam and Eve. The fact that it hangs in the "Escuela Preparatoria Nacional" ("National Preparatory School") illustrates my point that the selection of La Malinche and Cortés as the Mexican Adam and Eve reflects an official ideology of what is to be considered Mexican: and how men and women are meant to relate to one another. By means of this discursive strategy that focused on Adam and Eve as the narrative paradigm for the reading of the conquest and the attendant birth of the Mexican mestizo, the categories of Indian and Spaniard/European developed in which the Indian (read "La Malinche") was equated with betrayal, inferiority, unworthiness of respect. The fact that Malinche is symbol of the inferior Indian mother of the Mexican mestizo has become the primary "archetypal pattern" to be propagated, speaks more about the dominance of European discourse and hegemonic power than it relates to the inherent human condition. This paradigm still provides a serious negative influence. Research in the social community has shown that even in Mexico today, men act the role of the conquistador vis-à-vis their relationships with women and expect to impose their will on the subordinate, submissive woman; with regard to ethnic relations among the races, the Malinche-Cortés interaction constitutes a pattern of behavior in which the Indian is seen as inferior to the European. Remember how Paz sadly stated that as long as Mexicans repudiate La Malinche and their Indian past, they will remain orphans, wandering in the labyrinth of solitude. Yet Paz does not suggest another more positive way to read La Malinche. Perhaps what is necessary at this point is the possibility of finding another couple with more positive characteristics to serve as progenitors of the Mexican mestizo nation. I believe that I can suggest another possibility—a paradigm I shall save for my conclusion.

The very characteristics attributed to La Malinche-Llorona as mother of the commander's son, as the woman who serves as "spy and betrayer of her race to an alien power," and as the mother who causes the death of her children are also the very details that we find in the Greek myth of Medea. For writers like Jesús Sotelo Inclán (*Malintzin, Medea americana,* 1957) and Sergio Magaña (in his 1967 play *Los argonautas* renamed *Cortés y La Malinche*) both Medea and La Malinche share a similar experience of love, exile, betrayal and death. Nevertheless, by considering La Malinche as a Medea figure, these writers continue the legend that she was somehow guilty of guile, deceit, and a jealousy so great that she would be willing to kill her child out of vengeance. Or was it that she was guilty of guile and deceit so great that she was willing to kill her own people? Did she sacrifice her culture and peoples so that the foreign invader would triumph? Why not ask, "Did she have a choice not to obey the foreign invader?" In both these plays, Malinche's continued loyalty to Cortés is based on her carrying and caring for a mestizo child.

If La Malinche is related at all to the Medea myth, I would suggest that it is her own mother who can be considered a Medea figure. If we take the story of her early life as it is recounted in Bernal Díaz's version, we learn that La Malinche's mother, after her first husband dies, tried to get rid of her daughter. La Malinche's mother takes on a new husband and rids herself of this daughter whose heritage she does not want to perpetuate, just as Medea did not want to see Jason's blood perpetuated in her children. Betrayal, tortured love, and questions of inheritance all figure in the early life of Malinche and activate the decisive steps that lead her on the path to slavery and encounter with the "tribe" of Spaniards. Is that why La Malinche becomes in turn like her own mother, a Medea figure bent on revenge? From Bernal Díaz, we know that she reconciles herself with her family out of Christian love, and does not seek revenge since she is happy to be a Christian "doña," happy to have accepted her lord Cortés and his culture. So for the Spaniards she is ever an avatar of the Biblical Joseph, a good Mother Eve and not the traitorous Eve or a vengeful murderous Medea, associations proffered by post-Independence nationalist rhetoric.

La Malinche is also placed within the same paradigm as La Llorona, a syncretic figure with overtones of Medea (in her role as child-killer) and the indigenous figure of Cihuacoatl, an Aztec goddess. As José E. Limón reminds us, the figure of La Llorona is "a syncretism of European and indigenous cultural forms firmly grounded in the Greater Mexican cultural experience" (400). Indeed, the pre-conquest indigenous peoples, whose testimonies are recorded by Fray Bernardino de Sahagún, told the story of Cihuacoatl, who would appear at night crying out for dead children. So the idea of the "weeping mother" is not European alone.[5] However, by placing La Malinche within the paradigms of Medea and Llorona, she is blamed for the destruction of Indian society, or metaphorically, for "cultural infanticide," as Nicolás Kanellos calls it in his brief review of the use of La Llorona as a motif in Chicano poet Alurista's "Must be the Season of the Witch." Alurista's poetic vision notwithstanding, this charge ignores such facts of the historical record that other Indigenous groups, the Tlaxcalans notably, aligned themselves with Cortés against the Aztec overlords. To ascribe to La Malinche the deaths of all the indigenous peoples is an exaggeration of the historical record, but it clearly shows the need for a scapegoat on whom to transfer blame. As the presence of this Malinche-Llorona correlation shows, La Malinche is a negative icon in the representation of cultural identity and she is at the same time denied her positive role in the formation of the mestizo Mexican identity.

Those who pursue the relationship between Medea and La Malinche-Llorona proclaim in effect that the woman in the partnership is not to be trusted. Fear of women, distrust of the woman in a powerful position, envy of the woman as the procreator, all these features of masculinist attitudes are present in the origination of the Medea-Malinche-Llorona paradigm. My response to these associations embedded in the paradigm is, again, that it examplifies the imposition of the patriarchal model and a denigration of a pluricultural definition of Mexican identity.

Until the nineteen eighties, I would say, the majority of writers defined the contributions of La Malinche and the Indians in the formation of Mexican national identity based on the Eurocentric view that supported patriarchal ideas about women and race and symbolized by the Malinche-Cortés paradigm. However, theirs is not the only pattern of behavior for men and women in the formation of national identity. Documentation exists of another couple whose pattern of behavior subverts the supposed inferiority of the Amerindian culture that is read into the Malinche-Cortés relationship. Another cultural pattern can be symbolized by the behavior of an almost forgotten, emblematic couple, Gonzalo Guerrero and his Mayan wife. Beginning in the late seventies, novels by Mario Aguirre Rosas (*Gonzalo de Guerrero, padre del mestizaje iberoamericano,* 1975) and Eugenio Aguirre (*Gonzalo Guerrero* 1986), and studies by such critics as Rolando Romero and Manuel Medina, bring to light this forgotten, and contrastive, pattern of behavior. Gonzalo Guerrero was a Spaniard who came to the Yucatán peninsula as a conquistador, but because of a shipwreck, he wound up a captive among the Mayan Indians. Instead of returning to the Spanish ethnic group—(tribe)—when Cortés found him and offered to rescue him from his life among the Amerindians, Guerrero expressed a firm desire to remain with his Amerindian family and continue to live an "Amerindian lifestyle." I would like to emphasize what Guerrero offers as the explanation of his refusal to rejoin the Spanish forces: he shows not only his marked (tattooed) body, but also the products of his body: his mestizo children. He says he loves his children very much and he enjoys his social situation, and refuses to give it up. Pointing to his offspring, he tells the Spaniards, "Don't you see how lovely they are" (quoted by the contemporary historian Antonio Betancourt Pérez in *Historia de Yucatán*). These children could well have become the symbols of the Mexican mestizo, instead of the son of Malinche and Cortés, who arrives chronologically later but remains to this day the icon of mestizaje.

Another observation regarding the title "first mestizo" is warranted at this point. While many of us in this field may understand that Martín Cortés—the son of La Malinche and Cortés—unambiguously and unmistakably was not chronologically the first mestizo to be born in Mexico, since his date of birth is given as 1524 (and sometimes as late as 1532—clearly consensus is not easy to achieve), then why is it that he is so often regarded as the "first mestizo"? We may want to reply that he is the first symbolically, as the child of the pair selected as the founding couple, but for some publications and popularly on the Web, he has literally developed into the first in arrival. The historian Jesús Figueroa Torres, for example, comments that "Doña Marina fue la primera ciudadana, la primera cristiana y la primera mexicana que habló el español, la primera en mezclar su sangre con el conquistador para dar a luz un hijo, elementos que forjaron una patria y una nueva raza" (*Doña Marina: Una india exemplar* 75). No questioning takes the place of the reasons for Martín Cortés' designation as number one, and what that choice has meant and still means for Mexicans, or what ideological decisions underpin that selection. I would like to suggest that the preference of Cortés and Malinche's son Martín as *Mestizo #1* reflects the same ideological decisions that erased any other couple from consideration. Issues we can identify today that relate to gender, ethnicity, religion, and class are all relevant. The social standing of Martin's father, as opposed to Guerrero's position, has determined Martín's selection as number one mestizo. He is first in social rank as the son of a conquistador, and his Catholic religion, dress, and journey to Spain, all prove European male dominance over Amerindian women and European cultural dominance over Amerindian ways of life.

Guerrero's lifestyle and his adherence to his Mayan wife and children deconstruct the dominant culture's view of the Amerindians as inferior, unworthy of loyalty and respect. In contrast to that of the selected couple, the pattern that Gonzalo Guerrero provides indicates that the European can reject aspects of his heritage in favor of the Amerindian pattern provided by the woman. Yet the Guerrero paradigm has just not entered into Mexican consciousness and his wife's personal history has all but disappeared. Rather, La Malinche's negative image has remained powerful and continues to influence behavior.

On a positive note, over the past twenty years, a new Malinche paradigm has emerged that acknowledges the facts of the past yet places them within more appropriate contexts that account for ethnic, gender and class issues. Once again the body of La Malinche has become the territory of contesting representations that dramatize a struggle between regressive and alternative models of social institutions and values. Contemporary Mexican feminists and Chicana writers have re/viewed the figure of La Malinche and attempted to revise our perceptions of her.

An example of a contemporary Mexican woman's version of the historical events involving La Malinche and her negative role as "la Eva traidora" ("The Treacherous Eve") can be found in the essay, "El camino de las voces" by Martha Robles. Robles suggests a different perspective from which to interpret Malinche's role as guide and translator for Cortés. She affirms: "Malintzin no representa el sometimiento a lo extranjero como se ha insistido, sino el poder fundador de la palabra allí donde fueron enfrentados los lenguajes como armas enemigas en el campo de batalla" ("Malintzin does not represent submission to all things foreign as has been insisted, but rather the foundational power of the word—there where languages confronted each other as arms on the battle field" [18]). Robles does not belittle what La Malinche has accomplished, but rather, she offers her work with languages as a positive feature, a sign of her intelligence and agency. I bring out this rejection of Malinche's submission since that idea undermines the whole concept of "malinchismo" –Malinche's supposed rejection of her people in favor of the foreigner. Perhaps erasing this characteristic from her paradigm would also change the way she is viewed as Mother Eve, the traitor. There would be an opportunity to consider her as an activist and not subservient or "open" to foreign influences.

Brianda Domecq is another Mexican woman writer whose work uses the Malinche myth as a subtext in order to demythify her. Domecq's idea appears to build on Margo Glantz's essay, "Las hijas de La Malinche," in which Glantz also attempts to rescue La Malinche from the traitor's role (195); Glantz suggests that La Malinche is a "mother" to Mexican women writers in that they are carrying out the work she began in the public arena. Domecq uses humor in her essay and a colloquial tone to undermine one of the long-standing myths about Mother Malinche—and all women who work in public. Domecq offers a pun in the title of the collection, calling the anthology *Mujer que publica— mujer pública.* (México: Editorial Diana, 1994). Thus, the sign "publica" can be the verb, and the phrase means "the woman who publishes;" by adding an accent, the sign changes and the phrase is "mujer pública" or "public woman," another pun, since that is the colloquial Mexican expression for "putas," or prostitutes).[6] The essay that deals with La Malinche is entitled "Puta, re-puta, re-puta-ción" (37–51). By using references to "madres putativas," Domecq reminds us of La Malinche, often referred to in popular culture as "la puta de Cortés." Domecq declares that women writers are "madres putativas" (41) who offer "nuestras voces de mujeres públicas" as a way to allow all women to express their pain and frustration in a patriarchal society. Since La Malinche was the first "public voice" as a woman among the Mexicas and conquistadors, Domecq is using her legend as a subtext for her discussion of women writers and their role as rebels. In a thesis chapter on the uses of the Malinche image among contemporary Mexican women essayists, "Who is La Malinche in the Eyes of Contemporary Mexican Women Essayists?," Charlene Merithew, concludes that Domecq uses the term "puta" as a reference to La Malinche and also "to refer to all women whom society deems as 'bad,' whether they be sexually open women, counter-canonical women writers, or any others" (diss. 221). Merithew suggests that Domecq "uses the term 're-puta' to refer to the relationship between older and younger generations of Mexican women writers. "If society has considered the former to be 'putas,' traitors to the traditional codes, it will consider the latter to be 're-putas,' following in the footsteps of their predecessors" (221). The sign "re-puta" has a number of meanings, all of which are called into play by Domecq. First, as Merithew notes, as a noun, "re-puta" seems to indicate that the women are "putas again"; also, the verb "reputar" means to consider or deem, so that the idea is suggested that it is society that considers women who break tradition to be "putas." Further, the line of "putas" in Mexico, beginning with La Malinche, has continued as women continue to rebel against the strictures of the patriarchy. So that after La Malinche, each woman is a "reputa"—now in both senses of the prefix "re"—one as an emphatic, such as in "rebueno," ("very good") and also in the other use of "re" that forms when it is attached to verbs to mean repetition (such as "rehacer," "renacer," etc.) For Domecq, then, if women in Mexico who wish to exercise their public voice are considered to be of bad character, this "reputación" is based on society's construction of "good" and "bad" values and is not intrinsic to the woman herself.

By calling La Malinche a "madre putativa," Domecq proposes that her cohort of women writers are "madres putativas" too: here the adjective "putativa" is both a reference to puta and to the adjective meaning "supposed, presumed." Thus, Domecq implies, the supposed mother—the mother-whore—does not deserve the bad reputation she has received since it is a patriarchal construction and not a historical reality. Just as La Malinche has been maligned regarding her sexuality and her public persona, so, too, are her "daughters" suffering from the repetition of her unwarranted and disturbing reputation.

Just as Mexican women writers are concerned about the negative associations attached to the historical La Malinche, Chicana writers have been perhaps even more vocal about re-visioning La Malinche. In her indispensable essay, "Traddutora, Traditora: A Paradigmatic Figure of Chicana Feminism," Norma Alarcón traces the nature of the vindication of La Malinche by such Chicana writers as Adelaida del Castillo, Adaljiza Sosa Riddell, and Carmen Tafolla. They affirm that this Amerindian woman should be credited as the founder of a new race "la raza," a term incorporating Mexican Americans as well as Mexicans. For the purposes of this review, I would single out Tafolla's poem "La Malinche," in which Tafolla creates a subject position for La Malinche that subverts the masculine version of her dependent status. As Alarcón observes, "In Tafolla's poem Malintzin goes on to assert that she submitted to the Spaniard Cortés because she envisioned a new race. She wanted to be the founder of a people. There are echoes of Paz and Fuentes in Tafolla's view, yet she differs by making Malintzin a woman possessed of clear-sighted intentionality . . ." (73).

La Malinche's actions can be understood today within the context of the process of transculturation as proposed by Cuban sociologist Fernando Ortiz.[7] Transculturation, in opposition to acculturation, reflects a dynamic process as a means of resisting a dominant culture. La Malinche was indeed a mother of that philosophy of transculturation. She too often has been found guilty of colonial acculturation, but if we can believe the codices that portray her iconically, we note that she never accepted European dress but continued to wear her indigenous clothing, just as she continued to live in Mexico, and maintain all her languages. I can imagine that she would be very proud to be the mother of the mestizo progeny and their mix of cultures. Cortés, however, was not a worthy companion for La Malinche because he did not appear to value her or the mestizos as much as she did. I would like to follow the lead found in one of Elena Garro's texts and find a new (biological) partner for La Malinche. After all, Freudian theory suggests that in telling the family story, the mother is usually known but it is the father who is not always easily identifiable. Perhaps, then, Elena Garro's short story "La culpa es de los tlaxcaltecas" ("The Fault of the Tlaxcalans") offers us a new paradigm that will provide a more appropriate pattern for Mexico.

In my reading of Garro's story, the protagonist Laura is a Malinche figure.[8] At first, she too had chosen a white husband of the upper class, but he proved to be a "salvaje" from her point of view. Fortunately, Laura has the opportunity to correct her mistake, upon the arrival of her "primo marido," an indigenous figure from the conquest period who is also identified as her husband. The story ends when Laura decides to leave behind her white husband to follow the path offered by the indigenous mate. I have always read this as Garro's way of redesigning the outcome of the colonial period. Unlike La Malinche, Garro's Laura does have the opportunity to re-evaluate the behavior of the two husbands and the cultures they represent (Cypess, *La Malinche* 164-67). Garro reminds the reader through the experiences of Laura—and her other female characters of *Los recuerdos del porvenir* that "contemporary Mexican women are still associated with La Malinche's betrayal which determines how the men in society treat them" (166). However, by offering Laura the opportunity to choose a new husband in light of her re-awakened appreciation for indigenous civilization, Garro suggests that a new pattern of behavior for Mexican women is possible.

In the spirit of female possibilities of agency, I would like to refashion the first family of Mexican mestizaje. Since the dominant historical narratives posit the masculine side of the mestizo pair as a European figure, in this transcultural paradigm, the Euroepan male figure would appreciate and respect indigenous culture. For too long, traditional historical discourse has legitimized this "Adam and Eve" pairing that spawned the mestizo as one in which the male-European is read within the Cortés paradigm, that is, as the master figure who conquers the indigenous (female) side and dominates her (the inferior people) in all aspects—culturally, economically, politically. This image is not natural or biologically necessary, for the historical presence of Gonzalo Guerrero offers us a paradigm in which the European male celebrates difference and contributes to diversity and pride of identity. According to the documents we have, Guerrero respected indigenous culture as well as women, and shared a transcultural perspective with La Malinche. With regard to alterity, to the comprehension of "otherness," both Guerrero and Malinche are symbols of mestizaje, of fusion and union and tolerance to the detriment of uniformity, conformity, and bigotry. Therefore, let us not denigrate La Malinche in her role as Mother—progenitor—by equating her only with the negative role models of mothers such as Eve—in her treacherous guise, or Medea, in her murderous mask. Let us not forget or ignore Gonzalo Guerrero, either, since his actions prove that the European male can adapt to an indigenous and female model. I would like to think that with a revisioned Adam and Eve, of two individuals who are experts at transculturation, we have values that do reflect the Mexican mestizo nation.

As a final note, I join with the mexicanas and Chicanas who identify with La Malinche and recognize her accomplishments. La Malinche was at the least, trilingual; because of her intelligence and ability in languages she was able to learn Spanish quickly and add that European tongue to her mastery of Nahuatl

and Maya, the language spoken to this very day by Rigoberta Menchú, the
Nobel Peace Prize laureate. It is not an exaggeration to suggest that La Malinche
is one of the ancestors of this remarkable woman, since like Menchú, La Malinche began as a marginalized figure in a highly stratified society and was able
to break its structured patterns of power relationships and open a space previously closed for women as a spokesperson and as a leader among various male
figures. And like La Malinche, Menchú is being attacked today—"that mouthy,
presumptuous woman." La Malinche may have been a subaltern, but with regard
to alterity, to the comprehension of "otherness," she is the symbol of mestizaje,
of fusion and union and tolerance to the detriment of uniformity, conformity,
and bigotry. Therefore, let us not denigrate La Malinche in her role as Mother—
progenitor—by equating her only with the negative role models of mothers such
as Eve, in her treacherous mask, or Medea, in her murderous mask.

Notes

[1]For the reader who is not familiar with the various texts that have developed the legend surrounding the Malinche figure, detailed analyses of this material can be found in Cypess, Alarcón,
and Storm.

[2]The title "harlot or heroine" is used on an internet site hosted by "Mexico Connect":
http://www.mexconnect.com/mex_/history/malinche.html by Sheep Lintecs.

[3]A number of studies have centered on La Virgen de Guadalupe, see Lafaye and Rodríguez.

[4]For essays dealing in greater detail with conceptions of historical truth in the 16th and 17th centuries, see Adorno and Mignolo.

[5]See León Portilla. *La visión de los vencidos*. Also, the Biblical Matriarch Rachel, who died in
childbirth, is also considered a "weeping mother" who cries out for lost children. Limón adds that
the idea of the woman who is betrayed by an adulterous husband and is motivated by revenge so
as to kill her children are European add-ons (408). See Leal's essay in this volume for further
analysis of this figure and her association with La Llorona.

[6]See Debra A. Castillo for commentary on the idea of "mujer pública" and prostitution (13–14 et
passim).

[7]For a concise discussion of Ortiz's ideas, see Manzoni.

[8]See my "The Figure of La Malinche."

Works Cited

Castillo, Ana. "Extraordinariamente mujer." *La diosa de las Américas : escritos sobre La Virgen de
   Guadalupe*. Ana Castillo, ed. Mariela Dreyfus, trans. New York: Vintage Español, 2000. 24–32.

Cisneros, Sandra. "Guadalupe la diosa del sexo." *La diosa de las Américas:: escritos sobre La Virgen de Guadalupe*. Ana Castillo, ed. Mariela Dreyfus, trans. New York: Vintage Español,
   2000. 55–62.

Bartra, Roger. *La jaula de la melancolía Identidad y metamorfosis del mexicano*. México: Grijalbo, 1987.

Betancourt Pérez, Antonio. *Historia de Yucatán, Mérida*. México: Ediciones del Gobierno de
   Yucatán, 1970.

Cypess, Sandra Messinger. *La Malinche in Mexican Literature: From History to Myth*. Austin: UT
   Press, 1991.

Domecq, Brianda. *Mujer que publica/Mujer pública*. México: Editorial Diana, 1994.

Figueroa Torres, Jesús. *Doña Marina: Una india ejempla. Quince cuadros históricos que son un homenaje a la mujer mexicana.* México: B. Costa Amic, 1975.

Garro, Elena. *Los recuerdos del porvenir.* México: Mortiz, 1963.

Glantz, Margo. "Las hijas de La Malinche." *Esguince de cintura.* México: Consejo Nacional para la Cultura y las Artes, 1994. 178–197.

Janeway, Elizabeth. *Man's World, Woman's Place: a study in social mythology.* New York: Morrow, 1971.

Kanellos, Nicolás. "La llorona de Alurista." *Otros mundos otros fuegos: Fantasía y realismo mágico en Iberoamérica.* Donald A Yates, ed. East Lansing: Michigan State U, 1975. 261–264.

Merithew, Charlene. *What Do Mexican Women Say? Contemporary Essayists Fight For Women's Rights.* Ph.D. Diss. University of Maryland, College Park, 1999.

Robles, Martha. "El camino de las voces". *Espiral de voces.* México, UNAM, 1993. 13–22.

Rosenbaum, Brenda. *With Our Heads Bowed:: The Dynamics of Gender in A Maya Community.* Institute for Mesoamerican Studies, University at Albany, State University of New York: Distributed by UT Press, 1993

Foundational Motherhood: Malinche/Guadalupe in Contemporary Mexican and Chicana/Chicano Culture

Rolando J. Romero

Santa Malinche, madre de nos . . .

Malinche Global. La Malinche (Hernán Cortés's mistress and translator) has figured prominently in discussions of Latin American, Mexican, and Chicano identity. Appearing first in the sixteenth-century chronicles of conquest, she reappeared, according to Chicana critic Norma Alarcón, during the nineteenth century as Latin American intellectuals attempted (right after the successful movements of independence from Spain) to explain why a handful of soldiers were able to conquer the vast Aztec and Inca empires. Used as a scapegoat, the *Criollo* elite made La Malinche responsible for the conquest of the Americas.[1]

Malinche appeared again during the modern period in Mexico, used by Mexican Nobel Laureate Octavio Paz to explain the nature of Mexican identity and the Spanish cultural legacy. La Malinche (now cast as an Eve) became the prototypical mother of the new Mexican mestizo race. Mexican feminism, represented by Rosario Castellanos, linked Malinche's story, not to the events of the conquest but to the victimization of women by women. Castellanos recast La Malinche as a simple victim of patriarchal motherhood, sold by her Aztec mother who threw herself into the arms of the usurper and stepfather, after killing Malinche's father, "assassinated,/ ah, by poison, a dagger,/ a snare before his feet, a noose" (Castellanos 96). Though Castellanos herself does not register the birth of a stepbrother, much of subsequent criticism does, thus providing a motive for the staging of Malinche's death. Roger Bartra, in his "A la chingada" chapter of his famous *La jaula de la melancolía* describes the moment:

> Malintzin fue hija de los caciques de Painala; siendo pequeña murió su padre y su madre se casó con otro cacique, de quien tuvo un hijo. Aquí se inicia la historia de traiciones femeninas: la madre de Malintzin, para deshacerse de ella y asegurar la herencia del cacicazgo a su nuevo hijo, la regaló a unos indígenas de Xicalango aunque anunció que había muerto: los de Xicalango la dieron posteriormente a los de Tabasco, y éstos se la regalaron a Cortés. (Bartra 178)

Malintzin was the daughter of the lords of Painala; while still a child her father died and her mother married another man, with whom she had a child. Here the story of feminine betrayals starts: Malintzin's mother, to get rid of her daughter and to guarantee the inheritance of the lordship for the new child, gave her away to some Indians from Xicalango even though she announced that Malinche had died: the people of Xicalango later gave Malinche away to the people of Tabasco, and they in turn gave her to Cortés. (My translation)

Through readings of Rosario Castellanos, and in an attempt to reclaim positive cultural figures for women, Chicana critics and creative writers also came to the fore, re-interpreting Malinche as an archetypal figure who allegorized the Chicana and Chicano condition: bilingual, bicultural, racialized, etc.

Mexican writers continued thinking of La Malinche as a cultural figure manipulated by the power of the state. Willebaldo López, in his play *Malinche Show!* (1980) characterized La Malinche as a 400-year-old woman kept alive by the Revolutionary Party in Mexico (in power for over 70 years).

Te queremos, te queremos,	We want
Te queremos explotar	to exploit you,
Por eso es tonto que pienses	It's silly for you to think
Que nos podemos llenar.	we could ever have enough.
Te daremos mil cariños	We will pamper you,
Masajes y bienestar	Massage you and make you feel well
Vitaminas y calmantes	We'll give you vitamins and sedatives,
Para que puedas durar.	so you can remain alive.
Cuatro siglos tienes viva	You have been alive four centuries,
Y te bajamos la edad	And we lower your age
Pero mil años nosotros	but for a thousand years
Te debemos conservar.	we want to conserve you among us.
Te queremos, te queremos	We want
Te queremos explotar	to exploit you,
Por eso es tonto que pienses	it's silly for you to think
Que nos podemos llenar.	we could ever have enough.
Masajes, ajustes, chequeos y pastillas	Massages, adjustments, check-ups and pills,
Calmantes y alguna excitante inyección	Sedatives, and an exciting shot
Con gusto te damos Malinche querida	We will gladly give you, Malinche Dear,
Henchidos de gozo y veraz devoción	full of joy and devotion.
Somos todos tuyos	We belong to you,
Somos tu creación. (7)	we are your creation. (My translation)

For Willebaldo López, Malinche is literally a puppet of transnationalism, and globalization.[2] In his *Malinche Show!* one of the characters states:

¡Querídismos amigos! . . . Están ustedes de nuevo ante el programa que tanto han favorecido con su atención. ¡El Malinche Show! Un programa con todos los ingredientes extranjeros que usted necesita. Un programa para olvidar miserias que tiene a su alrededor. Piense en otro mundo ajeno al suyo, un mundo ajeno a su realidad. ¿Su realidad? ¿Para qué la quiere conocer? Es fea. Distráigase con la fantasía de otros países que le presenta la televisión, el cine, las fotonovelas, el teatro. Siempre que sean cosas que estén lo más lejos de la verdad. Y ese es precisamente el fin que nuestro programa tiene para con ustedes. . . . ¡Nada de realidad! Pero antes de inciar de lleno nuestro programa, tengo un importante mensaje para usted. Amigos inversionistas extranjeros, tiene aquí un campo abierto para invertir! Les damos todo, todo. . . . Y si les va muy mal, no se preocupen. Nosotros los subsidiamos. ¡Vengan! ¡Vengan! Yo les ayudaré a conquistar nuestra nación. (56)

(Dear Friends, you are now watching your favorite program, *Malinche Show*. A show with all the foreign ingredients you need. A program to forget the misery around you. Think of a world outside your own reality. Your reality? Why do you want to know it? It is ugly. Enjoy yourself with the fantasy of other countries brought to you by television, film, soap operas, theater. As long as they are things far from reality. And that is precisely the purpose of our show. No reality. But before we begin I have an important message. Foreign investors, you have an open field to invest. We give you everything, everything. And if things go bad for you, do not worry. We will subsidize you. Come! Come! I will help you conquer our nation.)

In retrospect, more than twenty years after the publication of the López play, Malinche appeared right at the moment of the José López Portillo (1976–1982) devaluation of the currency, when Mexico had experienced the first real post-oil boom economic crisis. In the United States we associate the era with Reaganomics, the rise of Madonna, and her "material girl" persona that unashamedly sought both wealth and gender equality. The era of globalization had begun, Mexico, self-sufficient no more, confronted the crisis by looking north, and privatizing many of the government owned companies (except for the most profitable one, PEMEX).

More recent texts, right after the approval of the North American Free Trade Agreement again used La Malinche to explain the "dilution" of Mexican cultural identity. Both Carlos Fuentes in "Malintzin de las maquilas" (1995) ("Malintzin of the maquilas") and Victor Hugo Rascón Banda in his play *Malinche* (2000) spoke of doña Marina as the archetypal person who would aid the enemy rather than protecting one's own culture. Again, the authors characterized her actions as treason under the tenets of globalization and the evils of the neo-liberal Mexican economy.

In Fuentes's short story, Malinche becomes one of the typical women workers in the border cities abused by the new economy of low wages, labor abuse, sexual harassment, substandard housing, and the dream of crossing over to the United States. The characters appear, disappear, and cross paths. Fuentes does not structure the story as an exacting historical allegory; Marina appears as a peon in the empire of Leonardo Barroso, while no personification of Cortés appears (is it perhaps Leonardo Barroso?, or the "gringos" with whom this border Artemio Cruz deals with?) nor does one find the dreams of conquest of territory, nor the quest for the riches of a new empire. The *prestanombres* here appear as in Fuentes's other work. And the narrator describes the maquiladoras for those who may not know exactly how a maquiladora functions:

> Las maquiladoras que le permitían a los gringos ensamblar textiles, juguetes, motores, muebles, computadoras y televisores con partes fabricadas en los EEUU, ensambladas en México con trabajo diez veces menos caro que allá, y devueltas al mercado norteamericano del otro lado de la frontera con el sólo pago de un impuesto al valor añadido: de esas cosas ellas no sabían mucho. (136)

> The outbound plants allowed the gringos to assemble textiles, toys, engines, furniture, computers and television sets with parts manufactured in the United States, assembled in Mexico with labor ten times less expensive, and returned to the North American market on the other side of the border with just payment of the value added tax: of those things they knew very little.

As in Fuentes's other texts ("El hijo de Andrés Aparicio" comes to mind about Tlatelolco and the 1968 student massacre) the Mexican elite abuses, manipulates, and discards the working class, when no longer needed. Most of the inhabitants of the colonias live in a deterministic world where eventually a sacrificial lamb will catalyze a resolution (remember the fire in *La región más transparente?*)

In Fuentes's "Malintzin" no Martín Cortés personifies the forging of a new race (". . . pero Marina no tenía hijos, un hijo, ésa era la diferencia" (133) [. . . but Marina did not have children, a child, that was the difference]. Marina, barren like the desert of Chihuahua, ". . . era sola y más valía seguir sola en esta vida que pasar las penas de los que tenían hijos y sufrían . . ." (157) [. . . she was alone, and better to continue living alone in this life than to undergo the sorrows of those who had children and suffered]. The author means for Marina's infertility to signify a loss. But another character, Dinorah, does have a child, a child she leaves at home, tied to the furniture since she cannot afford day care. The rope meant to keep the child tied to the house, the reader will find, will strangle this child.

This cord, the most prevalent symbol throughout the short story, becomes at once a symbol of tie to the mother, a symbol of loss, a symbol of nation, and consequently, a phallic symbol. This umbilical cord/rope binds the child to the house; the cord also ties the *hábito* that María Candelaria wears (again, around her waist), and ultimately the rope that strangles the child. It is as though the cord came full circle, at once giving life and taking it away. There is no mistaking this rope, insofar as the house also symbolized the mother, it is only when the rope turns phallic that the fragile situation becomes undone.[3] On a Friday, the women's night out, they attend a male strip show.

> . . . el muchacho empezó a jugar con el cordel . . . me lleva, se rió, pero el Chico Chippendale, bronceado, aceitado, maquillado, sin vello en las axilas, jugó con el cordón como si fuera una serpiente y él un encantador, levantando el cordón, le daba erección . . . pero las muchachas aullaban pidiéndole al boy que les tirara el cordón, el cordón, el cordón, y él se lo pasaba entre las piernas, se lo clavaba debajo del brillante de su ombligo, como un cordón umbilical . . . gritando todas ellas que les diera el cordón, que así se ligara a ellas, su hijo de unas por el cordón, su amante de otras por el cordón. . . . (153)

> (. . . the stripper started playing the cord . . . "you are pulling me," she laughed, but the Chippendale man, tanned, oiled, with make-up, hairless, played with the cord as if it were a serpent and me the charmer picking up the cord, it gave him an erection . . . but the girls screamed asking the boy to throw them the cord, the cord, the cord, and he would slide it under her legs, he would nail it under her belly ring, like an umbilical cord . . . all of them screaming for the cord, they wanted to be tied to her, their child because of the cord, their lover because of the cord . . .)

The cord landing on Dinorah's lap reminds the woman of her child tied to the furniture, upsetting her. A transference occurs here, since the narrator eroticizes the Chippendale dancer, feminizes him (hairless, using makeup, "clávandose el cordón en el ombligo"), thus turning the umbilical cord into the perfect symbol of sexual unity at this point, with male and female characteristics.[4] There is no mistaking the possibility, though, that the umbilical cord, by extension, also represents the very border between the United States and Mexico. Having the phallus in Mexico, means uniting the two countries, and anybody who dares think such thoughts must perish; unleash the God of the Old Testament onto the sinners of Juárez/Gomorrah. With this realization, the story unfolds into its dénouement. Dinorah will run home to find her son strangled. And of course, somehow the very search for a better life causes the tragedy: "Todos los rucos comentaron que en el campo no pasaría, las familias allí siempre tenían quién cuidara a los niños, no era necesario amarrarlos, las cuerdas eran para los perros, los marranos" (157). [All the men commented those accidents could not happen in the countryside, the families there always had someone to take care of the children, it was not necessary to tie them up, ropes were for the dogs and the pigs.]

The death of Dinorah's son will lead Marina to realize she cannot trust Rolando. She will run across the border only to find her man with another woman, only to find that the cellular phone Rolando uses is nothing but a front, it never has any batteries and thus was never functional. Rolando used the very instrument of communication to attract Marina, turning the cell-phone as a signifier of the connection it could not provide. Marina runs back to Juárez, and crosses paths with Leonardo Barroso:

> —Esta ciudad es el desmadre montado sobre el caos —le dijo Barroso a su nuera Michelina cuando se cruzaron con Marina, ella de regreso a Juárez, ellos a su hotel en El Paso. Michelina rió y le besó la oreja al empresario. (160)

> ("This city is chaos mounted upon chaos" Barroso told his daughter-in-law Michelina when they crossed paths with Marina, she coming back to Juárez, they returning to their hotel in El Paso. Michelina laughed and kissed the ear of the entrepreneur.)

In this story, all the liars live in the United States: Rolando, Barroso, Michelina, Rolando's gringa lover. Marina safely returns home, and while crossing the bridge, takes off her shoes. The narrator conveys to the reader how Marina connects to the earth; she likes the feel of her feet on the grass, on the pavement. Given the emphasis on the shoes at the point in which both countries unite, clearly shoes can be read as fetish. Shoes as fetish represent a transfer, the very realization of gender/national difference, "descalzarse" may symbolize truthfulness, but on the other hand we only need to remember Cinderella to understand that she releases the shoe in an exchange, a quid pro quo. Money for sex. In this context the maquiladoras' symbol may be the bordello, Leonardo as the pimp, the women workers as the prostitutes, the gringo entrepreneurs as the Johns. Fuentes echoes Roger Bartra: "La Malinche—en la leyenda mexicana—es la Gran Prostituta pagana . . ." (178) [Malinche—in the Mexican imaginary—is the Great Pagan Whore].

In most border stories, the line between the United States and Mexico functions as a geographical space in which the halves torn asunder reintegrate and reunite. Characters cross the border into the space of unleashed desire, the space in which intellect and emotion can reunite. In "Malintzin de las maquilas," though, the border functions as a space in which the two halves can safely separate and resolve the challenges to the nation. In the traditional fairy tale the reader would be witnessing the hero' return home after the slaying of the dragons to marry the princess and inherit the castle. After crossing the border back into Juárez, "Mexico is safe," Malintzin may be able to proclaim, "I have seen the light!" In his 1826 novel, Félix Varela structures a similar moment of repentance through republican motherhood after the birth of doña Marina's child:

> Con mucha sorpresa y no sin satisfacción del buen religioso, infierno, tormentos, escrúpulos, culpas, reparación, todo cede como por encanto al cariño maternal a la vista del hijo que acaba de nacer. Violenta en sus pasiones y viva y traviesa en sus talentos, esta Americana hubiera podido ser una mujer apre-

ciable sin la corrupción a que se le adiestró desde que se reunió a los españoles. Sin embargo, el tierno amor maternal derramó una dulce tinta sobre sus sentimientos. . . . (90)

(With much surprise and not without the satisfaction of the cleric, inferno, torment, scruples, blame and reparation, everything gives before the mother's love upon the sight of the just-born child. Violent in her passions and alive and mischievous in her talents, this American could have been a worthy woman without the corruption she was taught since she joined the Spaniards. Nonetheless, the tender motherly love spilled a sweet ink over her feelings . . .)

Fuentes redeems and reclaims La Malinche through Juaréz's "desmadre." With the nation at stake, we have gone full circle, from nineteenth-century republican motherhood to twentieth-century republican abortion; better to have no children than to have illegitimate children.

Rascón Banda's more recent play, *Malinche* (2000), was staged in Mexico City, Guanajuato, and the United States. The play was commissioned by Johann Kresnick, a German director, with specific instructions to Rascón Banda to not provide stage directions. Unwittingly, the author himself then becomes a personification of Malinche, serving as the intermediary between Mexican and German cultures. There is no mistaking that the negotiations between the director and the actors, as well as the playwright, become themselves clear allegories of the negotiations between Malinche and Cortés.

In this play, the audience will be hit by a multiplicity of signification, as though it were completely impossible to cast Marina in a single role (there are in fact three Marinas, a young one, an adult one, and an old one.) Since the play jumps back and forth between the past and the present, the Conquest and modern times, Malinche becomes the alter-ego of Mexican culture. In this play Malinche will go to the therapist to discuss her problems, especially the fact that her children hate her. Most of the chapters that provide the historical background on the play (what we would consider the historical information) are staged as a conversation between Marina and the psychoanalyst.

Rascón Banda will use information on La Malinche, from several sources, including Octavio Paz's infamous "Los hijos de La Malinche" from the *Labyrinth of Solitude*. The author will also use the song "La maldición de Malinche" 1975 by Gabino Palomares "se nos quedó el maleficio/ de brindar al extranjero/nuestra fe, nuestra cultura/nuestro pan, nuestro dinero" (20) [We retained the curse/of offering the foreigner/our faith, our culture/our bread, our money] in which the playwright casts doña Marina as "la enfermedad del presente" that Mexico needs to cure: "cuando dejarás mi tierra, cuando harás libre a mi gente" [When will you leave my land, when will you free my people] (Rascón Banda 21).

According to Rascón Banda the Mexican people, because of Malinche's legacy, prefer Halloween to the Day of the Dead, the Mall to the Market, the "Happy Birthday" song to Las Mañanitas (the Mexican happy birthday song), hamburgers to tacos, hot-dogs to tamales. The discussion on Mexican identity based on the easy cultural markers eerily reminds the reader of the time of the Mexican Revolution when the Contemporáneos argued over the notion of Mexico with Diego Rivera's group.

La Malinche, in the play, allegorizes contemporary issues: from the Americanization of Mexican culture, to the conflict in Chiapas, from the insertion of the Partido de Acción Nacional in Mexican politics, to the North American Free Trade Agreement. "Traeremos *La Malinche* al tiempo actual. Será una mujer adelantada a su tiempo, que intente conciliar dos mundos opuestos y construir uno nuevo" (160) [We will bring Malinche to the present. She will be a modern woman, a woman who will bridge opposite worlds and build new ones], declared Rascón Banda.

The "Corrido de Acteal," and subcomandante Marcos's voice in the chapter "El cerco de Tenochtitlán" will lead us directly to the conflict in Chiapas. The massacre of Acteal mimics the massacre when Cortés sends his soldiers to kill the indigenous people at the temple. "La fiesta interrumpida" (117) then becomes an allusion to the Free Trade Agreement. "Ni el aire nos pertenece" (123) also alludes to Chiapas. This play will provide the reader with a crash course in Mexican politics, from the "servilismo" of TELEVISA reporters to the fights between the PRI and the PAN, from Chiapas to Northern Mexico, from colonial times to the 21st century. Few things are left unsaid; in fact, the charge of signification far outweighed the vehicle in which it was presented. There will be no resolution, no attempt at conciliation: Malinche is at once an old lady, a reporter from Televisa, a PRD congresswoman. The incredible multiplicity becomes unbearable at times: corridos, stage props, the old and the new, politics, newspaper articles, critical essays, etc. The list goes on and on. And then came the controversy regarding the staging, the appearance of Vicente Fox in the diary that Rascón Banda puts together. When Fox was asked his opinion regarding the conservative walk-out during the staging of the play in Guanajuato (conservatives were upset over the nudity in the play), Fox answers: "pero ustedes mismos dijeron que la obra no era apta para menores."

Given the state of the scholarship at this point, and especially taking into account the new texts, are we seeing a new characterization of La Malinche, or simply a recasting of the figure within the old paradigms? Or better yet, are we seeing a distinct trend of characterization, a Chicano one, in which La Malinche becomes, in the words of Norma Alarcón, "Guadalupe's monstrous double"? Will Mexican culture then be presented through the Virgin of Guadalupe and Chicano culture through the figure of La Malinche? The revered one versus the outcast, the venerated one versus the treacherous one? The re-casting of La Malinche under the Free Trade Agreement falls back on the traditional

scapegoating of women, and actually continues in the tradition already established by Octavio Paz in the middle of the last century.

Like a Virgin. Contemporary Chicana culture has sought to demystify La
Virgen de Guadalupe. Considered a very positive figure, and the patron saint
of contemporary Chicano culture, she is ironically, Rebolledo writes, "a symbol of failure. In the personal relationship Chicano culture has with its saints,
the Virgin is often seen as not active enough . . . she is also clearly seen as the
image of the unattainable" (191). In Sandra Cisneros's essay, "Guadalupe The
Sex Goddess" the author states that the Virgin of Guadalupe has always been
used in Mexican culture to repress women's sexuality.

> What a culture of denial. Don't get pregnant! But no one tells you how not to.
> This is why I was angry for so many years every time I saw *La Virgen de
> Guadalupe*, my culture's role model for brown women like me. She was damn
> dangerous, an ideal so lofty and unrealistic it was laughable. Did boys have to
> aspire to be Jesus? I never saw any evidence of it. They were fornicating like
> rabbits while the Church ignored them and pointed us women toward our des-
> tiny—marriage and motherhood. The other alternative as *puta*hood. . . .
>
> As far as I could see, *la Lupe* was nothing but a goody two shoes meant to
> doom me to a life of unhappiness. Thanks but no thanks. (Cisneros 48)

Cisneros writes that when she sees the Virgin of Guadalupe, she wants "to
lift her dress as I did my dolls' and look to see if she comes with *chones* and
does her *panocha* look like mine, and does she have dark nipples too? Yes, I
am certain she does" (Cisneros 51). More than irreverence, the author puts
together all the different layers (including the sexual ones) that were repressed
by colonial discourse in the construction of the Virgin of Guadalupe.

As demonstrated by a very public controversy that erupted over Alma
López's painting "Our Lady" in the "Cyber Arte: Tradition Meets Technology"
exhibition at the Museum of International Folk Art in Santa Fe, New Mexico,
Chicanas have been trying to humanize the Virgin, to make her a representation
of their own experiences and their own personal relationship with her.

Alma López depicts the Virgin (Raquel Salinas, a performance artist) not
under the cloak and in a pious stance, but in a state of undress, with her hands
on her hips in seeming defiance of the viewer. One leg in front of the other, the
figure appears to have been caught in mid-step. Wearing a floral bikini she has
undone the cloak, a figuration of the Coyolxauhqui stone (not the cloak with
the stars and constellations that purportedly signal the date of the apparition to
Juan Diego). The Virgin now appears over the figure of a crescent moon being
held by a nude butterfly angel—modeled by Raquel Gutiérrez—(a symbol of
transformation). The church and Chicano activist José Villegas heavily criticized Alma López ("To depict the Virgin Mary in a floral bikini held aloft by
a bare-breasted angel is to be insulting, even sacrilegious, to the many thousands of New Mexicans who have deep religious devotion to Guadalupe," stat-

ed Archbishop Michael J. Sheehan),[5] and actual petitions started circulating to withdraw the painting from the exhibition, with such powerful cultural critics as Tey Diana Rebolledo coming to López's defense. Though Alma López clearly proclaims her intentions with the painting from a feminist perspective much of this intentionality is lost in all but the academic public. In a statement she entitles "Alma López's Respuesta," she writes:

> My intention as an artist was not disrespectful in any way. However, some people in Santa Fe feel offended. Who are those offended? Why do they feel more entitled to this cultural icon than the Chicana/Latina/Hispana women in the exhibition? Why are they unable to make a distinction between an image in a museum and an image in their church? Why is the church in New Mexico targeting this image when they have so many of their own issues?

López goes on to write:

> When [Sandra] Cisneros wonders if the Virgen has a dark Latina vagina and nipples underneath her dress, I imagined roses. Roses were the proof of her apparition to Juan Diego. Abstracted plants and flowers are imprinted on her dress. Among the other symbolism in her depiction and apparition, flowers and roses make the connection to the fact that she is a native. Xochitl is flower. Xochitlalpan is the flower earth place, which can be translated as paradise or heaven. When I imagined the image of "Our Lady," I saw a contemporary representation of a Latina woman covered with flowers.

By undressing the Virgin, López also uncovers the different layers of signification that colonial discourse tried to suppress: the cult of Guadalupe tied to indigenous reverence of Tonantzin, for example. Tey Diana Rebolledo writes that the Catholic Church dropped and denied those traits of Tonatzin it considered inappropriate for the mother of God, especially those "attributes of judging, creating, and destroying"; traits that would deny the centrality of the male figure. Rebolledo believes that "She was independent, wrathful, competent; her power to create and destroy was autonomous, as was that of most of the Nahuatl deities" (190).

By bringing in the cloak of Coyolxauhqui the artist also pays homage to the moon, the traditional feminist symbol supplanted by the sun, Huitzilopochtli. Though López credits Sandra Cisneros's essay on the Virgin of Guadalupe for her "Our Lady" painting, it is clear that it represents the aesthetics of Chicana feminism; especially Cherríe Moraga's "La fuerza femenina," in which, the figure of Huitzilopochtli's sister, Coyolxauhqui, decapitated by the god when Coyolxauhqui discovers that her mother Coatlicue is pregnant, rises up to the heavens as the moon.[6]

One of the most prominent artists to demythify the Virgin has been Yolanda López, whose "Portrait of the Artist as the Virgin of Guadalupe" (1978),

Figure 1. Yolanda López, "Portrait of the Artist as the Virgin of Guadalupe, 1978 Guadalupe Series." Printed with permission of the author.

Figure 2. Yolanda López, "Walking Guadalupe, 1978" *Fem* Cover (June–July, 1984). Printed with permission of the author.

and her 1984 cover of *Fem* are the most well known. (See figures 1 and 2.) The "Portrait" shows the figure of a woman in a running stance, wearing running sneakers, and stepping over the fallen angel whose wings represent the colors of the US flag. The figure now uses the cloak like a banner, and holds the snake in a grip. Though sometimes the snake is seen as a phallic symbol, in a lot of the pre-Columbian iconography, the serpent (as in Coatlicue) in reality represents the Earth and fertility. Thus, holding the snake in a grip actually indicates control of the power of creation.

López's most controversial works remains that of the cover that appeared on a special issue of *Fem*, in which the Virgin wears a shorter skirt and high heels, still with her hands held together as if in prayer. Lucy Lippard states that when the journal appeared in Mexico, the offices of *Fem* received death threats (42). The intention of the artist, as detailed by Lippard, also signals the artist's need to recast the Virgin "as an Indian, instead of a Mediterranean, a nice Jewish girl from the sixteenth century" (42). Ironically, Lippard does not get past López's intention, and does not explain the most visible changes in the figure, and what they may symbolize.

César Augusto Martínez's *Mona Lupe* (1992) decentralizes Western discourse by planting the face and posture of the Mona Lisa on the figure of the Virgin of Guadalupe.

Martínez's connection to the Mona Lisa comes both from the title of the painting and from the similarity in the position of the hands. Now it is an indigenous woman standing over the crescent moon, still blocking the rays of the sun. The cactus is positioned in the place of the angel, while the smile/smirk is gone. Most of the changes, in all of the recreations, have to do with the repositioning of the limbs: arms, legs and hands. The legs allow for the representation of movement. Agency, action, and determination seem to be the qualities artists are most looking for.

I must point out that México does not echo the rewriting of Guadalupe. Juan Francisco Urrusti's *A Long Journey to Guadalupe* (1996) for example, takes an anthropological look at the poor people's reverence of the Virgin, but does not engage at a revisionist history. Though it provides all the historical information concerning the construction of the myth, it re-affirms the virgin as mother, as protector, as symbol in what Norma Alarcón calls "Utopic moments" (Mexican Independence, Chicano Civil Rights Movement, etc.) (See "Traduttora").

In another instance, José Luis Barrios, writing about the election of Vicente Fox, states that ". . . on the day of his swearing in (December 1, 2000), the very first activity on his agenda was a visit to the Basílica de Guadalupe, where he kneeled before the Virgin prior to departing for the chamber of deputies in San Lázaro for the inauguration ceremony. The following day, the newspaper *La Jornada* published [the] images . . ." (33–34)

Monstrous Double. In her groundbreaking article "Traduttora, Tradito-

ra," Norma Alarcón writes that Malinche and Guadalupe represent different
versions of mediation:

> Guadalupe and Malintzin almost always have been viewed as oppositional
> mediating figures, though the precise moment of inception may well elude us.
> On the one hand, Guadalupe has come to symbolize transformative powers
> and sublime transcendence and is the standard carried into battle in utopical-
> ly inspired moments. Always viewed by believers as capable of transforming
> the petitioner's status and promising sublime deliverance, she transports us
> beyond or before time. On the other hand, Malintzin represents feminine sub-
> version and treacherous victimization of her people because she was a trans-
> lator in Cortés's army. Guadalupe and Malintzin have become a function of
> each other. (289)

Following Alarcón, it is clear that the revision of Malinche affects the
characterization of Guadalupe, since they are so intrinsically tied together.
Thus, as Mexico seeks to reify the reverence to Guadalupe while scapegoating
Malinche, the exact moment shows a concomitant reverence of Malinche and
irreverence towards Guadalupe in Chicano culture.

Cherríe Moraga writes in "A Long Line of Vendidas," "the sexual legacy
passed down to the Mexicana/Chicana is the legacy of betrayal, pivoting
around the historical/mythical female figure of Malintzin Tenepal" (99). Moraga goes on to argue that "the woman who defies her role as subservient to her
husband, father, brother, or son by taking control of her own sexual destiny is
purported to be a 'traitor to her race' by contributing to the 'genocide' of her
people—whether or not she has children" (113).

Opting for La Malinche as a mother becomes a conscious choice. "Yo soy
La Malinche," cries Carmen Tafolla:

> But Chingada I was not
> > Not tricked, not screwed, not traitor.
> For I was not traitor to myself——
> > I saw a dream
> > > And I *reached* it.
> > > > Another world . . .
> > > > > la raza
> > > > > > la raaaaa-zaaaaa (Rebolledo 1993).[7]

Tey Diana Rebolledo details the four ways in which La Malinche is represented in Chicana and Chicano culture: 1) La Malinche taken by the conqueror and
raped; 2) La Malinche representative of the conquest of the indigenous groups
by the Europeans; 3) La Malinche as language mediator; 4) La Malinche as
survivor (193). The articulation of these obvious connotations and historical
attributions to the figure guide the interpretion of La Malinche as allegorical

of contemporary culture. For example, in *American Me*, the initial sequence of the rape of the mother during the Zoot Suit Riots leads to the child's isolation. The father, who knows the child is the product of the rape, isolates him, pushing him into a life of crime. Rape begets rape. The central character will himself be raped in jail (*la maldición de Malinche*—as though the violation of the male body in a homosexual rape were any more violent than that of a woman). The ensuing hybridity, determinism, despair, and death, are all consequences of the initial rape. Thus, when Chicana and Chicano culture constructs Cortés as "White" (Moraga), then clearly the projection of culture to La Malinche describes Chicano culture as colonized, conquered, and "raped" by the Anglo-American culture.

The emphasis on La Malinche as *lengua* (the sixteenth-century term to refer to her translation skills), has now turned into a symbol for voice, for sexuality, and language mediation:

> la lengua que necesito
> para hablar
> es la misma que uso
> para acariciar (Moraga, *Loving* 149).

The question of "selling out" to the dominant culture reflects the Chicano cultural fear of assimilation, especially through education. Adaljiza Sosa-Riddell's "Cómo duele" clearly articulates this view as the poetic voice tries to reconnect with Chicano culture. The voice of a Berkeley student ("I was at Berkeley, where,/ there were too few of us") talks to a "you" who may be either a Chicano nationalist, or Chicanismo itself: "I found you, Chicano,/ but only for a moment,/ Never para siempre./ Temilotzin died the morning after,/ Malinche./ It's too late" (Rebolledo 214).

To conclude, one of the consistent Chicana anxieties regarding La Malinche, as in Moraga, is the question of the binds that tie Chicanos to Chicanas, brothers to sisters. Because of the exclusion of Latinas during the Civil Rights Movement, Chicano nationalism and feminism did not see eye to eye. Thus, if Bartra regroups the mother figure into what he calls the "ChingaLupe" (he put Humpty Dumpty together again), Chicanas have turned this "monstrous double" into "Malinche Coyolxauhqui."[8] Cerezita in Moraga's *Heroes and Saints* feminizes the decapitation as a symbol of loss of territory and Chicana and Chicano subject fragmentation. The myth of Coyolxauhqui also brings back the original sibling rivalry: the moon, and the sun, the daughter and the son, Huitzilopochtli. "My brother's sex was white, mine brown" writes Moraga (*Loving* 90). This original moment, though, can also be constructed as symbolic of a struggle between Euro-American and Chicana/Chicano cultures, between the English and Spanish languages, between identity and difference. The haves and have-nots has always cut in more than one-way.

Notes

[1]See especially *Jicoténcal* in the Arte Público edition that includes Luis Leal's attribution to Félix Varela. The English translation does not attribute authorship to Varela.

[2]Cypess does a tremendous job of interpreting the texts published prior to 1991, the publication of her book. My intent here is to simply add the most recent works to the discussion.

[3]Marjorie Garber writes in *Sex and Real Estate*: "The longstanding symbolic association between houses and women . . . is partly an extension of the cult of domesticity and partly a 'literal' reading of women's sexuality as something enclosed and interior." She continues later on in the same section: "In nineteenth- and twentieth-century novels the mother often becomes the home, to such an extent that when she dies the house itself seems to die as well" (59).

[4]The feminizing of the male body occurs at the point of contact between two patriarchal cultures.

[5]All of the information in this section comes from http://www.almalopez.net/ artist.html, Alma López's webpage. The artist states that the statement will be published in Aztlán.

[6]Alma López's "Lupe and Sirena" series could actually be construed as much more controversial. The "Lupe and Sirena" in Aztlán, for example, clearly depict the Virgin holding Sirena in a romantic/sexual embrace. In her "December 12, Iris print on canvas, 1999" the Coyolxauhqui stone stands behind the central figure.

[7]Judy Baca depicts hybridity in her "La mestizaje." The modern woman, who centers the painting, sheds masks that represent the indigenous and the mestiza, to reveal the precolombian behind her.

[8]Title of a painting by Cristina Cárdenas.

Works Cited

Alarcón, Norma. "Traduttora, Traditora: A Paradigmatic Figure of Chicana Feminism." Dangerous Liasons. . . .

American Me. Dir. [director] [distributor], [year].

Bartra, Roger. *La jaula de la melancolia: Identidad y metamorfosis del mexicano*. México: Grijalbo, 1987.

Barrios, José Luis. "Iconography Past and Present: Visual Constructions of Power in Post-PRI Mexico." *Discourse* 23.2 (Summer 2001): 26–43.

Castellanos, Rosario. "Malinche." *A Rosario Castellanos Reader*. Ed. Maureen Ahern. Austin: UT Press, 1988. 96–97.

Cisneros, Sandra. "Guadalupe the Sex Goddess." Ana Castillo, ed. *Goddess of the Americas: Writings on the Virgin of Guadalupe*. New York: Riverhead Books, 1997. 46–51.

Fuentes, Carlos. "Malintzin de las maquilas." *La frontera de cristal*. México: Alfaguara, 1995. 129–160.

Garber, Marjorie B. *Sex and Real Estate: Why We Love Houses*. New York: Pantheon Books, 2000.

Lippard, Lucy R. *Mixed Blessings: New Art In A Multicultural America*. New York: Pantheon Books, 1990.

López Guzmán, Willebaldo. *Malinche show!* Mexico: Ediciones del Sindicato de Trabajadores del INFONAVIT, 1980.

Messinger Cypess, Sandra. *La Malinche in Mexican Literature: From History to Myth*. Austin: UT Press, 1991.

Moraga, Cherríe. "A Long Line of Vendidas." *Loving in the War Years*. Boston: South End Press, 1983. 89–144.

_____. "La fuerza femenina." *The Last Generation*. Boston: South End Press, 1993. 65–86.

Rascón Banda, Víctor Hugo. *La Malinche*. México: Plaza y Janés, 2000.

Rebolledo, Tey Diana, and Eliana Rivero, eds. *Infinite Divisions: An Anthology of Chicana Literature*. Tucson: U of Arizona P, 1993.

Urrusti, Juan Francisco. *A Long Journey to Guadalupe*. México: Instituto Nacional Indigenista, 1996.

Varela, Félix. *Jicoténcal*. 1826. Houston: Arte Público Press, 1995.

_____. *Xicoténcatl : An Anonymous Historical Novel About the Events Leading Up to the Conquest of The Aztec Empire*. Trans. Guillermo I. Castillo-Feliú. Austin: UT Press, 1999.

Malinche's Revenge

Alicia Gaspar de Alba

> *The woman shrieking along the littered bank of the*
> *Río Grande is not sorry. She is looking for revenge.*
> *Centuries she has been blamed for the murder of her*
> *child, the loss of her people, as if Tenochtitlan*
> *would not have fallen without her sin. History*
> *does not sing of the conquistador who prayed*
> *to a white god as he pulled two ripe hearts*
> *out of the land.*[1]

In Chicano/a popular culture La Malinche is as much an iconic figure as the Pachuco or the *vato loco,* even though they embody diametrically opposite identity politics. Whereas the Pachuco in his stylized drapes, bilingual patois, and street-wise attitude came to signify Chicano pride and *carnalismo,* as well as resistance to assimilation and stereotyping, La Malinche, or people who are labeled Malinches or Malinchistas, signifies betrayal to everything that the *vato,* the Pachuco, the *carnal,* and the "homey" represent. In short, she is a traitor to Chicanismo.

Chicanos did not invent this treacherous view of La Malinche. That was inherited from Mexican patriarchy and its "colonial imaginary,"[2] to use the term coined by Chicana historian, Emma Pérez. Nowhere is there a better example of the colonial imaginary than Octavio Paz's interpretation of La Malinche. For Paz, the self-proclaimed guru on the Mexican mind, Malinche is "La Chingada," the violated mother, the seed of shame that every Mexican, but especially every Mexican male, carries inside him and which is, to a large degree, responsible for his Mexican fatalism and continued colonization. In her analysis of Paz's essay, "Sons of La Malinche,"[3] Emma Pérez refers to Paz as "el Chingón" (the great fucker) with a major castration complex, and reinterprets his interpretation of La Malinche (the primordial "Chingada" or fuck-ee) from a Chicana working-class lesbian vantage point.

To Paz, the Aztec princess Malinche "gave" herself to Hernán Cortés, the symbol of the Spanish Conquest, therefore, Paz charges her with the downfall of Mexico. In Paz, we have the symbolic son, the mestizo, repudiating the

symbolic father, Cortés. The Oedipal triangle is completed by *la india* that
they both raped and tamed, literally and metaphorically. . . . For Paz, *la india*
personifies the passive whore who acquiesced to the Spaniard, the conqueror,
his symbolic father—the father he despises for choosing an inferior woman
who begat an inferior race, and the father he fears for his powerful phallus.[4]

Thus, the Mexican mestizo son is as reviled by the European father as the
Pachuco is reviled by the Mexican father; the former because of his Indian (i.e.
inferior, uncivilized, licentious) mother, the latter because of the loss of language and culture that results from life in the belly of beast. In this case, the
Pachuco "becomes" in an existential way, like La Malinche, selling
herself/himself to the white conqueror and thereby betraying his Mexican patrimony. Despite the mestizo son's fear of the all-powerful white father, however, he is born with the father's gender privilege and the mother's racial stigma.

Let me attempt, here and in the triangulated figure below, to deconstruct
the Oedipal-conquest triangle that Pérez places as a template over Octavio
Paz's rendition of Malinche's history. At the pinnacle of the triangle, of course,
sits the white father, the colonizer, the political and ideological power of the
State symbolically represented in Mexico by the conquistador, Hernán Cortés.
At the bottom left and right sit, respectively, the Indian mother—La Chingada, the Mexican Eve, the conquered land that is the foundation of Mexican
nationalism—and the fruit of the union between the white father and the Indian mother—the bastard mestizo son. The son is the crossroads not only of two
races, but also of two mutually contradictory qualities: machismo, the power
of the phallus, and nationalism, the veneration of the mother, churn inside him
like cultural schizophrenia. Etymologically, the word nationalism springs from
nation, which itself springs from the Latin word *natio,* which means birth,
nation, and people. We could say, then, that while machismo is an overt manifestation of the Father's supremacy, i.e., patriarchy, nationalism is a fierce
allegiance to the womb (the land) that gave birth to the mestizo son. But the
mestizo son loves and hates his white father, loves and hates his Indian mother. Is loyal to both of them at the same time that he rejects their imposition on
his character: the father's rape which gave birth to him, the mother's passivity
and weakness in which he sees himself reflected. By choosing patriarchal privilege over racial roots, by promoting the white father's disavowal of that which
is indigenous and female or in any way open and penetrable, the mestizo son
attempts to become *like* the father, at the same time that he is spurned by the
father because of the marker of his inferiority, the color of his skin, the
intractable and irreducible trace of La Chingada. Hence, his phallus, though
strong in the service of patriarchy and in the domination of women, can never
compare to the father's, can never achieve the same level of power and privilege. As Emma Pérez explains:

Within a racist society, the mestizo male is a castrated man in relation to the white-male colonizer father. His anxiety is not only reduced to the fear of losing [the phallus], but also to the fear that his will never match the supreme power of the white man's. While the white son has the promise of becoming the father, the mestizo, even when he becomes the father, is set apart by his skin color and by a lack of language, the dominant language of the colonizer. Moreover, he must repudiate *la india y la mestiza* for fear that he could be like her, a weak, castrated betrayer of his people. Hence, he colludes with the white-colonizer-father as they both condemn la Chicana.

The conquest triangle dictates the sexual politics of miscegenation in the twentieth century.[5]

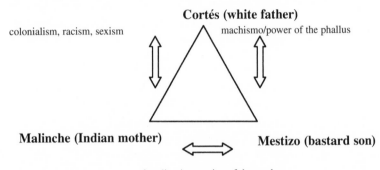

Cortés (white father)

colonialism, racism, sexism   machismo/power of the phallus

Malinche (Indian mother)   **Mestizo (bastard son)**

nationalism/veneration of the mother

The Conquest Triangle[5]

The Mexican Caste System

The Mexican colonial imaginary constructs betrayal to the culture as betrayal to the race, original sin *a-lo-mexicano*. In the popular 1997 telenovela, "María Isabel," for example, we find the story of a supposed Indian woman who falls in love with her "white" employer.[6] The Malinche, in this case, is not the Indian woman who is, after all, just looking to move up in the racial hierarchy, and thus, to improve the lot of her children by whitewashing the race; the real Malinche, or traitor, is the rich patrón who betrays his culture, his class, and especially his race by marrying someone lower on the totem pole of the racial caste system: a Huichol Indian woman.

We need not dwell on the fact that the actress chosen to portray the Huichol protagonist (Adela Noriega) has more of a European than an indigenous phenotype (the producers probably couldn't find any "real" Indian actresses to audition for the part).[6] What is significant here is the way this late 20th-century popular narrative illustrates the long-term legacy of the infamous "sistema de castas" by which racial relations were determined in colonial New Spain. As defined by R. Douglas Cope in his book, *The Limits of Racial Domination,* the "sistema de castas" was "a hierarchical ordering of racial groups according to their proportion of Spanish blood."[7] The taxonomy was based on 7 general racial categories (which included skin color, facial features, body types, and hair textures): thus, *criollo* was a Spaniard born in New Spain; an *indio* was a native of Mexico; a *negro* was an African; a *mestizo* was a product of Spanish and Indian miscegenation; a *mulato* was a product of Spanish and African miscegenation; a *castizo* was a product of Spaniard and mestizo mixing; a *morisco* was a product of Spaniard and mulatto mixing. From these 7 general categories, more than 40 different types of racial mixtures were traced, each one indicative of a different shading, or color, and given, as above, a separate name. The most removed from Spanish blood were, of course, at the bottom of the hierarchy, and this meant that Blacks were at the bottom of the scale, for it was believed that eventually the Indian castes would "whiten" up after enough generations of intermarriage, whereas the same was ostensibly not true of the Black castes. Even Blacks intermarrying with Spaniards (mulattos) would not "whiten" in the same way that Indians intermarrying with Spaniards would; as Blacks were the most cohesive of the castes, they tended to intermarry within their own category or with mulattos, metizos, and Indians—none of which really improved or "whitened" their status.

New Spain, upon which the Mexican nation was founded, operated under this caste system until Mexico's independence from Spain in the early 19th century, but even after Mexican independence, the caste system was in effect, that is to say, those in power were still the white-skinned, land-owning criollos and their servants were still the dark-skinned indios, mestizos, mulattos, and they continued to "own" black slaves until 1829. The fact that they were all "Mexican," that is, part of the sovereign nation of Mexico, did not liberate anybody from the racial ideology of the "sistema de castas." This ideology is still in effect, as we see amply represented in Mexico's cultural production, be that the writings of its Nobel Laureate, Octavio Paz, or the mass culture narrative of a telenovela.

In the Chicano colonial imaginary, on the other hand, betrayal to the culture is tracked along the axis of gender rather than race. As representatives of the new mestizaje, Chicanos inherited the colonial father's racial stigma against the Indian inside them, at the same time that claiming their Indian-ness was the very source of Chicano pride, a pride and a politics that were encoded into the Chicano label itself. Because the Indian-ness is associated with the feminine gender, however, and because Chicanos, too, are "hijos de La Chingada," it became necessary to transgender the Indian inside them, to transform the root of their pride from something passive and feminine, like Malinche, into something aggressive and masculine like an Aztec emperor, Moctezuma, or the Aztec god of war, Huitzilopochtli, or, the prototypical Chicano calendar image of an Aztec warrior named Popocatéptl carrying his fallen maiden, Ixxtacihuatl.[8] To this day, this iconography, overdetermined as it became in the

imagery of the Chicano Art Movement, continues to represent Chicano political beliefs and values. Embedded in that iconography is not only the repudiation of Malinche and her daughters, but also, the reenactment of the colonial
father's rape and the mestizo son's disdain for his Indian mother. Elizabeth
"Betita" Martínez, a hard-core *veterana* of the Movement, calls this "chingón
politics" in *De Colores Means all of us.*

> The concept of Aztlán has always been set forth in super-macho imagery. The
> Chicano activist today rarely sees taking Aztlán as a concrete goal but might
> like to imagine himself garbed in an Aztec warrior outfit, looking ferociously
> brave next to some red-lipped princess with naked breasts. If you note the
> whiff of sexual possession there, it's no accident. As often applied, the con-
> cept of Aztlán encourages the association of machismo with domination.[9]

What we need to remember, however, is that the image here is a Chicano
version of Michelangelo's "Pietà," which depicts the virginal blessed Mother
holding her fallen, sacrificial son. By changing the image of the son for that of
a bare-breasted Aztec princess, by reinscribing the bereaved mother into a brave
Nahua warrior, super-macho Chicano activists who find themselves represented by the image are, in reality, identifying with the mother rather than with the
son of the original image. The implicit and ironic message here: Chicanos/as
survive because the mother survives, not the other way around. Chingón politics are really the mother's politics, *la primera madre,* La Malinche.

Chingona Politics

Mujeres of the Chicano Movement had three roles to play, "the 'three' f's,"
as Cherríe Moraga has put it: "feeding, fighting, and fucking."[10] Their job was
to struggle beside, behind, and beneath their men in *la lucha* for race- and class-
consciousness in white "Amerikkka." The other job, of course, was procreation,
to breed more Raza for the struggle. "It reminds us painfully of how, within the
movement, Juana usually stayed home with the kids or typed the minutes or
nursed a domestic black eye while her *mero cabrón* played Aztec chieftain,"
writes Elizabeth Martínez."[11] Thus, *feministas* in the early days of *el* Movimiento—that is, women who believed they should have more of a role in *la* Causa
than typing up the minutes or making the food for the meetings, or having the
future Emilianos and Panchitos of the Movement—those *mujeres* were said to
be dividing the Movement and spouting Anglo middle-class beliefs that had no
place in the life of Raza. They were called men-haters and *agringadas* and sell-
outs because, in seeking equality with men and personal liberation for themselves as women, they were accused of putting the individual before the culture.
Rather than working toward cultural nationalism and the empowerment of the
Raza brotherhood, they were said to be polluting the Movement from within
and splitting up the Chicano Holy (not to mention heterosexual) Familia. For

this opposition they were ridiculed, humiliated, and consistently harassed by the men and their female loyalists. To make matters even more interesting, it was rumored among the more paranoid of the Chicano leadership that *feministas* were actually FBI infiltrators seeking to undermine the revolution.[12]

Traitors, infiltrators, wannabe *gabachas,* and reactionaries against the true goals of Chicano liberation—all Malinche traits ascribed to women who wanted their *hermanos* and *hermanas* of La Raza to practice the politics of liberation they were preaching to apply to all Raza. Did this make them *chingonas?* Possibly, but not in the "common" sense in which that term is understood when it applies to women; not in the sense that they had penis-envy and wanted to strap on a visible manifestation of male power.

The Laws of the Penis

Defined broadly, feminism is fundamentally a politics of resistance against patriarchy, and in a patriarchy, men are in power and women are their subordinates. If we break the word down, we get *Patri,* or Father, and *Archy,* or supremacy; thus patriarchy is a social organization based upon the supremacy of the Father. In a patriarchal social order, those who are like the Father— that is, male, but especially, white, rich, heterosexual males—are privileged over those who are unlike the Father—that is female, non-white, non-rich, non-heterosexual. What gives the Father his power is the phallus, the penis, which he passes on to his sons, and they to their sons, and so on across the centuries. The mother figures into the transaction, of course, but only as the carrier of the Father's seed, as the vessel through which the son (and future Father) comes into being. Because the mother has no penis, she is not allowed a leadership role in patriarchy, nor does she get to participate in the making of the laws that perpetuate that order, the laws of the Father.

Although the laws of the Father are inclusive and do not just pertain to family relations, it is the male-dominated family, in which the father is superior to the mother, the son to the daughter, the brother to the sister, the uncle to the aunt, the nephew to the niece, etc., which comprises the primary unit through which the laws of the Father become established as normative and natural. But because they are fundamentally about domination, the laws of the Father apply to every facet of the social system—from governance to education, from religion to popular culture, from foreign policy to fashion, from sex to gender, from class to race. Everywhere we look, in any page of Western history, we see the laws of the Father enacted.

Conquest of the so-called New World was the enactment of the laws of the Father, in this case, the European, capitalist-driven, Christian fathers of Western civilization. Colonization is also based on the laws of the rich white Father. So is Manifest Destiny. So is the Treaty of Guadalupe-Hidalgo. So is Operation Wetback. So is NAFTA. All of these are ways in which the white male penis perpetuates and enforces its power to rule over its subjects—be they women, or people of color, or indigenous inhabitants of the lands He wants to conquer, or the poor, or those whose sexual practices fail to conform to the symbolic order of reproduction. The importance of reproduction, we must remember, is not only to propagate the human race, but also to breed clones of the Father and thus assure that his laws are also proliferated. This is what feminism resists: the continued dominion of the Father and the rule of the white male penis.

Iconically, the white male penis is represented all around us. We see it in the shape of nuclear projectiles and spacecrafts. In cigarette ads and army recruitment posters. In church steeples and skyscrapers. The airplanes that plowed into the twin towers of the World Trade Center on September 11th showed us what happens when the white male penis gets hijacked and its power pointed back at itself by enemies intent on giving the world a demonstration of "Fuck You Back" politics. Look on the original cover of the *Little Mermaid* video and tell me that isn't a penis back there disguised as a tower of the prince's castle. Disney's big hit, *The Lion King,* is nothing but an ode to the laws of the white Father, epitomized by the big blonde feline king who rules over the lowly animals of the jungle, including the dancing, drum-beating Africans. And what about the Wicked Witch in all those fairy tales we grew up on? Who is she, but the aging stepmother narcissistically obsessed with her own image, jealous of the young and beautiful stepdaughter who threatens to take away the Father's attention. In league with powers beyond her domain as a woman, the Wicked Witch can never be a surrogate for the sweet and submissive Snow White. And Snow White, herself, even though she is taller and whiter than the seven dwarfs, nonetheless knows her place as the maid of the household until she reenacts Eve's original sin and bites into a bad apple. The only cure that can restore her back to the symbolic order is a heterosexual kiss from the manly prince. Appropriately married off to a good son of the Father (as opposed to living in sin among the seven deadly vices), she can now fulfill her role as a woman and begin the cycle of reproduction.

This is what is meant by the social construction of gender. "One is not born, but rather becomes, a woman," said the early French feminist, Simone de Beauvoir in *The Second Sex.*[13] Originally published in 1949, *The Second Sex* is considered the first manifesto of the liberated woman (although actually our Latina feminist foremother, Sor Juana Inés de la Cruz, wrote her feminist manifesto—"hombres necios que acusáis a la mujer sin razón"—two hundred fifty years earlier).[14] What de Beauvoir's famous premise means is that woman and female are two different things; woman is a gender while female is a sex. One is born male or female, says Beauvoir, that is, with a specific set of sexual genitalia, but one becomes constructed as a man or a woman by society and culture, by civilization as a whole—all of which have been dominated by the laws of the Father for over two millennia. In such a world, the sexes are conditioned socially to serve patriarchal interests and safeguard patriarchal power. "The child is persuaded that more is demanded of boys because they are superior," says Beauvoir. ". . . To give him courage for the difficult path he must follow, pride in his manhood is instilled into him; this abstract notion takes on for him a concrete aspect: it is incarnated in his penis."[15] Thus, the male child's gender is constructed: superiority, courage, competitiveness, pride, and reverence for the penis help him become a man. A female child's gender, on the other hand, is constructed as opposite a male's, as Other. She is inferior, weak, submissive; she lacks the organ that gives her brother, her father, the special privileges they enjoy. Like her genitals, the girl exists inside. Outside, where the penis is, is where the boys are. A boy's plaything and alter ego is his penis; a girl's is a doll. One is alive, autonomous, and active; the other is inert, dependent, and passive.

Such is the stuff that genders and inequalities are made of.

But there is more to patriarchy than sexual inequalities, and subordinates come in all sizes and colors. The laws of the Father upon which all other laws are based are primarily the laws of the white, heterosexual, land-owning Father. The Father, in other words, is inscribed with a sex, a race, a class, and a sexuality—all of which converge in the meaning of patriarchy. To fully resist patriarchy, then, one must go beyond gender inequalities—this is the message of Third World, Black, Latina, and Chicana feminists. Our genders, like our struggles, are colored and sexed and classed. We cannot and must not rank any of our oppressions; race above gender, gender above race, class above sex. And yet, we continue to see that tug-of-war, and meanwhile the stereotypes that define and degrade us get more and more entrenched in our collective unconscious.

We know that Mexican/Chicano patriarchy assigns three attributes to the feminine gender: *la madre, la virgen, y la puta,* iconographed by the image of the Virgin of Guadalupe (who is both virgin and mother) and La Malinche (the prototypical fucked-one). Chicana feminists label this the "tres Marías" syndrome, from the three Mary's in the life of Jesus: the Virgin Mary, who is both, paradoxically, virgin and mother, and Mary Magdalene, the reformed whore. For the mestizo son, the difference between the virgin/mother aspect and the whore aspect explains his own ambivalence toward the female sex, how he can venerate and denigrate women at the same time, a trait of Mexican machismo that Chicano culture has internalized and adapted to its own social construction of gender. Octavio Paz, in "Sons of La Malinche," explains the roots of this dichotomy thus:

> Guadalupe is pure receptivity, and the benefits she bestows are of the same order: she consoles, quiets, dries tears, calms passions. The *Chingada* is even more passive. Her passivity is abject: she does not resist violence, but is an inert heap of bones, blood, and dust. Her taint is constitutional and resides, as we said earlier, in her sex. This passivity, open to the outside world, causes her to lose her identity: she is the *Chingada*. She loses her name; she is no one; she disappears into nothingness; she *is* Nothingness. And yet she is the cruel incarnation of the feminine condition.[16]

Woman as nurturer, forgiver, and carrier of the race must be idolized and protected; woman as instigator of "original sin" (whether that sin is disobedience
or miscegenation), as willing or unwilling portal to enemies and conquerors
cannot be forgiven. In patriarchy, a woman's sex is the site of her deepest
power (creation, which must be controlled and monitored at all times) and her
deepest weakness (penetration, which must be punished). In between the
mother and the whore that is La Malinche, there is the virginal condition, that
ethereal state of womanhood, which can be owned, traded, and renamed.

The Dirty Name

One of the accusations launched at the feministas, apart from calling them
agringadas, Malinches, and FBI spies, was the term "lesbian." Because they
were believed to be *anti-familia,* they could be nothing but lesbians, according
to the machista logic, and the term "lesbians," of course, was a bad word, a
dirty name. Those of us who study the subject know that feminist and lesbian
are not synonymous terms. We know that in the early days of the Women's
Movement, lesbians were either ostracized or thrown out of organizations like
NOW, the National Organization for Women. It wasn't until the lesbian feminists started to organize on their own and devise agendas that directly critiqued
the mainstream feminist movement for its heterosexism and homophobia that
the lesbian voice started to be integrated into mainstream feminism. By the
same token, not all of the early feministas of the Chicano Movement were lesbians, despite being called that by the men who were suddenly forced to look
at, if not own up to, their own sexist politics. In fact, the main reason these
feminist-oriented Chicanas denied the term "feminist," apart from the fact that
they didn't want to be seen as wannabe white women, is that they did not want
to be associated with lesbianism, for they, too, believed that the Women's
Movement was not only white and middle-class, but also, that it was a lesbian
movement. Homophobia and heterosexism, in other words, did not just infect
the hijos de Cuauhtemoc; the straight women, too, were guilty of fearing
homosexuality and assuming that real Chicanas were straight Chicanas.

Chicana lesbians, seen as polluted by the sexual license of the white feminist movement to believe we can do what we want with our bodies, including
using them to pleasure or be pleasured by other women, are the most treacherous of all. As Cherríe Moraga tells us in her classic essay, "A Long Line of
Vendidas,"[17] a Chicana lesbian was considered the most extreme Malinche of
all, not only because she rejected heterosexuality, but also "refused the favor"[18]
of male domination and the biological destiny imposed by patriarchy that
ensures the perpetuation of the laws of the almighty Apá.[19] "The Chicana lesbian," says Moraga, "is the most visible manifestation of a woman taking control of her own sexual identity and destiny."[20]

In an article entitled "Chicana Lesbians: Fear and Loathing in the Chicano

Community," Carla Trujillo discusses four reasons that lesbians threaten the Chicano community: sexuality, identification, motherhood, and religion. All of these reasons are, of course, linked to patriarchy. Lesbians reverse the religious and cultural doctrine that sexuality—for women, anyway—is meant for reproduction, not for pleasure or self-fulfillment, and also they reverse the assumption that lesbians are just wanna-be men rather than women-loving women. To be a woman-loving woman means that men are not the object of desire, and this means that women cannot be controlled by what they are conditioned to desire, i.e., a good man or a heterosexual family. Lesbians show that there is another way that is not dependent on relations with men (as the terms "wife," "mother," "daughter," and "girlfriend" to identify women all suggest), that, in fact, women can have autonomous lives without needing to be seen as attachments to men, and thus, become the owners and creators of their own destinies. Lesbians either fail to propagate the race, and thus fail their calling as good Catholic women, if they choose not to bear children, or they subvert the sanctified male-female paradigm of "la sagrada familia" if they do choose to raise children, as indeed, more and more lesbians are doing.[21]

Patriarchy controls women primarily by controlling our bodies, by dictating what we can and cannot do with our bodies. Because reproduction is one of the primary mandates of patriarchy—both to produce sons and heirs for the Father and to perpetuate the laws and interests of the Father—the heterosexual imperative is one way of assuring reproduction. Dictating who and how women can love, and what legitimate forms our desire can take are ways in which the established social hierarchy gets perpetuated. Because lesbians refuse to participate in the heterosexual imperative, they threaten the patriarchal order. Cherríe Moraga says that our sexuality is both a form of oppression and a means of liberation; we are oppressed by practicing a sexuality that contradicts the patriarchal social order, and yet we are liberated from the restrictive and prescriptive roles that patriarchy imposes.[22]

In describing one of the main reasons that Malinche is called the betrayer, Sandra Messinger Cypess tells of an Amerindian male that Malintzin Tenepal is said to have rejected. "[This] is perhaps the most serious of the charges that cling to her image; it becomes a metaphoric act signifying the repudiation of the native in favor of the foreign."[23] Ultimately, the Chicana lesbian is charged with the same act: the repudiation of *el chingón* in favor of *la chingada.* For a mind that is socialized and conditioned to venerate *el chingón* and denigrate *la chingada,* what could be more insulting than this?

Malinchismo

I would like to close now by offering you a Chicana lesbian feminist revision of our infamous foremother. Chicana historian, Deena González, argues "Malinche was truly at the crossroads of all that the Spanish conquest had come to symbolize, mistress of conquerors, mother of their sons, and initiator as well of a new role for women."[24] It is that new role as intermediary, diplomat, and translator that eludes male interpretations of Malinche. In Nahuatl, the term "malinche" applied generically to outsiders (thus, Cortés was as much a "malinche" as Malintzin Tenepal, the Mayan noblewoman who belonged to Moctezuma's harem of slaves); in any culture, outsiders or strangers have always been seen as potential traitors, and the Aztecs were no different in that regard. Malintzin Tenepal, having been sold into slavery by her mother at a young age, owed no loyalty to the Aztecs. They were her conquerors, as well as the conquerors of all of the other native tribes who inhabited the valley of Anahuac, and who eventually teamed up with the foreigners on horseback in a bloody insurrection. Little did they know, of course, that the new empire would mean their own genocide as well as the Aztec's. The Aztecs knew; in fact, it was predicted in their prophecy of the Quinto Sol. And still, Moctezuma refused to see the writing on the pyramid. Malintzin Tenepal had already learned several Indian languages before she was given to Cortés as part of Moctezuma's tribute to the conquistador whom he believed to be the god Quetzalcoatl. She became Doña Marina to the Spaniards, and, because of her facility with languages, because of her translation and diplomacy skills in mediating between the Aztec emperor and the Spanish conquistador, because she became Cortés's lover and bore him children, was said to have become, like Cortés, a "malinche."

Ironically, 500 years of internalized racism and misogyny have transformed La Malinche from the great *Chingada* to the great *Chingona,* the woman with all the power to bring down the Aztec civilization. As my "Malinchista" poem says, "Centuries she has been blamed for the murder of her/ child, the loss of her people, as if Tenochtitlan would not have fallen without her sin." Curiously, no one ever accuses Moctezuma of betraying his people, of reaping the hatred of the subordinate tribes, of receiving the conqueror with open arms (or legs), of ignoring the prophecy that foretold of the collapse of the Aztec empire, of buying a malinche's favors with gifts and tributes worthy of a god. More than anything La Malinche could have done, it was Moctezuma's actions and inactions that facilitated the fall of Tenochtitlan. As Ana Castillo notes in *Massacre of the Dreamers:*

> [Moctezuma] called upon the thousands of dreamers who were sharing the same premonition: the prophesied arrival of Cortés and the subsequent annihilation of the Empire. Moctezuma's order to have the dreamers murdered en masse did not stop the landing of those alien ships that were already on their way with those whose intentions were to take whatever riches found at any cost.[25]

And yet, Chicano patriarchy has adopted Moctezuma's image as the symbol of indigenous pride while La Malinche is reviled as the eternal and unforgivable traitor.

Chicano patriarchy continues to evoke La Malinche's name to malign Chicanas who refuse to conform to their prescribed biological functions. In *Sister/Outsider* Audre Lorde warned that "the master's tools will never dismantle the master's house."[26] For all of its dissent against the domination of the white Father, the Chicano Movement used some of the Father's tools, including gender politics that not only privileged the men, but also perpetuated the *madre/virgen/puta* stereotypes of its women, which only served to fulfill the sexist fantasies of the Chicano penis. But Chicana feminists and particularly Chicana lesbian feminists have begun to transform the story of Malinche into a mirror of Chicana resistance against female slavery to patriarchy—be it the brown patriarchy of la Raza or the over-arching patriarchy of the white Father. Malinche also represents affirmation: of a woman's freedom to use her mind, her tongue, and her body in the way that she chooses and to cultivate her intellectual skills for her own survival and empowerment. From this mirror arises the vision of "Malinchismo," a new theory of Chicana identity politics that takes the pejorative term, "Malinchista," and turns all of its negatives into positives (just as "Chicanos" did in the 1960s and as "queers" did in the 1990s). "Our challenge," says Emma Pérez, "is to rebel against the symbol of the white father and affirm our separation from his destructive ideology to create a life-affirming *sitio*."[27]

If the best revenge, as they say, is living well—and I interpret that to mean not just economic wellness, but more importantly, the wellness of spirit that comes from loving ourselves and living true to our natures rather than embodying that "inert heap of bones, blood and dust" that Octavio Paz labeled "the cruel incarnation of the feminine gender"—then Malinche's revenge is upon us, and there is no turning back. Slouching toward the new Aztlán of the 21st century, Malinche's rebellious "Shadow Beast"[28] dares us to look in the mirror and experience what Gloria Anzaldúa called "the knowing," the inner power that results from our underworld journeys into consciousness. "Suddenly the repressed energy rises, makes decisions, connects with conscious energy and a new life begins."[29]

Notes

[1] Alicia Gaspar de Alba, section 5 of the poem, "Malinchista, A Myth Revised," *Beggar on the Córdoba Bridge in Three Times a Woman: Chicana Poetry* (Tempe, AZ: Bilingual Press, 1989), 17.

[2] See Emma Pérez, *The Decolonial Imaginary: Writing Chicanas Into History* (Bloomington: Indiana University Press, 1999).

[3] See Octavio Paz, *Labyrinth of Solitude,* trans. Lysander Kemp, Yara Milos, and Rachel Phillips Belash (New York: Grove Press, 1985).

[4] Emma Pérez, "Sexuality and Discourse: Notes from a Chicana Survivor," in *Chicana Lesbians: The Girls Our Mothers Warned Us Against* (Berkeley: Third Woman Press, 1991), 167.

[5] Pérez, "Sexuality and Discourse," 168.

[6] This essay was originally written for the Malinche conference at the University of Illinois, at Urbana-Champaign, which was held in 1999. Although the "María Isabel" example itself is dated, the case system as represented in Mexican telenovelas remains the same.

[7]R. Douglas Cope, *The Limits of Racial Domination: Plebeian Society in Colonial Mexico City, 1660-1720* (Madison: Wisconsin UP, 1994), 24.

[8]This is one of the stories associated with the Mexican volcanoes of the same name. Popocatéptl is the name of the active (thus, male) volcano, and Ixxtacihuatl is the name of the dormant (thus, female) one. Indeed, her name means Sleeping Lady.

[9]Elizabeth Martínez, *De Colores Means All of Us: Latina Views for a Multi-Colored Century* (Boston: South End Press, 1998), 175.

[10]Quoted in Cherríe Moraga, "Queer Aztlán: The Re-Formation of Chicano Tribe," in *The Last Generation* (Boston: South End Press, 1993), 157.

[11]Martínez, 166.

[12]See Alma García, ed. *Chicana Feminist Thought: The Basic Historical Writings* (New York: Routledge, 1997). See also chapter 3, "Out of the House, the Halo, and the Whore's Mask: The Mirror of Malinchismo" in my book *Chicano Art Inside/Outside the Master's House: Cultural Politics and the CARA Exhibition* (Austin: UT Press, 1998), 119–157.

[13]Simone de Beauvoir, *The Second Sex*, trans. H. M. Parshley (New York: Bantam Books, 1970), 249.

[14]"So in my case, it is not seemly/that I be viewed as feminine,/as I will never be a woman/who may as woman serve a man," wrote Sor Juana in her poem, "In Reply to a Gentleman from Peru, Who Sent Her Clay Vessels While Suggesting She Would Better Be a Man." See *Poems, Protest, and a Dream: Selected Writings of Sor Juana Inés de la Cruz*, trans. Margaret Sayers Peden (New York: Penguin Books, 1997), 141. See also my lesbian version of Sor Juana's life in *Sor Juana's Second Dream* (Albuquerque: UNM Press, 1999).

[15]de Beauvoir, 253.

[16]Octavio Paz, "Sons of La Malinche," reprinted in *Goddess of the Americas: Writings on the Virgin of Guadalupe*, Ana Castillo ed. (New York: Riverhead Books, 1996), 208.

[17]See Cherríe Moraga, "A Long Line of Vendidas," in *Loving in the War Years: lo que nunca pasó por sus labios* (Boston: South End Press, 1983), 90–144.

[18]See Deena J. González, *Refusing the Favor: The Spanish-Mexican Women of Santa Fe, 1820–1880* (New York: Oxford UP, 1999).

[19]This is an allusion to Helena María Viramontes's story, "Growing," in *The Moths and other stories* (Houston: Arte Público Press, 1995), 35–42, in which the female protagonist has to come to terms with the fact that growing up, or becoming a woman, automatically wins her the distrust of her machista 'Apá.

[20]Moraga, "Long Line of Vendidas," 112.

[21]Carla Trujillo, "Chicana Lesbians: Fear and Loathing in the Chicano Community, in *Chicana Lesbians: The Girls Our Mothers Warned Us About* (Berkeley: Third Woman Press, 1991), 186–194.

[22]See Moraga, "Queer Aztlán."

[23]Sandra Messinger Cypess, *La Malinche in Mexican Literature: From History to Myth* (Austin: UT Press, 1991), 35.

[24]Deena J. González, "Encountering Columbus," in *Chicano Studies: Critical Connection Between Research and Community*, Téresa Córdova, ed. (n.p.: National Association for Chicano Studies, 1992), 19.

[25]Ana Castillo, *Massacre of the Dreamers: Essays on Xicanisma* (New York: Plume Books, 1994).

[26]Audre Lorde, "The Master's Tools Will Never Dismantle the Master's House," in *Sister/Outsider* (Freedom, CA: The Crossing Press, 1984), 110–113.

[27]Pérez, "Sexuality and Discourse," 169.

[28]The "Shadow Beast" is Gloria Anzaldúa's term for a contradictory psychic energy that lives in all colonized peoples, but especially women and queers. It is a two-faced beast: one is the face of internalized hatred, the monster that aids our conquerors in keeping us oppressed by making us hate ourselves, our skin color, our sexuality, our desire; the other is the face of rebellion, the liberating force that gets us to rebel against the cultural tyranny of homophobia, linguistic ter-

rorism, racism, sexism, and other forms of bigotry. See Chapter 2, "Movimientos de rebeldía y las culturas que traicionan," in *Borderlands/La Frontera: The New Mestiza* (San Francisco: Aunt Lute Books, 1987), 15–23.
[29]Anzaldúa, 49.

Works Cited

Anzaldúa, Gloria. *Borderlands/La Frontera: The New Mestiza.* San Francisco: Aunt Lute Press, 1987.

Castillo, Ana. *Massacre of the Dreamers: Essays on Xicanisma.* New York: Plume Books, 1994.

Cope, R. Douglas. *The Limits of Racial Domination: Plebeian Society in Colonial Mexico City, 1660–1720.* Madison: Wisconsin UP, 1994.

de Beauvoir, Simone. *The Second Sex,* trans. H. M. Parshley. New York: Bantam Books, 1970.

de la Cruz, Juana Inés. "To A Gentleman From Peru Who Sent Her Clay Vessels While Suggesting She Would Better Be a Man." *Poems, Protest, and a Dream: Selected Writings of Sor Juana Inés de la Cruz.* Trans. Margaret Sayers Peden. New York: Penguin Books, 1997. 137–143.

García, Alma, ed. *Chicana Feminist Thought: The Basic Historical Writings.* New York: Routledge, 1997.

Gaspar de Alba, Alicia. *Chicano Art Inside/Outside the Master's House: Cultural Politics and the CARA Exhibition.* Austin: UT Press, 1998.

_____. "Malinchista, A Myth Revised." *Beggar on the Córdoba Bridge* in *Three Times a Woman: Chicana Poetry.* Tempe: Bilingual Press, 1989. 16–17.

González, Deena J. "Encountering Columbus," in *Chicano Studies: Critical Connection Between Research and Community.* Ed. Téresa Córdova. N.P.: National Association for Chicano Studies, 1992. 13–19.

_____. "Speaking Secrets: Living Chicana Theory." *Living Chicana Theory,* ed. Carla Trujillo. Berkeley: Third Woman Press, 1999). 46–77.

_____. *Refusing the Favor: The Spanish-Mexican Women of Santa Fe,* 1820–1880. New York: Oxford UP, 1999.

Lorde, Audre. "The Masters Tools Will Never Dismantle the Master's House," in *Sister/Outsider* Freedom, CA: The Crossing Press, 1984. 110–113.

Martínez, Elizabeth. *De Colores Means All of Us: Latina Views for a Multi-Colored Century.* Boston: South End Press, 1998.

Messinger Cypess, Sandra. *La Malinche in Mexican Literature: From History to Myth.* Austin: UT Press, 1991.

Moraga, Cherríe. "A Long Line of Vendidas." *Loving in the War Years: Lo Que Nunca Pasó Por Sus Labios.* Boston: South End Press, 1983. 90–144.

_____. "Queer Aztlán: The Re-Formation of Chicano Tribe." *The Last Generation.* Boston: South End Press, 1993. 145–174.

Octavio Paz. *Labyrinth of Solitude,* trans. Lysander Kemp, Yara Milos, and Rachel Phillips Belash. New York: Grove Press, 1985.

_____. "Sons of La Malinche." *Goddess of the Americas: Writings on the Virgin of Guadalupe,* Ed. Ana Castillo. New York: Riverhead Books, 1996. 197–208.

Pérez, Emma. *The Decolonial Imaginary: Writing Chicanas Into History.* Bloomington: Indiana UP, 1999.

_____. "Sexuality and Discourse: Notes from a Chicana Survivor." *Chicana Lesbians: The Girls Our Mothers Warned Us Against.* Berkeley: Third Woman Press, 1991. 159–184.

Trujillo, Carla. "Chicana Lesbians: Fear and Loathing in the Chicano Community," in *Chicana Lesbians: The Girls Our Mothers Warned Us About.* Carla Trujillo, ed. Berkeley: Third Woman Press, 1991. 186–194.

Malinche
Cuerpo de Mujer

Aesthetics of Sex and Race
Alfred Arteaga

There is an event in the history of the conquest of Mexico that transpires just before the fall of Tenochtitlan. It is a brief instance that focuses verbal energy on matters of the female body, on sex, on race, and, perhaps even a bit, on aesthetic selection. The event that constitutes the incident in Mexican history is a speech to Cuauthémoc that has been narrated by the "anonymous authors of Tlatelolco." They declare,

> The 'god' and La Malinche sent word to Cuauhtemoc and the other princes that there is no hope for them. Have they no pity on the little children, the old men, the old women? What more can they do? Everything is settled.
>   You are to deliver women with light skins, corn, chickens, eggs and tortillas. This is your last chance. The people of Tenochtitlan must choose whether to surrender or be destroyed.

Clearly, the demand for women says much about the ideology of conquest and the female body, and as the facts of that conquest have borne out, the imperialist, masculinist use of that body is implicated in matters of sex and race. That the conquistadors specifically demand "women with light skins," speaks, at least to a small degree, to matters of aesthetic concerns.

The general demand for women was an expression of the Spanish imperialist and masculinist project, which authorized the conquistador's use of the female body for sex and would ultimately render hybrid the subject of race. But the specification of "light skin" invests the demand for the female body with the element of aesthetic selection. The Spanish conquistadors demonstrated their taste by expressing preference, their color of choice, and in so doing, invested their project with matters of taste, beauty, discrimination.

The "anonymous authors of Tlatelolco" tell us that the actual demand for the female body passed through a series of interlocutors that linked Cortés, the demanding "god," to the besieged Aztec ruler, Cuauhtemoc, the falling eagle. The divine predilection for "women with light skins," as well as that for "eggs and tortillas," was transmitted to Cuauhtemoc by his so called "captain." Act-ing as Cuauhtemoc's representative, the Aztec "captain" ventured to the Spanish occupied Temple of the Woman and spoke to Xochitl, the priest held imprisoned there by the Spanish. Xochitl, in turn, passed on the demand that had originated with La Malinche and Cortés. The long line of command, the demand for "women with light skins" and the imposed choice "to surrender or be destroyed" originated with Cortés, with La Malinche close by. She must have been second in the chain, the first to receive divine word and an originator in her own right of the actual Nahuatl text transmitted to Cuauhtemoc.

There is, of course, much that can be made of the incident, of the content, of the demand, of the ideological underpinnings. It is a telling event in the series of events that constitute Mexican history and that shape Mexican and Chicano subjectivities. The brief speech act aimed at Cuauhtemoc figured as one successful imperial act. Its implications are huge and its ramifications, many. One could, for example, focus upon the problem of translation; upon the clash of machismos of Cortés and Cuauhtemoc; upon racial and even gastronomic taste.

I am more interested in sex. But the sex here is historical sex, narrated to us by the autonomous authors of Tlaltelolco or by Bernal Díaz del Castillo. It is textual sex rather than physical, and somehow I am left not satisfied.

The incident that contains the sex, that contains the matters of the female body, race, and aesthetics also contains La Malinche. And she too exists textually rather than physically. Yet she figures in the history; this is obvious. That she figures so prominently in such a discourse and that she remains persistent in our minds today is where my essay continues.

Contemplating La Malinche, I am confronted by a powerful conjunction of the textual and the physical. Textual, of course, because the story and image/icon, "La Malinche," occurs to me as I enact some textual act of reading history or relating myth. Yet that contemplation is somehow physical also, rendered corporeal because of the fact of her feminine and native body and the fact of its mestizo offspring.

The persistence of the corporeal "fact" of La Malinche rests on a line of descent that directly links her body with extant living and breathing bodies. The body of La Malinche attains reality for me, that is, attains a physicality beyond mere texuality, because of the "facts" of that line, the biological events in the sequence of heterosexual reproduction that tie contemporary mestizos with the originating indigenous mother.

Chicanismo and *mexicanidad*—to the degree that their fundamental paradigms is mestizaje, hybridity—embellish the textual history and myth with the corporeal, physical "facts" of sexual reproduction and racial miscegenation. In other words, the icon Malinche obtains a particular reality, a particular palpability, because of a line of facts, a sequence of real events, in this case, biological events, toward the origin.

That fact the Malinche story is history, rather than, say, fictional narrative or lyric, formally lends an element of palpability to her textual persistence. History, insofar as it is a sequence of "facts," is similar to the story of sexual reproduction. It is a real tie to the original. Or is it?

What if the facts were wrong, if they were not real after all? What if, for example, the physical Malinche bore no offspring, or what if she were a man? Or what if the textual Malinche was not completely an accurate representation, or if her narrative were somewhat lyrical, where "facts," as it were, were selected in part, for aesthetics?

This, I think, is somewhat the case. In other words, I think La Malinche persists because she is the first point, first body, first text, in a line of facts, biological and historical facts, that lead to this point, this place, today. And I think that that line, that corporeal and textual line, is not truly from first to now, nor is it constructed of real facts. Something other than a sequence of events participates in the persistence of La Malinche. The textual being, La Malinche, attains corporeality because it is not merely fact.

La Malinche persists for us today because the fairly vacant Malinche text is fleshed out. The real woman resists our knowing and is present in the histories only as a trace. But beginning with the imperial project, that trace is fleshed with meaning, made corporeal before our eyes and minds. The ideological work of empire, colony, nation-making, revolution, and the tools of patriarchy, Catholicism, machismo and even chicana feminism, have all rendered corporeal that fairly vacant text and have ensured the persistence of La Malinche.

In the demand for women with light skins, it is significant that Malinche is there with Cortés, at the source of the command. Whether or not true, this textual "fact" gains meaning for us because of her presence at the point of origin. Malinche persists because of this. This, to some degree, is an aesthetic choice, one shaped by ideology.

There at the founding speech acts that made modern Mexico, Malinche partook in the process. When Cortés wanted light women and tortillas, it was she who created the Nahuatl text for Cuauhtemoc and then created the Spanish text of reply for Cortés. It was she too who had a son with Cortés, having sex with the biggest Chingón Mexicans had seen.

Mother, traitor, Eve of the Raza Cósmica. She persists with a palpability that strikes us emotionally, ideologically despite the fact that factually she is hardly there at all. And just as Cortés aesthetically selected light women and tortillas and La Malinche, various groups select our Malinche of choice today. She attains corporeality, obtains a body, by our aesthetic fleshing out of a fairly vacant text.

It is aesthetically pleasing for most, for example, that she be a woman. But what is in a name? For the Spaniards, she was Doña Marina, and for the Aztecas, Cortés was "Malinche." But while the conquistador as Malinche may have pleased the Aztecs, it pleases few today.

That calls into question, what do we mean by Malinche? For if by "Malinche" we mean the vacant text, the sexually exploited, the first progenitor of mestizos, the slave, that title might better be applied to a Spanish man than a native woman. Of vacant texts, Gonzalo Guerrero is even more vacant than Malinche, more silent, absent. He shipwrecked in Yucatan years before Cortés arrived in Mexico. Guerrero, whose true name we do not know, was enslaved by the Maya, bore children, went native, and refused to return to aid the conquest.

But for a Christian, patriarchal, imperialist project, a woman Malinche is more pleasing than a man. The rape metaphor, the Eve analogy, the maternal harmony, the procreative balance to genocide, for example, all contributed to desire for the female body. The vacant text, so vacant that its genitals are absent, was given palpability by adding to bare fact female flesh.

Because the text is fleshed female, Gonzalo is cut out as a viable Malinche figure. That feminizing ensures the linking of Malinche with the markers woman, slave, mother, Eve, and object of male heterosexual desire. And because of the factual events in the relationship between the female Malinche and Cortés, the Malinche text is inscribed as translator and collaborator. This would not have been the case had the Malinche text been fleshed out in the image of the man. Guerrero not only refused to translate for the Spaniards, he refused to support the conquest, and quite possibly took up arms against the conquistadors.

Guerrero assimilated the culture of his slave-master wife and fathered mestizo children, probably before Cortés did. But the possibility of Guerrero as a progenitor of la raza, preceding Cortés as Adam and displacing Malinche as Eve, does not satisfy imperialist, patriarchal aesthetics; hence the virtually complete absence of Guerrero from history.

Absence from history means a lack of textual presence. This has nothing to do with the reality of the physical body. Assuming their reality, both Gonzalo Guerrero and La Malinche must have breathed air. The textual presence of each is small, but Guerrero further lacks the aesthetic and ideological palpability that has fleshed out the female Malinche.

History is a story made up of past events chosen in the present. It is a narrative and follows the order of narrative, including its aesthetic. Because of this construction, the events chosen to establish a line of causality are, in small part, aesthetic selections.

The history of Malinche has something of the lyric. The vacant text is fleshed out by flesh we choose because it satisfies our tastes. She is a product, perhaps of our desire, but certainly of our choice.

Canto Primero

Arrival

First, the island.
The cross of truth.
Another island.
A continent.
A line, half water, half metal.

An island of birds, "Ccollanan."
An island of birds, "Ccollanan Pachacutec!"
Sounds above an island, in
the air, trees, "Ccollanan Pachacutec!"
Female sounds. "Ricuy
anceacunac yahuarniy richacaucuta!"
An island of female birds, imagine
the sounds, the air, the trees, at times
the silence, the slither in thorns.

So perfect a shape, right
angles, the globe yields to so
straight a line, look. One
line, zenith to nadir, heaven,
precipitation. The only other,
straighter still than that horizon
we see at sea, perfect: paradise.
That horizontal line, from
old to new, he knew would yield,
yes, so perfect a move, he
knew, yes, so perfect a shape
yes.

Trees caught his thoughts.
Birds and onshores brought them
from the boats. She knew those
thoughts, heard those songs.
Could there be one more island?
Birds, sounds, perhaps pearls,
gold? Eden-Guanahani, perhaps
another? "O my Marina, my new
found island. License my roving
hands, and let them go, before,

behind, between, above, below."
West.

America, America. Feminine
first name, continent named
for him. America.
Here, Santa Fe. Here, the true
faith. I claim, in the name of
the father. Land of thorns,
in the name of the son.

The edge of this world
and the other, is marked
in water: ocean, river, wave to
her, she waits on the other
side. Aquí, se llama la Juana,
de apellido Juárez, india,
prieta y chaparra, la que le encanta
al gringo, al gachupín.

Island of cactus, genus
Cuauhtémoc. Island of rose,
land of thorns. Pedro de
Alvarado, an eagle, la
región transparente, a
night of smoke. Marina
Nightear, an ocean contained
in one *woman, as* it was in
the beginning, world
without end, fallen eagle.

So Feminine a shape. So female
a bay. Another shape: gliding
bird. Another: touching trees.
Trtze name of woman, Vera Cruz,
body of woman. "He named me
Xochitepec, yes so we are all flowers
of the mountain, all a woman's body,
that was one true thing he said in
his life." Above, birds,
leaves, above so woman a form.
Las quince letras: not the seven words:

Contestó Malintzin, "yes
I said yes I will Yes."

En el nombre
de la Virgen de las Espinas,
Ella que en buena hora nació,
This archeology is born: here
Tibia, here ball courts, codices,
teeth. Inside, the caves are
painted. Here is an architecture,
see, toco, toco,
tocotín:

Tla ya timohuica,
totlazo Zuapilli,
maca ammo, Tonantzin,
titechetnoilcahuíliz.
Mati itlatol ihiyo
Huel ni machicáhuac
no teco qui mati.

En la sangre, en las espinas
de la Virgen de Santa Fe,
these names are written:
America Estados-Unidos, née
Mexico. I name her
Flower of the Mountain,
Coatepec-Cihuatepec-Cuicatepec
Amor Silvestre,
Terra Nova,
Cuerpo de Mujer.

The edge of this world
and the other, is marked
in metal: on this side America,
on this side América.
Nights they spill from
San Diego and Los Angeles
threading the steel mesh
como nada, los verdaderos
alambristas, buscando el cuerpo
de mujer, buscando,
Xochitepec.

Coagulated Words: Gaspar de Alba's Malinche[1]

Debra A. Castillo

In the front matter to her poem, "Malinchista, A Myth Revised," Alicia Gaspar de Alba says it this way: "It is a traditional belief that La Malinche . . . betrayed her own people in exchange for a new life. It is said that La Malinche bore a son by Cortés, the first mestizo. . . . Some say that the spirit of La Malinche is La Llorona" (212). Here Gaspar de Alba succinctly summarizes a classic variation of the Malinche story/myth. The indigenous woman betrays her people to the Spanish conqueror by serving both as interpreter and mistress for Hernán Cortés; thereafter, "malinchista" in Mexican usage evokes the sense of an unpatriotic betrayal of the nation to foreign interests; as a consequence, the eternally frightening, uncanny, ghost/undead corpse, La Llorona, measures out her fit punishment. Nevertheless, the Texan poet cannily marks myth as myth by her insistent repetition of the crucial markers "it is a traditional belief," "it is said," and "some say." If the story of La Malinche has become petrified and monumentalized, it is also in Gaspar de Alba's account amazingly fluid, subject to the vagaries of gossip and oral storytelling. In these oral permutations of history, La Malinche becomes La Llorona, her son by Cortés becomes La Llorona's archetypal victim, as popular report and folklore shift and change historical record to fit different times, circumstances, and cultural needs.

Gaspar de Alba reminds us that the nebulous authority of rumor is all that substantiates a moral lesson derived not from knowledge of an event's historical accuracy or concern about actual ahistorical falsehood, but rather from human necessity for foundational models that fit understandings of contemporary circumstances. In this respect, La Malinche is that abject counterpart to the self that most clearly and precisely demonstrates "recognition of the *want* on which any being, meaning, language, or desire is founded" and as such lays bare what Kristeva calls the "nurturing horror" that undergirds "the cunning, orderly surface of civilizations" (5, 210). Figuring La Malinche as La Llorona, then, calls upon this composite feminine myth's abject and uncanny power, which might be said to lie in the very heart of the near oximoronic conjunction of "nurturing" and "horror" evoked in Kristeva's reading of abjection. She is horrible because she should be maternal and nurturing; by the same token, what she nurtures is, precisely, horror itself. At the same time, Gaspar de Alba's emphasis on what is said (as opposed perhaps, to what is, or was)—in its very insistence on conjectural saying—points to what is not said (the burden of the poem that follows), and hints too at alternative forms of expression (choked off words, the gestural economy of non-verbal communication). These issues of words and silences and significant gestures will lie at the core of all of Gaspar de Alba's rethinkings of the Malinche myth, both in her poetry and in her prose.

Octavio Paz's exceptionally influential discussion of Malinche as the icon of Mexicanness focuses on this psychological trauma of a national identity based on a foundational betrayal that is both political and sexual. We might even say, along with Kristeva, that for Paz her body "is a border that has encroached upon everything" (3). As Paz notes, the cry "¡Viva México, hijos de La Chingada!" recognizes the implicit underlying connection between the nation and Malinche as the figure of the raped indigenous woman, between the Mexican male force and the children born of violence. In this reading, Mexicans, metaphorically born to the rape victim ("la chingada"), wake up to find themselves victims of the evil betrayer, and so have no recourse but to commit violence, including sexual violence, against women and against their fellow man so as to shore up a sagging and threatened identity as the putative possessor of a powerful and inviolable male body. And yet, as Paz says, in these paranoid constructions of gender and sexual norms, while "La Chingada" is ineluctably associated with the mother, her very passivity leaches her identity and her name; she is nothing and no one; "es la Nada" (68; "she is Nothingness" [72]). If, in the complexities of national myth, the nation is both mother and whore, then national pride and perceived deficiencies in the national character derive from a common cause. Moreover, if racially inferior and sexually available women are to blame—literally or metaphorically—for society's problems, tacitly national pride is also bound up in the admission that nothing can be done to improve the situation since the powerful, handsome, yearned-for father is always already gone.

Chicano, and especially Chicana, critics and writers including Norma Alarcón, Gloria Anzaldúa, María Herrera Sobek, and Ana Castillo have turned this negative image of the indigenous woman on its head, rewriting her story as that of an empowered woman. Then too, they help us to remember that Paz's commentary is not the historical account for which it is so often mistaken, but rather a lyric reinvention of a national romance, a foundational myth, and in this respect no more authoritative than any other poetic effort. We might even say that here, if less apparently, Paz's tale and Gaspar de Alba's meet as alternative poetics.

While colonial chroniclers document that Cortés did indeed call Malinche "mi lengua" (my tongue), the Chicana recuperations of the power of the woman's native tongue and her indigenous body offer a twist on the old tale, refiguring the five-hundred year old history as an iconic example for the potentiality of a woman who escapes the confines of the home and allows herself to speak. Thus, the image that in Paz's Mexico figures shame and betrayal becomes in Chicana theory a figure of pride and empowerment, as well as a metaphor for the bilingual resistances of the contemporary Chicana woman who is faced with a second colonial threat through the pressures of US-Anglo culture and the English language that threaten to efface her from the national imaginary.

Alfred Arteaga sees this recuperation of a usable image for cultural consolidation as a particularly urgent project in the fraught cultural contact zones of the border region: "For Mexicans and for Chicanos subjectivity is reproduced anew in the self-fashioning act of heterotextual interaction. But this sense is more acute for the Chicano than for the Mexican because the Chicano derives *being* not only from the Spanish colonial intervention but also from Anglo-American colonialism: for not only was Mexico conquered by Spain, but Northern Mexico by the United States" (27). At the same time, Arteaga quite rightly points out the stress points in current poetic and theoretical re-elaborations of the Malinche legend, especially in its most celebrated forms where, ironically, prominent Chicana lesbians (Gaspar de Alba would also be included in this distinguished body) fall back into a heterosexual metaphor of national and textual production. Once again, as in Paz, textual production devolves back onto the absent authority figure, the white father.

"Malinchista, A Myth Revised" places the native woman in the context of an impossible power struggle between two figures of male domination, both of whom access speech by means of homicidal violence. On the one hand, the indigenous priest derives his power of sacred speech from the ritual sacrifice of human messengers who mediate between the gods and their earthly servants. For the priest, Malinche's unmediated power of speech is sacrilegious and incomprehensibly terrifying:

> The high priest of the pyramids feared La Malinche's
> power of language—how she could form strange syllables
> in her mouth and Speak to the gods without offering
> the red fruit of her heart. (212)

Strikingly enough, Gaspar de Alba's Malinche discerns no substantive difference between this literal sacrifice of human hearts on Aztec altars and the figurative ripping out of indigenous life by white men in their violations of body and soul following upon the successful conquest. On the contrary; the priest and the conquistador are strangely identified by the analogy in their violent practices, and, importantly, both are relegated to a secondary status in the history in which they imagined they would figure as central images:

> . . . history
> does not sing of the conquistador who prayed
> to a white god as he pulled two ripe hearts
> out of the land. (212–13)

Unlike her male counterparts, if ambiguously, La Malinche/La Llorona in this poem retains her power, no longer as the embodied Speaker, but as the haunting presence whose undecipherable shriek captures the imprinted cultural aftershocks of the violent convulsion that reshaped an American empire during the colonial period. She is both the nurturing mother who curves her body protectively around a much beloved newborn child, and the horrific ghost of a murderous child killer who returns to the scene of her crime to cry for vengeance. Malinchismo, Gaspar de Alba suggests in this moral tale, is redefined not as the act of a betrayer but as the reaction of one who has been betrayed; the horror that perverts the mother's nurturing instinct derives from another's violent action against her. Malinche is a potent force in this revised myth, but she is potent less as an embodiment of contemporary resistances to patriarchal power than as a historical reaction, as a figure of past abjection.

The short story, "Los derechos de La Malinche," picks up on and expands imagery the author had begun to explore in the more concise format of the "Myth Revised." From the poem, she draws the central thread of the tale, and also the imagery of heart and speech, and the metaphor of the cactus so crucial to both variations on the tale. In the story, however, the writer adds both a contemporary focus and a binational message, with her emphasis less on the act of betrayal (though, of course, the story cannot avoid this retelling) and more forcefully on the woman's proactive recognition and assumption of her rights.

"Los derechos de La Malinche" appears in Alicia Gaspar de Alba's collection of short stories, *The Mystery of Survival,* which she wrote in the 1980s as she moved from El Paso to Ciudad Juárez and to other cities in both Mexico and the US. Two of the eleven stories in *Mystery of Survival* are written entirely in Spanish, and the choice of language is not casual. While "Los derechos de La Malinche," offers a poetic meditation on that much discussed indigenous woman from the early sixteenth century conquest of Mexico by Spain, the other Spanish-language story, "El pavo" focuses on a child's anticipation of the mainstream US holiday of Thanksgiving. In effect, as the counterposition of the Thanksgiving and the Malinche stories suggests, at question in Gaspar de Alba's work is a deeper interrogation into the nature of historical origins for national and cultural identity claims (i.e., Pilgrims vs. *conquistadores*).

The twinned themes of memory and destiny are repeated over and over in the book, in Spanish and in English, often associated with some variation of the proverb that serves as epigraph to the collection and appears textually in the first story, stencilled onto a whitewashed wall in Querétaro: "el pueblo que pierde su memoria pierde su destino." The child narrator in that story asks her mother what it means, and her mother impatiently responds: "I don't know. . . Mexican proverbs don't mean anything anymore" (12). Pointedly, the loss of meaning has a good deal to do with the loss of language, and also with the willed memory loss involving the mother's refusal to acknowledge her daughter's abuse at the hands of her stepfather. This intentional forgetfulness, this encrypting of memory, results in the creation of the Pandora's box, or memory piñata that serves as one of the book's leitmotivs. By the end of the volume, with "Facing the Mariachis," one of the linked series of stories involving Estrella González, the author adds to this discussion the nuanced, and explicitly female, alternative genealogical tale involving a recuperation of memory through the deliberate creation of the child/future storyteller, Xochitl, implicitly conterposing Xochitl to Malinche as alternative textual strategies.

Gaspar de Alba's story "Los derechos de La Malinche" offers her take on the foundational moment in this vexed international and interlingual problematic genealogy, exploring the issue of a usable past by way of an aggressively feminocentric tale that nevertheless must cede its authority to the "barbudos," the Spanish and gringo male-dominant heterotexts. "Los derechos de La Malinche" opens in medias res with the voice of the female narrator, raising at the very beginning of the narrative the question that, while suppressed, will haunt and destabilize the whole of the succeeding text: "No me voy a disculpar. Después de tantos años, hasta nuestra lengua ha cambiado. Es posible que ni me entiendas. Es posible que mis palabras todavía estén coaguladas" (I am not going to ask for pardon. After so many years, even our language has changed. It is possible that you don't even understand me. It is possible that my words are still coagulated) (47). Economically, with these few and tightly constructed phrases, Gaspar de Alba outlines the central problematics and metaphorics of this story: the firm negative response to an implicit demand for contrition, the problem of communicating across languages, the image of the blood clot that stands in for a choked narration.

The narrative voice, abruptly interrupting the English flow of the majority of the stories in this volume, begins by aggressively refusing to ask for forgiveness. But forgiveness for what? For a traitorous reputation? A linguistic trangression? A sexual one? The uncontrite voice, in refusing to ask, nevertheless evokes an unstated history in which such forgiveness would more typically be begged—and perhaps grudgingly given. And yet, in the very next sentence, readers are invited to wonder if indeed "disculpas" are exactly at issue here—perhaps we misunderstand; after all, the language has changed: "our" language has changed. But which language? The historical Malinche originally translated Maya and Nahuatl, and later, as her abilities grew, Nahuatl and Spanish. The narrator in this story shifts to Spanish in an Anglophone context and a predominantly English-language collection. And yet, the story is there, on the page, stubbornly written in Spanish, defiantly non-US oriented in its metaphoric base; there—as María Lugones has said in reference to her own use of bilingualism in her theoretical texts—to be understood or to be missed, so that in both sharing an understanding and in having to skip over the text because of linguistic inability, there is an important meaning (46).[2]

This contestatory stance introduces a narrator who is simultaneously a contemporary woman and that much maligned and celebrated indigenous figure. In its historical evocation of the conquest tale, the story details a change of language and change of name through involuntary baptism and the imposition of a foreign spirituality: Malintzín becomes Malinche and then Marina in the wholly unwanted, terrified gesture of "el vendido" ("the sell out") who tosses his "gotas de ácido" ("drops of acid") in her direction in an attempt to control her (50-1). This cultural rape is paired with sexual abuse; indeed, sexual intercourse with the conqueror follows immediately upon baptism. Importantly, moreover, this doubled violence figures the narrator's entry into the space of narration. In the overlapping of colonial and contemporary times, of Malinche and her modern counterpart, these two elements of a spurious Catholicism and sexual abuse remain paired. Thus, the modern woman refers elliptically to sexual abuse by her father in the sordid surroundings of a movie matinee, through a parody of the Lord's Prayer: "tú, padre nuestro que estás en el cielo . . . me alzabas la falda y me dabas el pan de cada día." (you, our father who art in heaven . . . lifted my skirt and gave me our daily bread) (52). Likewise, the Spanish conqueror's entirely expected use of Malinche's body is paired with the modern woman's distaste for the pressured sexual relations with her gringo boyfriend, and both experiences are dismissed with the same phrase: "lo que pasó con ese barbudo no fue más que otro tributo a otro conquistador" (what happened with that bearded man was no more than another tribute to another conqueror) (52).

Yet, at the same time as the colonial Malinche and her Chicana counterpart dismiss complicity in their own abuse, they are profoundly aware of the social context in which the colonial woman, like the modern abuse victim, is made responsible for her victimization. The opening sentence of the story, with its implication that typically forgiveness would need to be given for the unstated offense, offers a clear index to this social construction by which the woman is sullied (in social terms) by the abuse visited upon her. Moreover, the bloody clot of words—an unspoken story, in another tongue—reminds us that at least at one level the rape victim is expected to keep silent and suffer in shame for her violation.

For both women, the first sign of this impending conquest is a linguistic catachresis followed by physical disgust and vomiting:

> Malintzín se empezó a marear. Le venía un ataque de palabras raras, palabras que no conocía, palabras secretas de las diosas. No quería que el extranjero escuchara su canto. . . . Se le convulsionó el estómago y echó un líquido amargo a los pies del barbudo. Ya le venían las primeras sílabas.
>
> (Malintzín began to get nauseous. An attack of strange words came upon her, words she didn't know, the secret words of the goddesses. She did not want the foreigner to hear her song. . . . Her stomach convulsed and she threw up a bitter liquid at the bearded man's feet. Then the first syllables came out.) (41)

Derridá is on the right track when he theorizes, in a discussion of Kant, the relation of the aesthetic category of the sublime and the physical experience of vomiting, and his conclusions are apposite for reading Gaspar de Alba's story as well. In his analysis, disgust in some sense stands in for that which is unassimilable. Vomit is the reappropriation of negativity by which disgust lets itself be spoken: "What it [the logo-phonocentric system] excludes . . . is what does not allow itself to be digested, or represented, or stated. . . . It is an irreducible heterogeneity which cannot be eaten either sensibly or ideally and which—this is the tautology—by never letting itself be swallowed must therefore *cause itself to be vomited*. Vomit lends its form to this whole system" (21). Derridá concludes: "The word *vomit* arrests the vicariousness of disgust; it puts the thing in the mouth" (25). Both literally and metaphorically, then, what the white man puts into the indigenous woman—his words in her ears, his water and semen in her body—provokes disgust at that unassimilable presence which nevertheless figures the hegemonic discourse that must somehow be taken in and made one's own. It is, as Derridá and Gaspar de Alba intimate, too much to be swallowed, and therefore must be thrown up.

At the same time, the colonial woman needs to hold back the pressure to give her words into the conqueror's ears, to give anything of herself or her culture to him. Thus, while disgust and vomiting give form to the system, the retention of some quality of the unassimilable creates blockages—the blood clots that choke narrative even while they retain the chameleonic power of the native woman's unspoken, unspeakable secrets. Derridá's analysis of the sublime strikes a chord with Kristeva's parallel reading of the coming into consciousness of the "I," which she sees as also constructed through the expelling of the sign of the other's desire. Thus, if Derridá's reading helps us to see how Malinche accesses her various languages, Kristeva defines the consolidation of the self through violaton:

> During that course in which "I" become, I give birth to myself amid the violence of sobs, of vomit. Mute protest of the symptom, shattering violence of a convulsion that, to be sure, is inscribed in a symbolic system, but in which, without either wanting or being able to become integrated in order to answer to it, it reacts, it abreacts. It abjects. (3)

Kristeva further notes the essential connection between this coming to consciousness of the self and an awareness of personal death: "it is thus that *they* see that 'I' am in the process of becoming an other at the expense of my own death" (3). Nevertheless, what "I" knows and what "they" see—the irreducibility of the body and the inevitability of its decomposition, both figured in the disgusting qualities of vomit—must be repressed (the exactness of the folk wisdom already adduced linking La Malinche and La Llorona is never clearer than in this respect). Fear too must be thrown up, driven out. And yet, of course, it always haunts us: "it shades off like a mirage and permeates all the words of the language with nonexistence. . . . Thus, fear having been bracketed, discourse will seem tenable only if it ceaselessly confronts that otherness, a burden both repellent and repelled, a deep well of memory that is unapproachable and intimate" (Kristeva 6).

While for the colonial woman, nausea is provoked by the need to contain the words of power in the face of an alien threat, in the modern woman's experience the immediate need is to eject the foreign presence from her body, to rid herself of an invader who is nonetheless at this point, nearly five hundred years after the conquest, deeply of her own body and blood—the father to whom this story is explicitly addressed:

> Te eché en seguida. Abrí la boca sobre el excusado y te dejé salir. . . . No me voy a disculpar. Cuando me avisaron de tu embolia, sentí una gran calma. El coagulo de palabras en mi garganta al fin se empezó a deslizar, al fin pude soltar la sangre de tu recuerdo.
>
> (I got rid of you immediately. I opened my mouth over the toilet and allowed you to leave. . . . I am not going to ask for pardon. When I was told about your stroke I felt a great calm. The clot of words in my throat finally began to break up, at last I was able to get rid of the blood of your memory). (50)

Here the death of the father, and the visit to the grave that frames the narrative, serves to free up, finally, the clotted narrative. The language may have changed from the words of power Malinche caught back in her throat, but in any case the vomiting up of that inassimilable presence of the disgusting allows narrative to take shape. Here again, Kristeva's reading helps to formulate more precisely the theoretical weight of this process. She says, "it is the brutish suffering that 'I' puts up with, sublime and devastated, for 'I' deposits it to the father's account," playing on the echo between "verse au père" and "père-version" (2). The father's account cannot be, in this abject vomiting out of the self, other than perverse.

Resistance to the master discourse takes another form, one even more closely aligned with the symbolic import of the story's title than the image of vomiting. Says the modern woman at her father's grave, "He venido a traerte tunas" (I have come to bring you prickly pears) (47). The prickly pear is, of course, a sweetly delicious native fruit, but one whose delicate heart must be carefully uncovered because of the cactus spines covering the protective outer peel. If, in this story, what is foreign and cannot be assimilated causes disgust and must be vomited, it would seem that the cactus fruit would stand at the opposite pole as a native source of pleasure and nourishment. Nevertheless Gaspar de Alba's use of this fruit, with its blood-red secret core and prickly exterior, rests on a different and feminocentric metaphoric turn, and one which echoes as well with the bloody hearts of her poem, "Malinchista: A Myth

Revised." At the end of the story the modern narrator clarifies: "Estas tunas son los derechos que me violaste, las palabras secretas que me tragué" (These fruits are the rights of mine which you violated, the secret words I swallowed) (52).

Here too, there is a carefully articulated genealogical thrust, as the modern woman's evocation of the blood-red fruits echoes the colonial woman's resistance to the force of the conqueror, her strategy for a silent opposition to his violation. The enforced silence, the secret that also becomes the defining quality of her identity and her resistance to co-optation, are figured in the internalization of the image of the prickly pear, by which the narrator and her foremother define those alienated rights, those coagulated narratives, that constitute them as excluded subjects from the masculinist-driven national enterprise. These women are raped and discursively rendered as abjectly apologetic or voiceless precisely so that their tongue will not be disseminated within this hegemonic structure. Yet, paradoxically, their exclusion creates the possibility not only for the rhetorical rendering of difference, but also for real oppositional strategy. Says Santiago Castro-Gómez:

> Observarse *como sujetos excluidos* conllevaba la posibilidad de desdoblarse, observar las propias prácticas y compararlas con las prácticas de sujetos distantes en el tiempo y el espacio, establecer diferencias con otros sujetos locales y producir estrategias de resistencia.
>
> (To observe oneself *as an excluded subject* carried with it the possibility of unfolding, of observing one's own practices and comparing them with the practice of subjects distant in time and space, of establishing differences with other local subjects and producing resistance strategies). (210)

If the prickly pear is what the modern woman swallows—and in the unclotting of the narrative also represents the blood she spills on her father's gravestone—this metaphorical connection becomes even more deeply layered through reference to the colonial tale. There is a homology of mouth and genitals in this story, already established in the parallels between rape and vomit, violation and secrecy. Both sites on the body become overdetermined loci of what is forced on the woman, what is resisted, what is spit out in silence. In this resistance narrative, the prickly pear serves an important function in a wincingly graphic attack on the master's power:

> La Malinche no dijo nada. . . . Esa noche, Marina se preparó bien. Con la ayuda de Coatlicue y Tonantzín, se irritó las paredes de su sexo con el pellejo espinoso de unas tunas, dejando que el jugo rojo de la fruta le chorreara las piernas. . . . Cuando él se encontró en aquella hinchazón, en aquel nido de espinas donde su miembro se había atrapado como una culebra, sus gritos le salieron a borbotones. Nunca se había sentido Doña Marina tan dueña de su destino.
>
> (La Malinche said nothing. . . . That evening, Marina prepared herself well. With the aid of Coatlicue and Tonantzín she rubbed the walls of her genitals

with the spiny peel of some cactus fruits, allowing the red juice to flow down
her legs. . . . When he found himself in that swelling, in that nest of spines
where his penis was trapped like a snake, his shouts escaped in torrents. Never
had Doña Marina felt so in charge of her destiny). (51-2)

This is not a utopic tale, however. Both for Malinche and her modern
counterpart, defiance is reactive: a refusal to submit passively to a conquest
that has already taken place. Sublime and abject at the same time, the self-cre-
ated through the abreactions of violent explusions cannot be otherwise. "Los
derechos de La Malinche" begins and ends at the father's grave, suggesting
that in this circular narrative the feminine voice, whether clotted or free-flow-
ing, is still doomed to repeat the structure of violation and vomit. Furthermore,
the unclotting of narrative offers purging (vomiting) of the father's memory—
but it is still the father's story, like the father's gravestone, that frames the tale
and dominates its telling. Survival, when that survival is marked by the
inescapable presence of the father's grave serving as the only opening onto
narration, offers no clear, proactive solution for the future.

How then do we get beyond the abject? How to break the folkloric link of
Malinche/Llorona, which discovers a perverse vomiting of the lover-father and
his words/works? Or, to put it in other terms, how do we rethink the heterotext
in the service of the feminine? Gaspar de Alba hints at one possible alternative
poetics in her much-anthologized poem, "Making Tortillas," which seems to
offer an implicit response to precisely the kind of blockage we have been track-
ing in her Malinche poem and story. The secret, she tells us, is to refuse the
premises of the patriarchal model, so damaging to women's self-construction:

> Tortilleras, we are called,
> Grinders of maíz, makers, bakers,
> slow lovers of women.
> The secret is starting from scratch. (*Beggar* 45)

"Starting from scratch," in genealogies as in cooking is in effect what Gaspar de Alba does in her most powerful Malinche poem, "Letters from a Bruja."
This poem in some sense restages the colonial encounter, echoing and giving
force to the mysterious "palabras secretas de las diosas" alluded to but repressed
under the father's narrative in "Derechos." Reading this poem, positioned from
the perspective and in the voice of La Malinche's mother, reminds us that the
ontological question undergirding our analysis to this point—Who or what is the
self?—is a question inevitably positioned from the perspective of the father's
law. It is, at base, a man's existential question, rooted in patriarchal concerns
about the integrity of the "I" and the primordial quality of the self's desires. Gaspar de Alba does not deny the power of this historically established framework,
but her *bruja* defamiliarizes it. In "Letters from a Bruja" Gaspar de Alba

estranges us from that male-oriented ontology and asks not "who am I?" but "who can I engender?" where the focus is not on the invasion of the self by the violating other and the vomiting out of the unassimilable foreign presence, but rather on the female genealogy that serves as patriarchy's necessary comple- ment: not father right, but the rites of the goddesses. What Gaspar de Alba pro- vides in this almost allegorical lyric recuperation of the female genealogy is not just another renegotiation of tired concepts but a strategic operation to usher in a reconceptualization as well as a reinscription of the linguist/cultural project.

The *bruja* in this poem is terrifying and wonderful. She forces us to rethink the hoary legend of La Malinche from the perspective of deliberative, feminocentric action, as part of a resistant heritage of strong women, neither self-abnegating nor abject. Following Natalie Melas, we could say that Mal- inche's witch-mother's poem, when (dis)placed into the context of a patriar- chal model, "produces a version of incommensurability which differs from our received definition of the incommensurable as 'that which cannot be measured by comparison for lack of a common measure,' suggesting instead a definition along the lines of 'that comparison which cannot measure because its equiva- lences do not unify" (275). The unity here is not that of spiritual or physical violation, but rather of blood and bone, of women physically conceived and spiritually engendered in women's bodies and from women's knowledge.

There are two parts to the "Letters from a Bruja." The first "letter" is addressed "to my daughter," explicitly identified as Malinche:

> But tonight my scorpion's blood boils
> with the heat of the lion . . .
> and you are conceived, hija,
> from the worm of incest,
> Already your seed bears the gift of darkness.
> Already your name washes up
> on the salty foam
> between my thighs: Malinche . . . (46)

The second "letter" is addressed to Malinche's daughter who, five hundred years after the Spanish conquest, has learned to speak in yet another tongue, neither native American nor imposed Spanish, but the English of the new con- quest. This girl child will inherit the grandmother's words and powers, which will spill forth from her mouth not as vomit, but as generative potential:

> I wind stories in your native
> tongue to frighten you . . .
> We are together only
> to hunt each other down.
> I have waited five hundred years for this.
> In fifty more my bones will rattle

around your neck. My words will foam
from your mouth. (47)

The bruja in this poem is something other than and beyond conventions of
either the abject or the beautiful. Even sitting in the mud, she cannot be mistaken
for anything except a figure of enormous potency, akin perhaps to the goddesses
Coatlicue and Tonantzín who are evoked only parenthetically in "Los derechos de
La Malinche," but are here given voice and centrality. Likewise, if abjection and
vomit is a form of rejection of death, an expelling of fear, here the strong woman
makes fear an integral element of the learning process; death is not bracketed off
as the uncanny presence of a monstrous decomposition, but brought home and
made part of the self in the homely/uncanny string of bones around the grand-
daughter's neck. The scorpion that accompanies the women in this family line
may sting, but the poisoned words carry weight and power. The women in this
poem do not wait for phallogocentric authorization to enter the symbolic realm;
that patriarchal trap has been long since recognized. Instead, they draw from "the
gramarye of your blood" (47) an alternative sacred and erotic structure.

Anne McLeod describes the effects of feminism for women as a process of
unhinging, of imagining "antithetical relations between the parts in such a way
that the ontological framework within which they have been thought comes
unhinged" (159). Likewise, Gaspar de Alba's inquiry into the twists and torsions
of a Mexican-American woman's narration of her doubled and duplicitous histories point toward an unhinging of both US- and Mexican-based masculinist
ontological frameworks. To take this step runs the risk of becoming unhinged
in its second sense as well: thus the continual flirting with madness, the association with scorpions, the foaming at the mouth. Gaspar de Alba's literary practice challenges readers to rethink the category of the woman as discursive sub-
ject/object outside the essentialist frame into which she has so traditionally
been cast, as she also forces us to return to a question relative to the field of literary study at large, that of the struggle with and against the power of words. In
putting pressure on ignored and reinscribed histories of origins, she suggests
not only a model for revitalizing national and cultural mythic structures, but
also a method for dislocating the hinge between linguistic and extralinguistic
binaries such as the one that has exercised us over the last few pages.

David Johnson describes the process by which Octavio Paz's definition of
Mexicanness is produced by crossing the border into the United States and
fetishizing that act of crossing as a psychic journey in understanding the
national and personal self as a cultural product. Says Johnson:

> On either side of the border, on both sides of the border, there is one cultural
> identity; however it is defined, in whatever terms it is disclosed, it is never-
> theless *one*—it is *our* identity. And even if on either side of the border there is
> more than one cultural identity, each one will be located within the horizon of

a certain discretion; each will be found in its own place, bordered by the dream of its proper univocity. Such is the effect of Paz's border . . . "we" will only find ourselves there, awaiting us on the other side of the border. (133–4)

Johnson's reading of Paz reminds us of striking similarities between the Mexican thinker's 1950s meditation on Mexicanness and Mignolo's 1990s discussion of border epistemology as a play of self and other. Despite generational and ideological differences, for both Paz and Mignolo the most salient quality of the border is that the act of crossing serves the psychic function of reflection. The border itself becomes a mirror exacting knowledge of the self and the other, but most importantly, as a reinscription of the self in the other, generating knowledge of the self.

Gaspar de Alba too, uses the traversal of the border to rethink knowledge of self and other, but she does so as a feminine process of unhinging the political and linguistic univocity of "we" and "us," rejecting, in the final analysis, the old comfortable clichés of mirrored self-reflections for a productive, if destabilizing, witchy heritage. We need not wait another five hundred years to attend to the rattling of La Malinche's bones.

Notes

[1] An earlier version of part of this essay has been published with the title, "Border Theory and the Canon," *Post-colonial Literatures: Expanding the Canon* ed. Deborah L. Madsen. (London: Pluto, 1999).

[2] "If you do not understand my many tongues, you begin to understand why I speak them. . . . It [introductory monologue in Spanish] is here to be appreciated or missed, and both the appreciation and the missing are significant. The more fully this playfulness is appreciated, the less broken I am to you, the more dimensional I am to you" (46).

Works Cited

Arteaga, Alfred. *Chicano Poetics: Heterotexts and Hybridities.* Cambridge: Cambrige UP, 1997.

Castro-Gómez, Santiago. "Modernidad, Latinoamericanismo y globalización." *Cuadernos americanos* 12. 1 (1998) 187–213.

Derridá, Jacques. "Economimesis." *Diacritics* 11.2 (1981): 3–25.

Gaspar de Alba, Alicia. *Beggar on Cordoba Bridge.* Eds. Alicia Gaspar de Alba, María Herrera Sobek, and Demetria Martínez. *Three Times a Woman.* Tempe: Bilingual Review Press, 1989.

_____. "Malinchista, A Myth Revised." eds. Tey Diana Rebolledo and Eliana S. Rivero. *Infinite Divisions: An Anthology of Chicana Literature.* Tucson: U of Arizona P, 1993: 212–13.

_____. *The Mystery of Survival and other Stories.* Tempe: Bilingual Press, 1993.

Johnson, David E. "The Time of Translation." Eds. Scott Michaelson and David E. Johnson. *Border Theory: The Limits of Cultural Politics.* Minneapolis: U of Minnesota P, 1997. 129–65.

Kristeva, Julia. *Powers of Horror: An Essay on Abjection.* Trans. Leon S. Roudiez. New York: Columbia UP, 1982.

Lugones, María. "Hablando cara a cara/Speaking Face to Face: An Exploration of Ethnocentric Racism." Ed. Anzaldúa, Gloria. *Making Face, Making Soul: Haciendo Caras: Creative and Critical Perspectives by Women of Color.* San Francisco: Aunt Lute, 1990. 46–54.

McLeod, Anne. "Gender Difference Relativity in GDR-Writing or: How to Oppose Without Really Trying." *Oxford Literary Review* 7 (1985): 41–61.

Melas, Natalie. "Versions of Incommensurability." *World Literature Today* (Spring 1995): 275–280.

Mignolo, Walter D. "Posoccidentalismo: El argumento desde América Latina." *Cuadernos americanos* 12.67 (1998): 143–165.

Paz, Octavio. *El laberinto de la soledad.* 1959. México: Fondo de Cultura Económica, 1980. Trans. Lysander Kemp as *The Labyrinth of Solitude.* New York: Grove, 1961.

Malinche et al.

Malinche, Calafia y Toypurina: Of Myths, Monsters and Embodied History

Antonia I. Castañeda

"Peínate que pareces India."
(Comb your hair, don't be looking like an Indian.)
"Arréglate, que te toman por India."
(Fix yourself up, lest you be mistaken for an Indian girl.)

Do this, that, or the other to your appearance to avoid being perceived as Indian—familiar, familial admonitions for Mexicana/Chicana (meaning mestiza), women and girls on the nineteenth and twentieth century Borderlands. Unspoken, but understood, in exhortations to mestizas to erase all cultural, and wherever possible, "racial," traces of Indigenous ancestry, is the underlying equation of Indian womanhood with devalued sexuality.[1]

This equation, as historians, feminist theorists, and other scholars have shown, is rooted in the gendering of the "New World" as female, in the sexualizing and eroticizing of its exploration and conquest, and in the erasing of its subjugated indigenous populations.[2] This equation is equally grounded in the gendered, sexualized, racialized, cultural, and economic violence of colonial domination. It is fixed in the history of Indian-woman-hating that Gloria Anzaldúa, Norma Alarcón, Deena González, and Inés Hernández-Avila theorize.[3] It is premised in the multi-layered strategies of Mestizas' survival, and in the practice of everyday life under conditions in which the Indian in us, always subject to attack, is to be denied, erased, extirpated.

My work, which moves Indigenous and mestiza women's bodies and sexuality in 18th and 19th century Alta California to the center of historical inquiry, draws on scholarship that theorizes gender and sexuality as dimensions of subjectivity that are both an "effect of power and a technology of rule," and that analyzes colonial domination in relation to the construction of subjectivities—meaning forms of personhood, power, and social positioning.[4] Relying too on studies analyzing the body as a trope that is key to the configuring of domination, subjugation, and resistance, I explore how women articulated their subjectivitiy and identity/ies within the confines, conflicts, and contradictions of a frontier colonial order—where Indias were under colonial domination, and Mestizas, initially among the colonizing forces, also became the colonized in the post-U.S. Mexican War era.[5] Mestizas, then, are both dominated and dominating historical subjects whose multiple identities, polyvalent locations, and agency I examine as part of the ongoing debate in Chicana/o Studies about our indigenous identities and selves.[6]

Calafia: The Body of Myth

In California, the myth and paradigm of the historical Malinche has significant antecedents in the myth of Calafia, the beautiful but wild and ferocious black Amazon Queen of the the *novelas de caballería,* from which the name California is derived.[7] Though initially a construct of the medieval Spanish literary imaginary, Calafia and the Amazons, the monstrous women of medieval Europe's mythic geography, formed an integral part of the New World historical imaginary and imperial archives from the sixteenth through the eighteenth centuries.[8]

The myth of Calafia and California first appeared in *Las sergas de Esplandián,* the chivalric novel by Garcí Rodríguez (Ordóñez) de Montalvo, published in 1510 for distribution in America, had significant currency at the beginning of the subjugation of Mexico.[9] In this male fantasy, the Amadís de Gaula and his son Esplandián, the Christian heroes of the novel, first meet Calafia in combat, when the Amazons join Aramato's struggle to capture Constantinople from the Emperor's Christian allies.

In the fashion of Amazons everywhere, Calafia rules a tribe of women without men in California, a remote island next to the earthly paradise. Calafia and her army of black women warriors tame and mount fearsome flying griffins, wield weapons of pure gold, and battle their male opponents while mounted atop the backs of these fearsome creatures. The women feed the enemy men captured on the battlefield to the griffins, sparing a few for purposes of procreation. When the children are born, Amazon mothers keep the females and immediately kill the males. In this myth of women living with women who kill their male infants at birth, Western constructs of the polluting female body, the "monstrous feminine," converge with fears and fantasies of New World monsters.[10]

Calafia's Amazons and Amadís's Christian troops (male Europeans) fought a ferocious battle. For a while it seemed that the magnificently wild, black warrior-women would triumph; but the wild beasts turned on their mistresses and devoured them. At tale's end, the mighty Calafia is subdued, tamed, dominated. Like infidel queens in most other *novelas,* Calafia converts to Christianity and offers herself—body, soul, and worldly goods—to the hero-object of her desire, even though he rejects her. Moreover, she resignedly accepts Espandián's marriage to the *infanta* Leonorina, and weds Talanque, another victorious Christian, whom the splendid hero bestows upon her.[11]

In this story, published ten years before the conquest of Mexico and the appearance of the historical Malinche, the black Amazonian queen Calafia, like the land that is named for her, is militarily conquered, Christianized, and married to one of her captors. She relinquishes her authority, sovereignty, religion, and her life among women without men. In the male imaginary, Calafia/the land is tamed, husbanded, seeded.

Myth and History: Archiving the Body

Mythic legends of Amazons, and the quest for women reigning in a land of untold riches, ripe to be dominated, who offer themselves to their conquerors, existed not only in the *novelas de caballería,* or "Books of the Brave."[12] Rather, these accounts persisted in the journals and reports of Spanish explorers, *conquistadores,* and colonizing expeditions. The myth, and search for the Amazons, traveled with the explorers, from the Yucatán in the South to far northern waters in the futile search for the Northwest Passage to India. The search for the Amazons, and near sightings, were consistently documented mapped, and archived.

From Juan de Grijalva's expedition of 1518, one account notes "This Isle of Women is a small island north of Cozumel off the east coast of the Yucatán that, according to López de Gómara, . . . was named for the women-like dolls or idols supposedly found there."[13] A Spanish map of 1526–30 identifies an islet lying off the northwest tip of the "island" of Yucatán, as "Amazonas." A similar map shows both an islet of "Amazonas," and an "isla de mujeres," named Ciualtán (also spelled Cigualtán, Igualtán).[14]

In the North, the myth begins with Hernán Cortés, who sent out the exploring expedition that first landed in Baja California and who came to the peninsula himself in 1535. Cortes writes, in his fourth *Carta de relación* to the Catholic monarchs, ". . . he [Cristóbal de Olid] likewise brought me an account of the chiefs of the province of Ciguatán who affirm that there is an island inhabited only by women, without any men. . . and that this island is ten days travel from this province. . . ."[15]

Nuño de Guzmán, Cortés bitter rival and sadistic explorer of Nueva Galicia, also competed to be the first to find the Amazons. In his letter-report, Guzmán writes that: "From then [Azatlán] ten days further I shall go to find the Amazons which some say dwell in the sea, some in an arm of the sea, and that they are rich, and accounted of the people for goddesses, and whiter than other women. . . ."[16] Here, Guzmán invokes Aztlán, the ancient homeland of the Aztecs, and skin color, both themes which I discuss in other essays.

Peter Martyr, who interviewed Juan de Rivera, Cortés' representative at the Royal Court in 1522, quotes Rivera's discussion about "a region inhabited only by women, in the mountains situated toward the North. . .[by] the name of Igualtan, which in the language of the country, means "region of women," from "iguatl," "woman" and "Lan," "Lord."[17] In his recounting, Martyr fixes the virgin-whore binary for American Amazons—noting that in one account the companies of women are reputedly a group of vestal virgins, and "a pack of harlot amazons" in another.[18]

Literary and historical fusions are evident in another stock female character from the chivalric novels, including *Las Sergas de Esplandián* and its multiple sequels, the *maga enamorada*—the enamored woman.[19] This deceiving, lustful woman uses magic and witchcraft to ensnare the hero—who, finding her neither attractive nor desirable, if not downright repellent, rejects her. Invariably, the *maga enamorada* is a pagan and most often, is Muslim. *La mora encantada*, the enticing Moorish enchantress, is but another representation of the lusting, complicitous, alien-female Other.[20]

Thus, the sexualization, eroticization, racialization, and devaluation of Indian women's bodies symbolized by the Malinche myth during the conquest of Mexico, is here seen within the discourse of the Crusades—the Reconquest of the Peninsula from Muslim rule that ended in 1492—and of Christian orthodoxy of the Inquisition with its extirpation of the religious and racial Other.

In sixteenth century Spain, black was a symbol for non-Christian. Calafia, as a non-Christian woman of dark skin and a politico-military-religious foe, is the consummate symbol of the alien "Other." These are political representations of women native to the contested land—the space of war, conquest, and nation building. In the Western imperial gaze, the women of the enemy, of the land under attack or conquest, are anxious to be delivered from their own men, to deliver themselves unto the conqueror, and to be complicit in the conquest.[21]

These politics inform the military-religious conquest and colonization of Alta California in the latter third of the eighteenth century. Though the myth of Calafia and the Amazons faded from the historical record, eventually to be replaced by the Malinche paradigm, the archival record documenting this conquest consistently constructs Indian women in sexual, erotic, and racial terms.[22]

Mexico's independence from Spain in 1821, and the liberalization of trade and colonization policies launched a new *entrada* (incursion), of single males—especially of Euro-American entrepreneurs, merchants, traders, and trappers—into the borderlands region (Alta California, Nuevo Mexico and Tejas).[23] Their arrival, and corolllary discourse of U.S. political, national, and capitalist formation set in motion a new wave of sexualized, eroticized and racialized representations of Californian Indian women, and of Californiana mestizas.

In Euro-American fiction, memoirs, historical documents, and interpretive histories of nineteenth century California, Californianas, particularly those of landed families, appeared as anxious accomplices to the Euro-American takeover. Their greatest desire, according to Bancroft and echoed by Bolton, was to "marry a blue eyed stranger."[24] Thus, Caiforniana marriages to Euro-Americans have, until recently, been interpreted within the terms of one aspect of the Malinche paradigm—*traidoras, vendepatrias* (traitors) who gave themselves over to the conquest. While elite mestizas, or Californianas, were deracinated and represented as eagerly complicitous with the conquering white males, non elite mestizas were constructed as Mexican-Indian prostitutes, monte-dealers, and fandango-dancers in another battlefield, now between Catholicism and Protestantism.[25] They represented the other side of the Malinche paradigm—the "conquered," sexually, racially, and socially devalued Indian woman.

India/Mestiza Bodies: *La Historia Encarnada*

The arrival of Euro-Americans from the new Protestant nation initiated still another re-enactment of the ongoing ideological/epistemological contest in which native women's bodies were the battlefields. In Alta California the battle began in 1769, when on arriving here, Spanish colonial authorities (church, military, colonial state), confronted the reality of Amerindian societies in which women not only controlled their own resources, sexuality, and reproductive processes, but also held religious, political, economic, and sometimes, military power.[26] The patriarchal church and state sought to eradicate native traditions that were centered on and controlled by women

In the confessional, priests queried both women and men about their sexual lives and activities and meted out punishment accordingly. While prohibitions against fornication, adultery, masturbation, sodomy, incest, bestiality, and coitus interruptus applied to all, abortion and infanticide—violations of the Fifth Commandment which condemned killing—applied specifically to women and were harshly punished.[27] Hugo Reid writes that the priests at Mission San Gabriel attributed all miscarriages to infanticide and that Gabrielino women were punished by "shaving the head, flogging for fifteen subsequent days, [wearing] iron on the feet for three months, and having to appear every Sunday in church, on the steps leading up the altar, with a hideous painted wooden child (*a monigote*) in her arms" representing the dead infant.[28]

The imperative to control and remake native sexuality, in particular to control women's procreation, was driven as much by material interest as by doctrinal issues. California needed a growing Hispanicized Indian population as both a source of labor and as a defense against foreign invasion, and thus missionaries might take extraordinary measures to assure reproduction.

Father Olbes at Mission Santa Cruz ordered an infertile couple to have sexual intercourse in his presence because he did not believe they could not have children. The couple refused, but Olbes forcibly inspected the man's penis to learn "whether or not it was in good order" and tried to inspect the woman's genitalia.[29] She refused, fought with him, and tried to bite him. Olbes ordered that she be tied by the hands, and given fifty lashes, shackled, and locked up in the *monjero* (women's dormitory). He then had a *monigote* made and commanded that she "treat the doll as though it were a child and carry it in the presence of everyone for nine days."[30] While this woman was beaten and her sexuality demeaned, the husband who had been intimate with another woman, was ridiculed and humiliated. A set of cow horns was tied to his head with leather thongs, thereby converting him into a "cuckhold," and he was "herded" to daily Mass in cow horns and fetters.[31]

Franciscan priests also prohibited initiation ceremonies, dances, and songs in the mission system. They sought to destroy the ideological, moral, and ethical systems that defined native life. They demonized non-complying women, especially those who resisted openly, as witches. Indeed, Ramon Gutiérrez argues that, in the borderlands of New Spain, "One can interpret the whole history of the persecution of Indian women as witches . . . as a struggle over [these] competing ways of defining the body and of regulating procreation as the church endeavored to constrain the expression of desire within boundaries that clerics defined proper and acceptable.[32]

Until recently, literary and historical writings about native women in California history, meaning Indias and mestizas, were informed by the Calafia and Malinche myths, and variations on this theme. More recently, cultural and oral historians, feminist theorists, religious scholars, and cultural critics, among others, are examining the daily lives of California Indian women.[33] They are, to quote feminist theoriest Emma Pérez, "excavating words and their inherited meanings," digging in the silences, gaps, and interstitial spaces, of historical documents and other sources for the thoughts, words, actions and forms native women used in shaping multiple, complex, and changing identities across time and space.[34]

These works have concluded that while colonizing males constructed Indian women's bodies, both symbolically and materially, as a site to effect territorial and political conquest, women constructed and used their bodies, both symbolically and materially, as instruments of opposition, resistance, and subversion of colonial domination.[35] In California, as elsewhere in the Americas, Indigenous women countered the everyday violence inflicted upon them with gender-centered strategies that authorized them to speak, to act, to lead, and to empower others. They fought the ideological power of the colonial church and state, which subordinated women to men and sought to control their bodies and their sexuality, with equally powerful ideologies that vested women with power and authority over their own sexuality.[36]

Accordingly, historian Nancy Shoemaker concludes that the central signifier of gender identity among native societies was the kind of work one performed. Religious scholars Inés Talamantes and Mary Riojas Muñoz analyze puberty ceremonies and ritual menstrual seclusion to theorize how Apache and Yurok women fit into the symbolic order of the sacred in their respective cultures.[37]

Native systems of gender included gender parallelism, matriarchal sociopolitical organization, and matrilineal forms of reckoning and descent. Some Indian societies had an institutionalized acceptance of gender variation, which scholars refer to as a third gender, or more commonly *berdache,* and which Native Americans refer to as "Two Spirit."[38] Within these diverse cultures, women's power and authority could derive from one or more elements: the culture's basic principle of individual autonomy that structured political relationships, including those between men and women; women's important productive or reproductive role in the economy; and the authority accorded women by their bearing and raising of children.[39] Further, women's power and authority were integral to, and also derived from, their people's core religious-spiritual beliefs, values, and traditions, which generally accorded women and men equivalent value, power, and range of practices.

As part of the natural world, sexuality, for many indigenous peoples, was related to the sacred and, as such, was central to the religious and cosmic order and was celebrated in song, dance, and other ritual observances. Accepted practices included premarital sexual activity, polygamy, polyandry, homosexuality, transvestitism, same-sex marriage, and ritual sexual practices. In general, consent, not contractual obligation, defined marriage, and divorce was easily attainable.[40]

Woman—the female principle—was a pivotal force in Native American origin stories, cosmologies, and world views. Woman, whether in the form of Grandmother, Thought Woman, White Buffalo Calf Woman, or other female being, was at the center of the originating principle that brought the people into being and sustained them. Muñoz recontextualizes the origin myth of the Yurok in which women "in payment for all the things that humans were going to gather from the land . . . offered to menstruate as a way of making payment for all the blood human beings were going to have to spill in order to feed the people."[41] Interpreting Apurowak ritual menstrual seclusion within the concept of balanced reciprocity and rites of reciprocity, Muñoz concludes that women chose self-isolation in order that they might shape the symbolic order established in the beginning. In doing so she calls up a new subject position that decenters Christian concepts of the body as base and vile, of menstruation as a signifier of societal ills, and corollary anthropological interpretations of the "menstrual taboo."[42]

Toypurina's Line: Oppositional Bodies

Toypurina, the medicine woman of the Japchavit *ranchería*, used her power and authority to lead Gabrielino armed opposition to Spanish colonialism.[43] In 1785 she recruited 6 of the 8 villages that attacked mission San Gabriel, an attack she and two male companions organized and led. Toypurina, the other two leaders, and twenty other warriors were captured. After a three-year imprisonment at San Gabriel, in 1788 she was exiled to the far northern regions of Alta California to Mission San Carlos Borromeo. The twenty warriors captured with her were sentenced to between twenty and twenty-five lashes plus time already served. This punishment was levied as much for following the leadership of a woman as for rebelling against Spanish domination. Governor Pedro Fages stated that their public whippings were "to serve as a warning to all," for he would "admonish them about their ingratitude, underscoring their perversity, and unmasking the deceit and tricks by which *they allowed themselves to be dominated by the aforesaid woman*"[44] (emphasis added).

Toypurina's power and influence derived from a non-Western religious-political ideological system of power in which women were central to the ritual and spiritual life of the tribe.[45] California Indian women continued to resist colonial domination with a range of actions and activities, including a religious-political movement that vested power in a female deity and placed the health and well-being of the community in the hands of a female visionary.

In 1801, at the height of an epidemic ravaging the Chumash in the missions and the *rancherías*, a Chumash woman at Mission Santa Barbara launched a clandestine, large-scale revitalization movement.[46] Drawing her authority from visions and revelations from Chupu, the Chumash earth goddess or diety, this neophyte woman—who remains unnamed in the documents—called for a return to the worship of Chupu. Almost all the neophytes, Alcaldes included, went to the visionary's house to present beads and seeds and to go through the rite of renouncing Christianity.[47]

While historical documents portray both Toypurina and the Chumash visionary of 1801 as "witches and sorceresses"—and ecclesiastical and civil officials dismissed, discredited, exiled, or sometimes put to death non-white women charged with witchcraft—women themselves used witchcraft as a means of subverting the sociosexual order sanctioned by religion and enshrined in the colonial honor code as an ethical system.[48] Ruth Behar argues that women used sexualized magic to control men and subvert the male order by symbolically using their own bodies and bodily fluids as a source of power over men.[49]

Other women resisted in less visible, day-to-day practices: they poisoned the priests' food, practiced fugitivism, worshipped their own deities, had visions that others believed and followed, performed prohibited dances and rituals, and refused to abide by patriarchal sexual norms, as well as continued to participate in armed revolts and rebellions against the missions, soldiers, and *ranchos*.[50] Participants cited the priests' cruelty and repression of traditional ceremonies and sexual practices among primary reasons for the attacks on the missions, for the assassination of the friar Andrés Quintana at Mission Santa Cruz in 1812, and for the great Chumash *levantamiento* of 1824.[51]

That colonialism, for all its brutal technologies and distorted narratives, could not completely destroy native women's historical autonomy is something native peoples have always known, but scholarly researchers are just beginning to learn.[52] Through oral and visual traditions, and other means of communicating counter-histories, native women's power, authority, and knowledge have remained part of their peoples' collective memory, historical reality, and daily struggles of "being in a state of war for five hundred years."[53] Tribal memory and what anthropologist Ana María Alonso terms "ideology of resistance based on social memory," preserve and reinscribe native women's subjectivity."[54] Elaborating the concept of third space feminism, subjectivity, and women of color, Chela Sandoval, in *Methodology of the Oppressed*, theorizes the state of being in resistance and opposition as a

> . . . mapping of consciousness. . . . a topography of consciousness in opposition. . .[that] represents the charting of psychic and material realities that occupy a particular cultural region. This cultural topography delineates a set of critical points within which individuals and groups seeking to transform dominant and oppressive powers can constitute themselves as resistant and oppositional citizen-subjects."[55]

Thus, Vera Rocha, a Gabrielino elder whom I interviewed in 1996, related how her own and other Gabrielino children's resistance to the educational systems' unrelenting efforts to de-Indianize them, led to their dropping out of school at very early ages.[56] Rocha, who lived the terrors of the federal government's post-World War II Indian policies, known as the "termination laws" of the Truman and Eisenhower administrations, had received the story of Toypurina and the Gabrielinos as a very young girl from her great-grandmother, who received it from her mother.[57] Rocha, in turn, transmitted the story to her children and grandchildren and, more recently, to the world in general in the form of a public monument—a prayer mound dedicated to Toypurina developed in conjunction with Chicana artist Judith F. Baca.[58] In preserving and retelling the history of Toypurina and her people, Rocha claims and embodies her "right to history," her authority and sources to claim and to speak come not from Western academic fronts.

> The Great Spirit has given me the right to say what comes through my ancestors. My genes are from my ancestors and on to my children . . . The history is coming through me . . . That's why I honor Toypurina. Toypurina has given me the instrument to fight.

The histories remain archived in tribal, family, and individual memory, as well as in other texts—some written, most not. Drawing on literary, linguistic, and performance methodologies and theories, feminists and other scholars are learning to read and interpret the ways in which American Indian women, and their mestiza daughters, have constructed identities in daily opposition to assaults on their sexual, social, and cultural bodies within the gendered, sexualized, and racialized politics of colonial and nationalist domination and histories.

Malinche's Tongues

Let me return to Malintzin/Marina/Malinche/La Lengua, the young Mexica multilingual translator/diplomat who entered the Valley of Anahuac with Cortés in 1519–1521 and who bore Cortés's son.[59] Chicana scholars and writers, whose research and writing has re-membered Malintzin/Malinche since the early 1970s, have reclaimed this symbolic mother of mestizo peoples from the opprobrium of patriarchal Mexicano/Chicano history that condemned her sexuality, devalued and dismissed her as Cortes' "Indian whore."[60]

Most recently, linguist Frances Karttunen extends literary critic/Conchero dancer Ines Hernández's early discussion of Malintzin as the symbolic path-opener, the vanguard, the person in command who leads the way in "La danza de la Conquista," a reenactment in dance performed in native communities since the conquista itself.[61]

Karttunen examines the representation of Malintzin in codices, dance and other cultural representations. She draws on the long Mesoamerican tradition of two-headed and two-faced figures and the Aztec tradition of IXIPTLAY-OTL, "representation," in which chosen human beings served as temporary embodiments of deities, providing them a conduit through which to speak and act in the world inhabited by humans, to rethink Malinche. Noting that much has been made of the notion that the indigenous peoples perceived the Europeans as Gods, she inverts the position of deity-or representation of deity (European and male)—and argues that the Aztecs may have perceived Malintzin/the interpreter as an IXIPTLA of a supernatural force. Faced with circumstances unlike any other in the history of her people, Malintzin/Malinche, here interpreted as the embodiment of a IXIPTLA, used the language and skills she needed to live each day, performing her role to perfection.[62]

Conclusion

Having gone unspoken and unthought in Borderlands historiography until very recently, to recover, claim and re-member the historical bodies of Indias y Mestizas is critical to researching, writing, and interpreting Chicana history. As recent scholarship reveals, Native Women's bodies—their gender, race, and sexuality—are pivotal to the politics, policies, and cultures of colonialism, nationalism, and transnationalism—from the basic core of family life to contemporary structures of globalization.[63] We need only to read the politics and policies of gender, sexuality, and reproduction in the 1996 immigration law and in the draconian "Welfare" reform measures of 1996-1997 to know the

contemporary significance of these politics and policies. The horrendously
brutal unsolved murders of over three hundred Mexican women, and disap-
pearance of over five hundred, on the U.S.-Mexico border—most of whom
worked in the U.S.-owned *maquiladoras* (assembly plants)—tells us that Malinche's daughters can still be viciously raped, sexually tortured, mutilated, and
killed, with impunity.[64] It tells the world that young, poor, brown-skinned
Mexican women, have no value. The sexual nature and utter viciousness of
these murders is, I argue, part of a historical continuum of unrelenting sexualized violence against Indian/Mestiza on the Spanish/Mexican/U.S. borderlands from the 16th century to the present.[65]

It is within these historical and contemporary contexts that we historicize,
analyze, theorize, and interpret the gendered, racialized, and sexualized meanings of oft-heard exhortations, "péinate, que pareces India;" "arréglate que te
tienen por India." It is from historical memory of Malinche and Toypurina
among countless others, and examination of how native women have deployed
their bodies across time, space, condition, and location, that we reconstitute
the female body and knowledge of history. It is from knowledge of native
women's resistance that Chicanas affirm their oppositional legacy and refuse
familial and others' exhortations to disavow our India/Malinche selves with
"Si mamá, somos!" Or, in Chicano Spanish, "Si mamá, semos!"

Notes

[1]Antonia I. Castañeda, "Sexual Politics in the Politics and Policies of Conquest: Amerindian
Women and the Spanish Conquest of Alta California," eds. Adela de la Torre and Beatriz M. Pes-
quera, *Building with Our Hands: New Directions in Chicana Studies* (Berkeley: U of California
P, 1993) 15–33.

[2]Virginia Marie Bouvier, *Women and the Conquest of California, 1542–1840: Codes of Silence*
(Tucson: U of Arizona P, 2001); Richard C. Trexler, *Sex and Conquest: Gendered Violence, Political Order and the European Conquest of the Americas* (Ithaca: Cornell UP, 1995); Louis Mon-
trose, "The Work of Gender in the Discourse of Discovery," *New World Encounters,* ed. Stephen
Greenblatt (Berkeley, Los Angeles, London: U of California P, 1993) 177–217.

[3]Deena J. González, "Lupe's Song: On the Origins of Mexican/Woman-Hating in the United
States," in Curtis Stokes, Theresa Meléndez, Genice Rhodes-Reed, eds. *Race in 21st Century
America.* (East Lansing: Michigan State UP, 2001) 143–158; Inés Hernández-Avila, "An Open
Letter to Chicanas: On the Power and Politics of Origin," *Without Discovery: A Native Response
to Columbus.* Ray Gonzáles, ed. (Seattle: Broken Moon P, 1992) 153–166; Norma Alarcón,
"Chicana Feminism: In the Tracks of 'The' Native Woman," *Cultural Studies,* 4–3, (October,
1990): 248–256; Gloria Anzaldúa, *Borderlands/La Frontera: The New Mestiza* (San Francisco:
Aunt Lute Press, 1987).

[4]Chéla Sandoval, *Methodology of the Oppressed* (Minneapolis and London: U of Minnesota P,
2000); Deena J. González, *Refusing the Favor: The Spanish-Mexican Women of Santa Fe,
1820–1880* (New York, Oxford: Oxford UP, 1999): Deena J. González, "Juanotilla of Cochiti,
Vecina and Coyota: Nuevomexicanas in the Eighteenth Century," *New Mexican Lives: Profiles
and Historical Stories,* ed. Richard Etualain (Albuquerque: U of NM P, 2002); Teresa de Lau-
retis, *Technologies of Gender: Essays on Theory, Film, and Fiction* (Bloomington: Indiana UP,

1987) 2–3. Rosaura Sánchez, *Telling Identities: The Californio Testimonios* (Minneapolis: U of Minnesota P, 1995).

[5]For feminist theories of the body and subjectivity, see: Barbara Brook, *Feminist Perspectives on the Body* (London and New York: Longman, 1999); Radhika Mohanram, *Black Body: Women, Colonialism and Space* (Minneapolis and London: U of Minnesota P, 1999); Janet Price and Margrit Shildrick, eds., *Feminist Theory and the Body: A Reader* (New York and London: Routledge, 1999); Paula M. Cooey, *Religious Imagination and the Body: A Feminist Analysis* (New York and Oxford: Oxford UP, 1994); Elizabeth Grosz, *Volatile Bodies: Toward A Corporeal Feminism* (Bloomington and Indianapolis: Indiana UP, 1994); Elizabeth Grosz, "Bodies and Knowledges: Feminism and the Crisis of Reason," in Linda Alcoff and Elizabeth Potter, eds. *Feminist Epistemologies* (New York, London: Routledge, 1993): 187–216.

[6]Emma Pérez, *The Decolonial Imaginary: Writing Chicanas into History* (Bloomington: Indiana UP, 1999); Linda Tuhiwai Smith, *Decolonizing Methodologies: Research and Indigenous Peoples* (New York and London: Zed Books Ltd., 1999); Florencia E. Mallon, "The Promise and Dilemma of Subaltern Studies: Perspectives from Latin American History," *American Historical Review* 99 (1994): 1491–1515; "Founding Statement: Latin American Subaltern Studies Group," *Boundary* 2 20 (Fall 1993): 110–21; Hernández-Ávila, "Open Letter to Chicanas"; Jack D. Forbes, *Aztecas del Norte: The Chicanos of Aztlán* (Greenwich, CT: Fawcett Publications, 1973). For discussion of Latinos and indigenous identity relative to the 2000 U.S. Federal Manuscript Census, see: Jack D. Forbes, "2000 Census Will Effect All Persons of Pre-Columbian American Ancestry," and Patrisia Gonzales and Roberto Rodríguez, "On the Census of Being," *Column of the Americas* 15 October 1999 Xcolumn@aol.com.

[7]The myth of Calafia is related in *Las Sergas de Esplandián,* whose author is sometimes identified as Garcí or García Ordóñez de Montalvo and at other times as Garcí or García Rodríguez de Montalvo. See Garcí Ordóñez de Montalvo, *Las Sergas Del Muy Esforzado Caballeo Esplandián,* in Don Pascual de Gayangos, ed., *Biblioteca de autores espanoles, Libros De caballerías,* vol. 40 (1857; reprint, Madrid: M Rivadeneyra, 1874/1880): 403–561. In this essay, which uses English translations, the author of *Las Sergas de Esplandían* is referred to as Garcí Ordónez de Montalvo when I cite Dora Beale Polk, *The Island of California: A History of the Myth* (Spokane: The Arthur H. Clark Company, 1991); Irving I. Leonard, whom I also cite, identifies the author of as Garcí Rodríguez de Montalvo, see Irving A. Leonard, *Books of the Brave: Being an Account of Books and of Men in the Spanish Conquest and Settlement of the Sixteenth Century New World* 1949. (Berkeley, Los Angeles: U of California P, 1992). See also Irving Leonard, *Romances of Chivalry in the Spanish Indies* (Berkeley: U of California P, 1933). See also, Bouvier, 3–17.

[8]Leonard, *Books of the Brave* 38–41. For sustained discussion of medieval mythology and the conquest of the Americas, see Luis Weckmann, *The Medieval Heritage of Mexico,* trans. Frances M. López-Morillas (New York: Fordham UP, 1992) 46–71.

[9]Weckmann 51.

[10]Weckmann 46-7; María Helena Sánchez-Ortega, "Woman as a Source of 'Evil' in Counter-Reformation Spain," Anne J. Cruz and Mary Elizabeth Perry, eds. *Culture and Control in Counter-Reformation Spain, Hispanic Issues* 7 (Minneapolis: U of Minnesota P, 1992). I draw upon feminist film criticism for the concept and term "the monstrous feminine". See Barbara Creed, *The Monstrous Feminine: Film, Feminism, Psychoanalysis* (New York: Routledge, 1993). For feminist theories of the body, see Note 5.

[11]Ordónez de Montalvo, 554–56.

[12]Irving Leonard used this term to refer to the chivalric novels, or books of fiction, with which Christopher Columbus, Hernán Cortés, Bartolomé de las Casas, and their contemporaries would have been familiar as they stepped ashore in the "New World." See, Leonard, *Books of the Brave* xlii–xlvii.

[13]As quoted in Polk, *The Island of California* 77.

[14]Polk 78.

[15]As quoted in Leonard, *Books of the Brave* 48–49.

[16]As quoted in Polk, 93.

[17]Polk 83.

[18]Polk 78.

[19]For gender theory and interpretation of the image of women in the novels of chivalry, most particularly non-Christian women, see Judith Whitenack, "Don Quijote y La Maga: Otra Mujer Que 'No Parece,'" ed. Juan Villegas, *La Mujer y su representación en las literaturas hispánicas, Actas Irvine-92: Asociación Internacional de Hispanistas* (Irvine: Regents of the U of California P, 1994): 82–96; Judith Whitenack, "Conversion to Christianity in the Spanish Romance of Chivalry, 1490–1524," *Journal of Hispanic Philology* 13 (Autumn, 1988): 13–39; For discussion of medieval mythology and the conquest of the Americas, see Weckmann 46–71.

[20]George Mariscal, "The Role of Spain in Contemporary Race Theory," 2 (1998): 7–22.

[21]For a discussion of native women (California Indian and Mestiza women) and the issue of complicity in eighteenth and nineteenth century California, see: Antonia I. Castañeda, "Gender, Race, and Culture: Spanish-Mexican Women in the Historiography of Frontier California," *Frontiers: A Journal of WomenStudies* XI (1990): 8–20; Antonia I. Castañeda, "The Political Economy of Nineteenth Century Stereotypes of Californianas," ed. Adelaida R. Del Castillo *Between Borders: Essays on Mexicana/ Chicana History* (Los Angeles: Floricanto, 1990): 213–236.

[22]Antonia I. Castañeda, "Sexual Violence in the Politics and Policies of Conquest: Amerindian Women and the Spanish Conquest of Alta California," eds. Adela de la Torre and Beatriz M. Pesquera, *Building With Our Hands: New Directions in Chicana Studies* (Berkeley, London, Los Angeles: U of California P, 1993): 15–33.

[23]For nineteenth century New Mexico and California, respectively, see: González, *Refusing the Favor*, and Sánchez, *Telling Identities*.

[24]Castañeda, "Spanish Mexican Women in the Historiography of California."

[25]Castañeda, "The Political Economy of Nineteenth Century Stereotypes of Californianas."

[26]Weckmann, 49–50; Antonia I. Castañeda, "Engendering the History of Alta California, 1769–1848: Gender, Sexuality, and the Family," eds. Ramón A. Gutiérrez and Richard J. Orsi, *Contested Eden: California Before the Gold Rush* (Berkeley: U of California P, for The California Historical Society, 1997) 230–259.

[27]Harry Kelsey, ed., *The Doctrina and Confesionario of Juan Cortés* (Altadena: Howling Coyote, 1979): 112–16, 120–23; Madison S. Beeler, ed., *The Ventureno Confesionario of José Senan, O.F.M., U of California Publication in Linguistics* 47 (Berkeley: U of California P, 1967): 37–63.

[28]As quoted in Castañeda, "Engendering," 234–356.

[29]Castañeda, "Engendering" 235.

[30]As quoted in Edward D. Castillo, "The Native Response to the Colonization of Alta California," Edward D. Castillo, ed. *Native American Perspectives on the Hispanic Colonization of Alta California, Spanish Borderlands Sourcebook 26* (New York: Garland, 1991), (New York & London, 1991) 426; Edward D. Castillo, "Introduction," Castillo, ed., *Native American Perspectives on the Hispanic Colonization of Alta California*, xvii–xlv.

[31]Bouvier, 127–28.

[32]Ramón A. Gutiérrez, "Sexual Mores and Behavior: The Spanish Borderlands," Jacob Ernest Cooke, et. al., eds. *Encyclopedia of the North American Colonies*, vol. 2 (New York: Charles Scribner's Sons, 1993): 700–710. Quote is from p. 701.

[33]See Greg Sarris, *Mabel McKay: Weaving the Dream* (Berkeley: U of California P, 1994); Greg Sarris, *Keeping Slug Woman Alive: A Holistic Approach to American Indian Texts* (Berkeley: U of California P, 1993); Greg Sarris, "'What I'm Talking about When I'm Talking about My Baskets': Conversations with Mabel McKay," in Sidonie Smith and Julia Watson, eds. *De/Colonizing the Subject: The Politics of Gender in Women's Autobiography* (Minneapolis: U of Minnesota P, 1992); Castillo, Victoria Brady, Sarah Crome, and Lyn Reese, "Resist! Survival Tactics of Indian Women," California History 63 (Spring 1984).

[34]Pérez, xviii.

[35]Castañeda, "Engendering" 237.

[36]See Laura F. Klein and Lillian A. Ackerman, eds., *Women and Power in Native North America* (Norman: U of Oklahoma P, 1995); Nancy Shoemaker, ed., *Negotiators of Change: Historical Perspectives on Native American Women* (New York: Routledge, 1995); Kevin Gosner and Deborah E. Kanter, eds., *Women, Power, and Resistance in Colonial Mesoamerica*, spec. issue of *Ethnohistory* 42 (Fall 1995); Carol Devens, *Countering Colonization: Native American Women in the Great Lakes Missions, 1630–1900* (Berkeley: U of California P, 1992); Gretchen M. Bataille and Kathleen Mullen Sands, eds., *American Indian Women: Telling Their Lives* (Lincoln: U of Nebraska P, 1984); Beatrice Medicine and Patricia Albers, eds., *The Hidden Half: Studies of Plains Indian Women* (Lanham: U of America P, 1983).

[37]Shoemaker; Ines Talamantez, "Images of the Feminine in Apache Religious Tradition," *After Patriarchy: Feminist Transformations of the World Religions* eds. William R. Eakin, et. al. (Orbis Books, 1991) 131–145; Mary Virginia Rojas Muñoz, "'She Bathes in a Sacred Place': Rites of Reciprocity, Scratching Sticks and Prestige in Alta California," M.A. thesis, U of Santa Barbara, 1997.

[38]Sabine Lang, *Men as Women, Women as Men: Changing Gender in Native American Cultures* (Austin: UT Press, 1998).

[39]Klein and Ackerman, see especially Klein and Ackerman's introduction and essays by Victoria D. Patterson, Mary Shepardson, Sue-Ellen Jacobs, and Daniel Maltz and JoAllyn Archambault; Shoemaker, especially Shoemaker's introduction, and essays by Lucy Eldersveld Murphy and Carol Douglas Sparks; Gosner and Kanter, especially the essays by Alvis E. Dunn, Martha Few, and Irene Silverblatt.

[40]Antonia I. Castañeda, "Marriage: The Spanish Borderlands," *Encylopedia of the North American Colonies*, eds. Jacob Ernest Cooke, et. al. 3 vols. (New York: Charles Scribner's Sons, 1993) 2:727–38.

[41]Muñoz, 18–19.

[42]Muñoz.

[43]"Ynterrogatorio sobre la sublevación de San Gabriel, 10 octubre de 1785," Archivo General de la Nación, Provincias Internas, tomo I (Californias):120, Microfilm Collection, Bancroft Library, Berkeley, California; See also, Castañeda, "Engendering" 235–238.

[44]"Ynterrogatorio."

[45]Alvis E. Dunn, "A Cry at Daybreak: Death, Disease, and Defense of Community in a Highland Ixil-Mayan Village," and Martha Few, "Women, Religion, and Power: Gender and Resistance in Daily Life in Late-Seventeenth-Century Santiago de Guatemala," *Women, Power, and Resistance in Colonial Mesoamerica*, spec. issue *Ethnohistory* eds. Gosner and Kanter 595–606 and 627–639, respectively.

[46]Robert F. Heizer, "A California Messianic Movement of 1801 among the Chumash," *American Anthropologist* 43 (1941, reprint, 1962): 128–29; Dunn, "A Cry at Daybreak." For discussion of the warrior woman tradition, women's councils, religion, and spirituality as a source of women's power and resistance, and of women's cultural mediation and resistance in Native American history, see Elizabeth Salas, *Soldaderas in the Mexican Military* (Austin: U of TX P, 1990) 1–10; Clara Sue Kidwell, "Indian Women as Cultural Mediators," *Ethnohistory* 39 (Spring 1992): 97–107; Beatrice Medicine, "'Warrior Women'—Sex Role Alternatives for Plains Indian Women," *The Hidden Half*, eds., Medicine and Albers, 267–80.

[47]Heizer, "Chumash visionary."

[48]Antonia I. Castañeda, "Witchcraft on the Spanish-Mexican Borderlands," *The Reader's Companion to U.S. Women's History* eds. Wilma Mankiller, et.al. (New York: Houghton Mifflin Company, 1998) 638–39; Ruth Behar, "Sexual Witchcraft, Colonialism, and Women's Power: Views from the Mexican Inquisition," *Sexuality and Marriage in Colonial Latin America*, ed. Lavrín, 178–206; Ruth Behar, "Sex and Sin, Witchcraft, and the Devil in Late Colonial Mexico," *Amer-*

ican Ethnologist 14 (February 1987): 344–54; Ruth Behar, "The Visions of a Guachichil Witch in 1599: A Window on the Subjugation of Mexico's Hunter-Gatherers," *Ethnohistory* 34 (Spring 1987): 115–38; see also Solange Alberro, "Herejes, brujas, y beatas: Mujeres ante el Tribunal del Santo Oficio de la Inquisición en la Nueva España," *Presencia y transparencia*, ed. Escandón 79–94; Henry Kamen, Inquisition and Society in Spain in the Sixteenth and Seventeenth Century (Bloomington: U of Indiana P, 1985); Henry Kamen, "Notes on Witchcraft, Sexuality, and the Inquisition," *The Spanish Inquisition and the Inquisitorial Mind* ed. Angel Alcalá (Boulder: Social Science Monographs, 1987) 237–47; Sánchez-Ortega, "Woman as a Source of 'Evil' in Counter-Reformation Spain," *Culture and Control in Counter-Reformation Spain*; Marc Simmons, *Witchcraft in the Southwest: Spanish and Indian Supernaturalism on the Rio Grande* eds. Cruz and (Lincoln: U of Nebraska P, 1980).

[49]Behar, "Sexual Witchcraft, Colonialism, and Women's Power."

[50]Bouvier, 133–39; Edward D. Castillo, trans. and ed., "The Assassination of Padre Andres Quintana by the Indians of Mission Santa Cruz in 1812: The Narrative of Lorenzo Asisara," *California History* 68 (fall 1989): 117–25; Edward D. Castillo, "Introduction" and "The Native Response to the Colonization of Alta California," in Castillo, ed., *Native American Perspectives on the Hispanic Colonization of Alta California*, xvii-xlv, and 423–40; Antonia I. Castañeda, "Comparative Frontiers: The Migration of Women to Alta California and New Zealand," *Western Women: Their Land, Their Lives* eds. Lilian Schlissel, Vicki L. Ruiz, and Janice Monk (Albuquerque: U of NM P, 1988) 283–300, especially 292–94; James Sandos, "Levantamiento! The 1824 Chumash Uprising," *The Californians* 5 (January-February 1987): 8–11; Bruce Walter Barton, *The Tree at the Center of the World: A Study of the California Missions* (Santa Barbara: Ross-Erickson Publications, 1980) 185; Sherburne F. Cook, *Conflict between the California Indian and White Civilization* (Berkeley, Los Angeles: U of California P, 1976) 56–90.

[51]Sandos.

[52]Greg Sarris, "What I'm Talking About When I'm Talking About My Baskets."

[53]Paula Gunn Allen, *Spider Women's Granddaughters: Traditional Tales and Contemporary Writing by Native American Women* (New York: Fawcett Columbine, 1989) 2.

[54]Alonso 7.

[55]Sandoval 53.

[56]Vera Rocha, personal interview. 5 July 1996.

[57]Laurence M. Hauptman, "Congress, Plenary Power, and the American Indian, 1870 to 1992," *Exiled in the Land of the Free: Democracy, Indian Nations, and the U.S. Constitution* eds. Oren Lyons, et.al. (Santa Fe: Clear Light Publishers, 1992) 318–36.

[58]Judith F. Baca, personal interview. 8 October 1995.

[59]Sandra Messinger Cypess, *La Malinche in Mexican Literature: From History to Myth* (Austin: UT Press, 1991)

[60]Cordelia Candelaria, "La Malinche, Feminist Prototype," *Chicana Leadership: The Frontiers Reader*, eds. Yolanda Flores Niemann, et. al (Lincoln and London: U of Nebraska P, 2002) 1–14; Deena J. González, "Malinche as Lesbian," *Culture and Conflict in the Academy: Testimonies from the War Zone*, 14 spec. issue *California Sociologist*, (Winter/Summer 1991); Adelaida R. Del Castillo, "Malintzin Tenepal: A Preliminary Look into a New Perspective," *Essays on La Mujer* eds. Rosaura Sánchez and Rosa Martínez Cruz, (U of California: Chicano Studies Center Publications, 1977) 124–149; Hernández-Ávila, "Open Letter to Chicanas"; Alarcón, "Chicana Feminism: In the Tracks of 'The' Native Woman, Cultural Studies; Anzaldúa, *Borderlands/La Frontera*. For an excellent cross-section of Chicana poets writing on Malinche, see: Lucha Corpi, "Marina," Carmen Tafolla, "La Malinche," Angela de Hoyos "La Malinche a Cortez y Vice Versa/La Malinche to Cortez and Vice Versa," Margarita Cota-Cárdenas, "Malinche's Discourse," Erlinda Gonzales-Berry, "Malinche Past: Selection from Paletitas de guayaba," Alicia Gaspar de Alba, "Malinchista, A Myth Revised," *Infinite Divisions: An Anthology of Chicana Literature* eds. Tey Diana Rebolledo & Eliana S. Rivero (Tucson: U of Arizona P, 1993).

[61]Frances Karttunen, *Between Words: Interpreters, Guides, and Survivors* (New Brunswick: Rutgers UP, 1994) 1–22; Hernández-Ávila, "Open Letter to Chicanas."

[62]Karttunen, Between Worlds.

[63]See notes 1–3.

[64]For recent coverage of the unsolved murders of Mexican women on the U.S.-Mexico border, see Ginger Thompson, "Wave of Women's Killings Confounds Juárez," *The New York Times*, December 10, 2002: A1 and A14.

[65]For discussion of sexual violence in 18th and 19th century California, see: Castañeda, "Sexual Politics in the Politics and Policies of Conquest: Amerindian Women and the Spanish Conquest of Alta California"; Bouvier, Women and the Conquest of California"; Albert Hurtado, *Intimate Frontiers: Sex, Gender, and Culture in Old California* (Albuquerque: U of NM P, 1999); Clifford E. Trafzer and Joel R. Hyer, eds., *Exterminate Them! Written Accounts of the Murder, Rape, and Enslavement of Native Americans during the California Gold Rush* (East Lansing: Michigan State UP, 1999).

Agustín Víctor Casasola's *Soldaderas:* Malinchismo and the Chicana/o Artist

Guisela Latorre

Evoking images of home and hearth amidst the scorched battlefields of the Mexican Revolution, Agustín Víctor Casasola's photographs of *soldaderas* depicted indigenous and *mestiza* women in the uncertain territory between documentary photography and pictorial desire. Active between 1910 and 1938, history books and texts have used Casasola's work as primary visual resource material and have inadvertently equated it with the very essence of this event rather than as a visual representation saturated and informed by various ideologies. The *soldadera* in Casasola's visual narrative of the revolution was a mother, a wife, a cook, a warrior and even a lover, yet her presence, unlike that of her male counterparts, slipped from the grasps of historicity and fell into the ambivalence of myth.

It was precisely in the transition from history to myth that the *soldadera* became the Adelita, the romantic yet anonymous female figure that joined armed revolutionary struggles out of her love for a male soldier, as it was later popularized in music and literature. María Herrera-Sobek, in her analysis of female archetypes within the *corrido* musical narratives, stipulates that behind this construct there was the urge "to neutralize the woman by making her a love object and thus presenting her in a less threatening manner" (104). After all, beginning with La Malinche during the conquest, the *soldadera* joins a pantheon of feminine historical figures that have challenged their prescribed patriarchal function (mythification and all) as peripheral entities in the construction of historical narratives. As such, the *soldadera* joins the ranks of what Cherríe Moraga calls a "long line of *vendidas*" (117).

The visual representations of *soldaderas* in Casasola's photographs, however, would be taken up by Chicano, and in particular, by Chicana artists working from the 1970s to the present. By paraphrasing or directly transcribing Casasola's *soldadera* iconography, these artists deconstructed and exposed the seams of this archetype. These artists subjected the *soldadera* image to complex transformations that pointed to the ways in which Chicanas/os redeployed

98

material that was already circulating in the mass media in order to recycle and reformulate it with renewed meaning. Thinking of the relationship between Casasola iconography and Chicana/o creative expressions as a dialectic can provide a fluid model of analysis for the works of art discussed in this essay. Anthropologist Charles W. Nuckolls has described cultural systems as being dialectical in that they are "made up of dynamic conflicts between the whole and its parts" (xxiv). Drawing from Bakhtian ideas, communication studies scholars Leslie Baxter and Barbara Montgomery, in discussing the nature of interpersonal exchanges, commented on how forces of unity and difference (or *centripetal* and *centrifugal* forces) often collaborate in the formation of social relations (25). The relationship between the Casasola canon and Chicana/o art can be described as an interdependent yet conflictive and oppositional dialogue. These works of art are conversant with Casasola's visual repertoire, but often in a critical and contesting fashion. Though a visual dialogue is established, it is often a multi-vocal process whereby dissenting and contesting voices contribute to the creation of a unified cultural product. Chicana/o artwork containing Casasola's iconography can be regarded as that product given that it simultaneously embraced and rejected imagery from the Mexican Revolution of 1910. This element of "contradiction" and "opposition," however, does not point to stagnation in the cultural process, but instead it ushers in the creation of an emerging new cultural system.

Chicana/o artists established a dialectic relationship with Casasola's work, in part, because of his photography's close association with institutionalized history of the Mexican Revolution. Drawing on Roland Barthes' statements on the relationship between photography and the construction of history, Scott McQuire emphasized the medium's potential to transform collective memory and to "blur the sharpness of the line thought to divide past from present, then from now" (109). Casasola's photography, as a source for Chicana/o artists, offered them the opportunity to employ a legitimized historical document that nevertheless allowed them to breach the gap between Mexican and Chicano history, that is, between the past and the present. In spite of the photograph's fixation on the *moment* of representation, its capability to change the way the past is perceived prompted these artists to adapt the Casasola vocabulary to more current concerns. Chicana/o artists were keenly aware of the positionality and "constructedness" of history and saw in Casasola a tool by which they could write themselves into its narrative.

Women artists, in particular, have sought out Casasola's representations of *soldaderas* to retrieve them from the vaults of Mexican revolutionary history and to recast them in the role of the liberated Chicana. In the same manner in which Latina feminist writers and activists found in La Malinche, in both her historical and mythical form, an allegory of their own predicament as women of color, Chicana artists saw in the *soldadera* a malleable symbol capable of re-adjusting itself to their heterogeneous reality. Moreover, numerous Chicana intellectuals have taken on the task of uncovering both La Malinche and the *soldaderas*'s ignored or displaced contributions to Mexican and U.S. history. In her essay entitled "Malintzin Tenépal; A Preliminary Look into a New Perspective" first published in 1974, Adelaida del Castillo offered detailed accounts of her life along with the historical events in which she was an active participant by way of clarifying that "here, woman acts not as a goddess in some mythology, but as an actual force in the making of history" (125). Elizabeth Salas in her monograph *Soldaderas in the Mexican Military* (1990) undermined the anonymity *soldaderas* had suffered in photography, literature and music by revealing their identities with the help of oral histories and archival information.[1] Not only did Salas discuss the role they had in the Mexican Revolution, but she also traced their lineage back to the Mesoamerican period in addition to underscoring their subsequent importance to Chicanas. But rather than furnishing our present knowledge of *soldaderas* with more historical nuances, in what follows, I will reevaluate the significance of the *soldadera*, both as she appears in Casasola's oeuvre and as she is reformulated in the work of Chicana/o artists, closely analyzing her category as myth. In the process, I will argue that the mythification of *soldaderas* follows a long tradition of female archetypes beginning with La Malinche who, rather than representing an unmitigated vision of history, personify the anxieties generated by the active participation of women in critical historical events.

Mexicanas and Chicanas often played a complex and debated role during nationalist struggles in Mexico and the United States which has lead them to call for renewed feminist analyses focusing on race and bordered identities as central loci of critique. Chicana/o artists, who looked to the Mexican Revolution as a historical precedence for their own struggles in the Civil Rights Movement, included the *soldadera* in the pantheon of Chicano historical figures, which also encompassed individuals from both sides of the border like Emiliano Zapata and César Chávez. Books about Mexican modern history, usually illustrated with Casasola photographs, provided these artists with seemingly unquestionable sources of revolutionary imagery. However, the *soldadera*, as an icon of cultural resistance, became a contested territory of representation for these various artists, many of whom were informed by male-centered ideologies while others were more concerned with feminist critiques of Chicano nationalism. Chicana/o history scholar Vicki Ruiz reiterated the contested nature of this archetype:

> The idea of a strong courageous woman garbed in the iconography of the Mexican Revolution was not a threatening image to Chicano nationalists; it implied that the woman fights beside her man and cares for his needs. . . . The soldadera embodied a conflicted middle ground between loyalists and feminists, one that could be fiercely independent, yet strongly male-identified.[2]

But the epistemological ambivalence that arose from this figure was indicative not only of the dynamic and sometimes paradoxical nature of the emerging Chicano identity of the 60s and 70s, but also of the disputed site that was the indigenous or mestiza female body in the history of the Chicana/o visual arts. On the one hand, images of scantly clad, voluptuous and often submissive Aztec princesses were not uncommon sights in Chicano community murals, but, on the other, Chicana artists were offering alternative visions that depicted women as vital architects of Chicano nationalist identity. Santa Barraza's oil painting entitled *Malinche* (1991) was indeed an example of the latter. In this work La Malinche takes up most of the picture plane as she is closely watched by Hernán Cortés from behind. Black silhouettes representing episodes of Mexico's conquest slip far into the background like ghosts from a distant past. Barraza puts great emphasis on the child revealed through La Malinche's chest whose hair and skin color more closely resembles Cortés's. While he represents the birth of the mestizo race, his emergence from La Malinche's bosom as well as from within the core of a maguey plant, firmly ground him in Mexican soil. Barraza's monumentalization and soft rendering of La Malinche denotes a desire to circumvent the traitorous legacy ascribed to her in the past and to temper her despised role in history with smooth brushstrokes and vibrant colors. Moreover, the small size of the painting (8 by 9 inches) and media (oil and enamel on tin) are both direct references to the Mexican devotional *retablo* tradition, as Barraza once commented to me: "[*Malinche*] is actually a retablo painting and this format of the *retablo* then brings into play another phenomenon—that of producing an iconographic painting of a revolutionary figure within the space of the 'sacred' and 'miraculous.' This image becomes 'subversive' within the religious format of the retablo."[3] In the same manner in which Chicana poet Sylvia Gonzáles called for La Malinche's return to recover the dignity and pride of her Chicana daughters (Alarcón, "Traduttora" 288), Barraza imbued her with religious overtones, motherly attributes and primordial virtues. Here she also stands as an allegory of women's inclusion back into Chicano history.

Both Salas and Herrera-Sobek have conveyed that the various perspectives on La Malinche's role in history provide an appropriate template for deconstructing representations of women in the Mexican Revolution. While Salas emphasized La Malinche's role as military advisor to Cortés (15), thereby making her a precursor to the *soldadera*, Herrera-Sobek pointed out how her *traidora* legacy was later revisited in revolutionary *corridos* (68). Though the *soldadera* was not as radically charged with the treacherous allegations directed against La Malinche, she was indeed not only de-historicized and mythicized, but she was also recruited into a discourse that simultaneously excluded her. Casasola's photographs have contributed much to that discourse by not only endowing the representations of the *soldadera* with an aura of anonymity and romanticism, but also by providing one of the first visual representations of *sol-daderas* thereby establishing an iconographic canon of representation. His image entitled *Soldaderas* (ca. 1914) is perhaps one of his most cited and repro-duced photographs depicting women in the Revolution. Situated within the domain of a train station, Casasola saturates the scene with a compelling feel-ing of urgency and a captivating sense of dynamic motion, rare qualities in early twentieth-century Mexican photography. This image's apparent spontaneity and presumed transparency of reality provide the scene with an essence of his-torical accuracy and precision. However, the written historical narratives do not seem to be consistent with Casasola's visual accounts. Salas recounts how many of these *soldaderas* were forced to ride on train rooftops, rather than inside the wagons, an activity that would often cost them their lives when these trains would speed through the menacing ravines and cliffs of Mexico's coun-tryside (43). Casasola's carefully crafted scenes and mindfully chosen moments coupled with the *soldaderas*'s purported anonymity undermined the hopes for a comprehensively feminist interpretation of this photograph.

Nevertheless, this particular image by Casasola provided Chicana/o artists with a fertile ground of possibilities for a dialectic exchange. This figure of the distraught *soldadera* acts as what Roland Barthes termed the photograph's *punctum,* that is, "that element which rises from the scene, shoots out like an arrow, and pierces" the spectator (26). Moreover, the vividness and dramatic attributes of this image's *punctum* prompted Wayne Alaniz Healy, prominent member of the legendary muralist collective the East Los Streetscapers, to fix-ate on the figure of this *soldadera* descending the train and to remark on how it seemed to him that the Revolution was "taking place in her (very) eyes" (Sorell 26).[4] This figure, however, appears in the work of Chicana/o artists only after being repeatedly reproduced in the public sphere, including every-where from history books to bottles of tequila.[5] But, in the process of re-visit-ing this *soldadera* image, Chicana/o artists were also engaging the various meanings attributed to her throughout history. Beyond her visual attributes, these artists were also addressing her various roles as mother, prostitute, romantic heroine and/or commodified object.

Rather than engaging in a nationalist interpretation of this photograph by Casasola, Chicano artist Larry Yáñez opted to comment on the image's treat-ment as a commodity. In his photocopy composition entitled *Adelita* (1981) (figure 1) he put together mass produced objects such as a post-card image of the Virgin Mary, a Mexican flag and a large *tostada,* all elements commonly associated with "Mexicanness" by commercial media. His use of photocopies as an artistic medium further emphasized the irreverent tone of the work while also reiterating society's continuous craving for reproduced material. Yáñez's visual construction made of discarded cultural paraphernalia resonates with the *rasquache* aesthetics described by Tomás Ybarra-Frausto (157) while also

Figure 1. Larry Yáñez, "Adelita" (1981) Xerox composition. Used with permission by the artist.

recalling Laura Alisa Pérez's reference to the "recycled, transformed and recirculated components found in the crevices of the symbolic and social order" that make up the Chicano Nation (20). Yáñez and many other Chicana/o artists have employed these mass produced objects in their work as a way to denounce their inherent absurdity. For instance, painter Yolanda López directly addressed the detrimental aspects of this type of commodification:

> I find [these mass produced objects] to be a revealing expression of how American culture perceives Mexicans and by extension Mexican Americans. I find what we have visible in mass culture is a corrupted artifact passing itself as Mexican culture. And this false Mexican culture . . . lives in the everyday items we consume with our eyes, ears and culture-hungry minds. It runs parallel to Chicano culture. (3)

While Yáñez in his *Adelita* was ridiculing these objects that have come to symbolize Mexican identity in our market economy, the central placing and larger scale of the *soldadera* in the composition reveals a more ambiguous attitude toward this icon on the part of the artist. Rather than mocking this one figure as he did with the elements surrounding her, he appeared to be underscoring her displacement and dislocation amidst these vestiges of consumer culture. The *soldadera's* historical character and cultural significance here had been purposely undermined and diminished to make them more digestible for public consumption. Using humor as a lure, Yáñez conscientiously constructed this configuration as a metaphorical mirror being placed before the face of market interests.

Though Yáñez used commodified imagery as a starting point for parody, other artists have directly tapped into the nationalist potential of this Casasola photograph. While critical of the gendered biases of Chicano Nationalism, Chicana artists also sought ways in which to situate the presence of women within discourses of racial consciousness. But these artists sought to take up radical postures toward *el movimiento* thereby revealing a desire for reformation rather than eradication of Chicano nationalism. To cite Yolanda López's experience as an artist once again, the creation of her now-classic *Guadalupe Series* (1978) was prompted by a need to critique, in her own words, even "progressive Chicanos."[6] López was preempting an image that symbolized for her the colonization carried out by the Catholic Church in Mexico, but subverted its religious significance and transformed it into an icon of feminist liberation. Chicana artists have often formulated strategic schemes to modify canonic imagery as can be see with Carolina Flores's oil painting entitled *La Revolución no ha terminado* (The Revolution is Not Over) (1976). Utilizing Casasola's dynamic image of the *soldadera* descending from the train, Flores was nevertheless particular about the nationalist connotations she chose to adopt from the original photograph. Flores uprooted this *soldadera* from the purely feminine sphere depicted in the Casasola image and relocated her amidst the presence of two men who gaze at her from below. Flores modified her facial expression from that of urgency and consternation to that of contempt and confrontation. This Chicana *soldadera* appeared to briskly walk past her male counterparts, acknowledging them only to challenge their nationalist stance.

But Casasola's *soldadera* underwent a transmutation in *La Revolución no ha terminado* that not only occurred in the subject matter and iconography, but also transpired in the painting's style and execution. Flores converted the sharp outlines and stark contrasts of the photographic medium into a turmoil of gestural brushstrokes and uncertain spaces. In the process of subjecting the Casasola image to this metamorphosis, Flores was eradicating the claims of truth behind his photography, which often rendered a masculinist perspective of the Revolution. Aside from engaging in a dialectic exchange with Casasola's *soldadera*, Flores also engaged in a feminist translation that reveals itself in several layers of meaning: from photography to painting, from canonic history to feminist revision, from official discourse to counter-hegemonic affirmation.

Norma Alarcón identified women's translation as historically transgressive and tainted by accusations of treason. Chicanas—as social, political and cultural translators—have become part of an extended lineage of *vendidas* that originated with La Malinche whose activities as translator to Cortés gained her ill fame:

> In such setting to speak in one's behalf of the group's perceived interest and values is tantamount to betrayal, the assumption of an individualized non-maternal voice, such as that of Chicanas during and after the Chicano Movement has been cause to label them as *malinches* or *vendidas* by some, consequently prompting Chicanas to vindicate Malinche in a variety of ways. ("Traduttora" 281)

Flores's translation can be regarded as more than just a mere straightforward or objective transcription of Casasola's photography; it can also be viewed as a vehicle for the artist's creative expression. Among certain Chicana poets and writers, the use of both English and Spanish in their texts is a proclamation of linguistic freedom while, for others, engaging in translation prompts them to re-think the meaning of the "original." Chicana poet Gloria Enedina Álvarez, for instance, initially began translating her own work from English to Spanish and vice versa as a personal challenge to herself and to expand her audience, but later found that this very act took on a life of its own.[7] For Álvarez, the experience became so fulfilling and indicative of her bordered identity that she began using translation in dynamic and unexpected ways within single poems, as in "Vende Futuro":

> I saw him handcuffed, the Caminante,
> El sol amaneciendo en sus ojos cafés,
> Matizando la sonrisa,
> Muy esperanzado hace un día,
> consiguiendo sólo para otra caja de naranjas a cinco dólares
> confiscadas hoy como evidencia
> Making enough for another five-dollar box of oranges. (124)[8]

Álvarez and Flores, though resorting to translation in very different contexts, used it as a strategy of empowerment for them as Chicanas who navigate through a world impregnated with sexism, racism and *malinchismo*.

The *soldadera,* as a symbol of nationalist zeal, offered Chicana/o artists a multiplicity of possibilities allowing for a somewhat plastic interpretation of her significance. In many cases, however, artists opted to directly address the ambivalence this figure could elicit. This untitled drawing by Santa Barraza from 1976 (—a work that drew part of its iconography from a Casasola photograph of a *soldadera* standing next to a wagon (ca. 1915–20)—can be said to embody the ambivalence felt by many Chicanas who transgress prescribed roles. Like Flores's *La Revolución no ha terminado,* Barraza was also selective about the aspects of the Casasola image she chose to use. Removing her rifle and long sleeves to reveal a robust arm carefully placed behind her back, the artist was able to remove this *soldadera* from the context of warfare and military participation yet still retain the commanding and powerful character of the figure. Barraza included two other female figures in the composition, an older woman and a young girl and, as such, construed a generational bond that united these three figures under the roles of daughter, mother and grandmother. Barraza said that she envisioned this image "as a child looking back into the past to retrieve information on his or her identity and discovering the roles of the Adelitas in the Mexican Revolution."[9] This type of familial narrative places women as architects and conveyors of culture through the passage of time. Chicana writers and artists certainly have established a tradition in their work that traces their lineage through the women in *la familia.* Yolanda López's *Guadalupe Series,* for example, reinforced this tradition of female genealogy by casting the artist, her mother and grandmother as the Virgin of Guadalupe. But Barraza's composition is more ambiguous, fragmented and in a state of disarray with figures drawn to different scales and overlapping one another. Despite the importance of the women in their family, Chicanas who came to age during the period of the Civil Rights also experienced episodes of incomprehension with the older generations, as elucidated by historian Ramón Gutiérrez:

> The generational conflict took on its most confrontational and accusatory tones when daughters, be they lesbian or heterosexual, started to assert their sexuality. . . . For mothers such behavior was tantamount to the abandonment of *mexicano* cultural values and the acceptance of the Anglo ways. Mothers thus accused their daughters of assimilationism; daughters accused their mothers of accommodationism—and here was the problem (58).

In spite of the bifurcated character of Barraza's drawing, the *soldadera* nevertheless stood as a pillar of strength amidst the chaos imposed on Chicana creativity by pressures to assimilate, fulfill and comply with assigned gender roles. Moreover, the artist in this work reveals the malleability and symbolic potential of this revolutionary icon, originally the product of an ideology far removed from the one Barraza was endorsing yet nevertheless used to convey the power of Chicana feminist discourse.

But, as is common in the development of Chicana/o history and culture, different currents and tendencies overlap, intersect, pass and/or contradict one another as they make their way through the debris of excluded histories. While artists like Flores and Barraza offered different ways to incorporate Chicanas into discourses of nation, women's exclusion and objectification was and still is a common recurrence in Chicano art. The *soldadera* has also served as a fitting icon representing a more peripheral view of women in Chicano history. Despite the attempts by Chicana artists and writers to rescue the *soldadera* from the process of mythification she had experienced in Mexico at the hands of novelists (such as Mariano Azuela in *Los de abajo,* 1917) and *corridistas,* she too became a nationalist symbol devoid of agency in U.S. soil. From misogynist constructions depicting her in revealing clothing and provocative poses that left her "open to sexual exploitation," as Norma Alarcón once remarked about La Malinche (Alarcón, "Chicanas" 184), to romanticized and ahistorical representations of the Adelita as wife and mother. Falling within this second category of archetypal construction, Carlos Almaraz's mural entitled *Adelita* (1976) (figure 2), located in East Los Angeles's Ramona Gardens Housing Project, exemplified common illustrations of woman and nation in Chicano community murals. In addition to employing the name "Adelita" in the title with its connotation of anonymity, the mural presents her as a transnational symbol of idealized femininity and motherhood. The text included on either side of this figure attests to the specified roles she would fulfill during the construction of the imaginary nation. To her right, Almaraz inscribed the lyrics of the famous *corrido* "La Adelita": "Adelita se llama la joven a la que quiero y no puedo olvidar, en el mundo yo tengo una rosa y con el tiempo la voy a cortar" (Adelita is the young woman's name of whom I want and cannot forget, in this world I have a rose and with time I will eventually cut it). In this text, Adelita exists only as the male revolutionary's love interest and in function of his desire. Moreover, Herrera-Sobek interpreted the words in this strophe as a metaphor for the impending loss of her sexual purity in the hands of the author of the *corrido* (105). As a counterpart to these lyrics, the text written to Adelita's left pleads for her maternal embrace amidst the chaos of

Figure 2. Carlos Almaraz, "Adelita" (1976), mural, Ramona Gardens, East Los Angeles. Used with permission by Elsa Flores.

Chicano reality extending her relevance from Mexico to the United States while, paradoxically, locking her within a lover/mother dichotomy:

> Madre de la tierra y de la libertad
> has perdido tus hijos en guerras extranjeras y en las calles de nuestros barrios
> has visto lo que nos hace esta maldita pobreza, este racismo
> esta conquista que sigue . . .
> danos la fuerza para perseguir, para combatir contra nuestras condiciones
> para poder ver que verdaderamente somos carnales
> Adelita no me vallas [sic] por Dios a olvidar

> [Mother of earth and liberty,
> you have lost your children in foreign wars and in the street of our barrios,
> you have seen what this cursed poverty has done to us, this racism,
> this continuing conquest . . .
> give us strength to persist, to fight against our conditions
> to see that we are truly brothers
> Adelita, by God, don't forget me]

In this mural, the Mexico/U.S. duality is then reaffirmed visually by the Adelita's presence before rows of neatly stacked Mexican revolutionary soldiers who, at the same time, symbolically stand for Chicano militants. While she commands the mural's composition, her standardized military clothing and archetypal indigenous features identify her more as an allegorical entity than a historical figure. She wears a simple dress adorned with the characteristic revolutionary bandoleers criss-crossing her torso yet any signifiers of warfare are mitigated by the *rebozo* demurely draped over her head provoking closer associations to the Virgin Mary. While these attributes distance her from the loose morals and unrestrained sexual conduct identified with women in the battlefields of the Mexican Revolution, the artist has diluted her historical importance both to Mexico and to the United States opting instead to depict her as a secular icon of nationalist devotion. While this mural places her among revolutionary ranks, both the text and image situate her in positions detached from active participation and relegate her to the role of the less relevant male's lover or mother. As such, her placement becomes indicative of the gendered constrictions of women in moments of national and cultural crisis.

The uniqueness of the *soldadera*, together with all her different manifestations, rests with her capacity to either uphold or disrupt Chicano nationalism depending on how she was represented and who articulated her role in history. Likewise, Sandra Messinger Cypess reminded us that "culture and gender shape experience . . . ; [thus] the actions of La Malinche were influenced by those two key factors, just as our readings of her actions are affected by our culture and gender" (142). The fluidity of the soldadera's metaphorical capabilities makes itself even more palpable in its visual form. As she is formulated and re-formulated, the impact of her visual representation in Casasola or in the Chicana/o art, as opposed to her references in oral and written texts, resonate with a seemingly unambiguous conviction. The accessibility and immediacy of these images, in particular those forming part of community street murals, provided these constructions of the *soldadera* with the necessary means by which to most effectively and pragmatically impress public opinion. As we re-think and re-inscribe the role of women in history, we are simultaneously reconsidering and evaluating the role of women in the here and now. So asking how these visual representations of *soldaderas* are perceived by their audience is tantamount to asking whether women of color are currently regarded as legitimate political and social beings. As we witness the opening and, more often, the closing of physical and metaphorical spaces available for the assertion of Chicana identity, the *soldadera* continues struggling to find her voice amidst the annals of *malinchista* history and tradition.

Notes

[1]Though Elizabeth Salas has put together the most rigorous and ambitious historical account on *soldaderas*, the Instituto Nacional de Estudios Históricos de la Revolución Mexicana in Mexico City published the volume *Las Mujeres en la Revolución Mexicana 1884–1920* (Mexico City: Honorable Cámara de Diputados, 1992) which contains hundreds of brief biographies and photographs of women who participated in the Revolution either politically or militarily including many *soldaderas*.

[2]In her monograph *From Out of the Shadows,* Ruiz also noted that the female members of the Brown Berets, a militant Chicano organization during the 1960s and 70s, were seen as modern-day *soldaderas*. When they appeared in public, they would often wear the *soldaderas'* clothing as a form of performative activism (111). In her book *Soldaderas in the Mexican Revolution,* Elizabeth Salas reproduced a picture of an unidentified Brown Beret woman dressed in this manner taken by an unknown photographer for the *Chicano Movement Newspaper* (81). This photograph too was appropriated by Chicano artist Carlos González in his mural entitled *Heroes* (1994) in which she was included amidst a pantheon of other celebrated figure of Chicano history. González employed an economy of pictorial means that further underscored the anonymity of the Brown Beret woman in the original photograph, and stressed her category as symbol.

[3]These comments were made by Santa Barraza to the author via an e-mail conversation, March 16, 2001.

[4]Alaniz Healy and David Rivas Botello would also use that famous *soldadera* photograph by Casasola in their East Los Angeles mural entitled *Chicano Time Trip*. The artists used this figure, however, to underscore the importance of Chicana/Mexicana women within *la familia* and within nationalist struggles such as the Chicano Movement.

[5]A more recent example of the *soldadera's* commodification by the mass media and of her popularity as a signifier of cultural identity was the July 1999 cover of *Latina* magazine, a bilingual publication geared toward young Latinas in the United States. In it, famous Mexican actress Salma Hayek appeared wearing *soldadera* clothing with the inscription "*Libertad, maternidad, felicidad:* Salma's *Revolución*" below. This cover attests to the currency and power this iconography still holds in the collective memory of the U.S. Latina/o community, even if Hayek was visibly wearing make-up and a lingerie-like dress along with her bandoleers.

[6]This information was obtained during an interview between the author and Yolanda López on August 10, 1999.

[7]These statements were made by Alvarez during an interview with the author on August 10, 1999.

[8]Álvarez has long collaborated with several Chicana visual artists such as Alma López and Yreina Cervántez. An excerpt of "Vende Futuro" was included in Cervántez's 1989 mural entitled *La Ofrenda* as a large inscription placed at the base of the composition.

[9]E-mail conversation with Santa Barraza, March 16, 2001.

Works Cited

Alarcón, Norma. "Chicana's Feminist Literature: A Revision Through Malintzin/or Malintzin: Putting Flesh Back on the Subject." *This Bridge Called My Back: Writings of Radical Women of Color.* Cherríe Moraga and Gloria Anzaldúa, Eds. Watertown, MA: Persephone P, 1981. 182–190.

_____."Traddutora, Traditora: A Paradigmatic Figure of Chicana Feminism." *Dangerous Liaisons: Gender, Nation and Postcolonial Perspectives.* Anne McClintock, Aamir Mofti and Ella Shohat, eds. Minneapolis: U of Minnesota P, 1997. 278–297.

Álvarez, Gloria Enedina. "Vende Futuro." *Chicana Creativity and Criticism: New Frontiers in American Literature.* Eds. María Herrera-Sobek and Helena María Viramontes. Albuquerque: U of NM P, 1996. 124–125.

_____. Personal Interview. 10 August, 1999.

Barraza, Santa. E-mail Interview. 16 March, 2001.

Barthes, Roland. *Camera Lucida.* New York: Hill and Wang, 1981.

Baxter, Leslie A. and Barbara M. Montgomery. *Relating: Dialogues and Dialectics.* New York: The Guilford P, 1996.

Del Castillo, Adelaida. "Malintzin Tenépal: A Preliminary Look into a New Perspective." *Essays on la Mujer.* Eds. Rosaura Sánchez and Rosa Martínez Cruz. Los Angeles: Chicano Studies Center, U of California P, 1979. 124–149.

Gutiérrez, Ramón. "Community, Patriarchy and Individualism: The Politics of Chicano History and the Dream of Equality." *American Quarterly* 45.1 (March 1993): 44–75.

Herrera-Sobek, María. *The Mexican Corrido: A Feminist Analysis.* Bloomington: Indiana UP, 1990.

López, Yolanda M. *Cactus Hearts/Barbed Wire Dreams: Media Myths and Mexicans.* San Francisco: Galería de la Raza, 1988.

_____. Personal Interview. 10 August, 1999.

McQuire, Scott. *Visions of Modernity; Representation, Memory, Time and Space in the Age of the Camera.* London: SAGE Publications, 1998.

Messinger Cypess, Sandra. *La Malinche in Mexican Literature: From History to Myth.* Austin: UT Press, 1991.

Moraga, Cherríe and Ana Castillo, eds. *Loving in the War Years: Lo que nunca pasó por sus labios.* Boston: South End Press, 1983.

Nuckolls, Charles W. *The Cultural Dialectics of Knowledge and Desire.* Madison: U of Wisconsin P, 1996.

Pérez, Laura Elisa. "El desorden, Nationalism, and Chicana/o Aesthetics." *Between Woman and Nation: Nationalisms, Transnational Feminisms, and the State.* Eds. Caren Caplan, Norma Alarcón and Minoo Moallem. Durham, London: Duke UP, 1999. 19–46.

Ruiz, Vicki L. *From Out of the Shadows: Mexican Women in Twentieth Century America.* New York: Oxford UP, 1998.

Salas, Elizabeth. *Soldaderas in the Mexican Military: Myth and History.* Austin: UT Press, 1990.

Sorrell, Victor. "The Photograph as a Source for Visual Artists: Images from the Archivo Casasola in the Works of Mexican and Chicano Artists." *The World of Agustín Victor Casasola. Mexico 1900–1938.* Washington: Fondo del Sol Visual Arts and Media Center D.C., 1987. 35–47.

Ybarra-Frausto, Tomás. "Rasquachismo: A Chicano Sensibility." *Chicano Art: Resistance and Affirmation, 1965–1985.* Eds. Richard Griswold del Castillo, Teresa McKenna and Yvonne Yarbro-Bejarano. Los Angeles: Wight Art Gallery, U of California P, 1991. 155–162.

Malinche Myth and Metaphor

In Search of La Malinche: Pictorial Representations of a Mytho-Historical Figure

María Herrera-Sobek

Marina/Malintzin/Malinche. There was no one remotely like her, nor has there been since in the semi-millennial history of the Americas after Columbus. Pocahontas and Sacajawea run distant seconds. Like these other women, she is now enclosed within an edifice of myth, a construction all the more fantastic and obscuring because it has had more centuries to develop and because many groups have an investment in it. (Karttunen 291)

Malinal, Malintzin, Malinche, Marina, Ce-Malinalli, doña Marina—the multiplicity of names indicates a multiplicity of identities. Many Mexicans associate with these multiple identities an equal or even greater number of controversies all connected to the famous or more precisely, infamous, Aztec woman who was directly involved in the conquest of Mexico and with its conqueror Hernán Cortés. Sandra Messinger Cypess in her detailed study *La Malinche in Mexican Literature: From History to Myth* points out how La Malinche has been since the conquest "the subject of biographical, fictional, pictorial, and symbolic interpretation . . ." (2). Messinger Cypess approaches the study of La Malinche by underscoring the transformations this woman has undergone: "from historical figure to literary sign" encompassing multiple transformations (2). Her study is the first to "identify the formation of a Malinche paradigm, characterize its features, and show the changes that have occurred in the use of the sign through the impact of sociopolitical events on the literary expression"(2). The extensive bibliography on La Malinche details how she has been studied as a historical figure and as a literary figure. However, in the numerous books I consulted—codices, book covers, and paintings throughout Mexico and most recently in the United States—I did not find an analysis of the pictographic representation of this important historical figure. In this study, I focus my analysis on a substantial number of the most significant iconographic or pictorial representations of Malinche extant since the sixteenth century and posit how these portraitures reinforce and encapsulate the verbal representations found of this extraordinary woman in narrative texts. That is to say, textual descriptions of Malinche since the Colonial period portray her as a beautiful, powerful, vivacious, young woman of superior verbal skills and intelligence. The pictorial renderings project this same image and substantiate the written texts depicting this famous Native American woman of Mexica-Nahua ancestry and Mayan cultural upbringing.

Mariano G. Somonte in his 1969 book *Doña Marina: "La Malinche"* cites a wide compendium of voices lauding the virtues of La Malinche. Some of the early chroniclers singing bountiful praises of La Malinche include Bernal Díaz del Castillo, Fernando Ixtlixochitl de Alba, Alfonso Herrera, Fray Bernardino de Sahagún, Tezozomoc, Fray Juan Torquemada and others. Later in the nineteenth century the highly respected scholar and educator Justo Sierra as well as the North American historian William Prescott II join the chorus praising La Malinche. Throughout the centuries the discursive layers have structured a mythical image of Malinche. The pictorial representations provide a visual reality to the words woven in the construction of the Malinche richly embroidered tapestry.

Who was Malinche? The 1990 *Diccionario Enciclopédico de México Ilustrado (M-Q)* provides us with basic data: she was born in Painala, the daughter of a *cacique* near Coatzacoalcos (Veracruz) about 1501 and died around 1528, the dates of birth and death not being exactly known. Ce-Malinalli was her birth name and Malintzin was the reverential form of addressing her. From thence comes the word Malinche, a variant of Malintzin. When the Spaniards received her she was baptized and given the Christian name Marina; she was later reverently called Doña Marina, a sign of respect and homage. Of course, the above is one version, and as scholars know, everything related to Malinche's life, including her name, is surrounded by controversy, both as to its meaning and when she received the name Malintzin, i.e. whether it is actually a derivation of Marina. The theory related to the name "Malinche" being derived from Marina is linked to the characteristics of the linguistic system of Nahuatl, the Aztec's language. Since the indigenous languages did not distinguish between the "r" phoneme and the "l" phoneme Marina became Malina. The morpheme "-ztin" was used as an honorific title and thus the two joined words together became Malintzin and later Malinche (Karttunen 292).

Bernal Díaz del Castillo in his *Verdadera historia de la conquista de la Nueva España* written in 1568 explains that Malinche's mother, after the death of her husband, married another man, and had a son by him. She then sold young Malinalli to the Mayas. Malinche's mother, wishing for her son to inherit their estate got rid of the young girl and in this manner the child ended up as the slave of a Mayan *cacique*.

Andrés Tapia and Francisco Gómara provide a different version. Their variant of the Malinche narrative has her being stolen by merchants who sell her to the Mayans (see Karttunen 299). Frances Karttunen in her article

"Rethinking Malinche" gives credence to some of Bernal Díaz del Castillo's assertions as stated in his *Verdadera historia de la conquista de la Nueva España,* particularly the issue associated with Malinche's noble birth. Karttunen bases her conclusions regarding Malinche's noble birth on her linguistic dexterity since she could communicate in a multiplicity of local dialects as well as with the lower and upper strata of indigenous society.

> . . . [T]hat doña Marina could communicate with Moteuccoma's representatives, negotiate with the lords of Tlaxcala, investigate a plot in Cholula, and ultimately interpret between Cortés and Moteuccoma himself supports the claim of Bernal Díaz, López de Gómara, and others that she had been born and raised within a Nahua noble family before people began to hand her around as a piece of disposable property. (301)

When Hernán Cortés arrives at Tabasco on March 12, 1519, he is given twenty young indigenous women; among them is Malinche. Cortés distributed the young maidens among his soldiers giving Malinche to Alonso Hernández Puertocarrero after baptizing her as Marina. However, when Cortés became aware of Malinche's linguistic abilities he sent Puertocarrero on an errand back to Spain and kept the young woman for himself both as an interpreter and as a lover. Malinche eventually had a son by Cortés named Don Martín Cortés.

The union between Cortés and Malinche did not last, for when Cortés's wife arrived in Mexico in 1524, he married Malinche to his soldier Juan Jaramillo, with whom she had a daughter named María. She was given land and an *encomienda* (a group of tribute-paying indigenous people) as a reward for her services but Malinche died shortly thereafter of mysterious and unknown causes at an unknown date while still in her twenties.

In the *Diccionario Enciclopédico de México Ilustrado* we encounter the visage of a young woman, perhaps twenty or so years old. This contemporary drawing, evidenced by her modern, europeanized physiognomy, is not derived from the sixteenth century. The portrait shows a pleasant round face surrounded by long braided hair and marked by wide, large eyes; it is rendered in a frontal position facing the reader—her eyes do not look straight at the reader but are turned slightly outward looking into the distance. The picture does not offer any visual clues as to her Native American background. Since it is a head and shoulders photograph-like rendition of Malinche, the viewer only sees the bare shoulders of the young woman with a pleasant disposition and a line above her breasts demarcating a dress or blouse. There is a Mona Lisa-like smile on Malinche's face; it is not a full smile but a very sweet, almost shy smile. The face, however, does not project shyness; indeed, the overall composition of Malinche's portrait suggests a confident young woman. The drawing is a contemporary visualization of what Malinche looked like and is an artistic rendition taken from the artist's imagination. In a similar manner, all the iconography related to Malinche found in the paintings, chronicles and historical books is derived from the imagination of the artist since there does not seem to be an actual drawing of Malinche while she lived.

Much of the iconography extant on Malinche has been reproduced from the Lienzo de Tlaxcala, a tapestry-like cloth in which the events of the conquest were painted in 1575–1577. The Lienzo encompasses eighty-eight scenes related to Cortés and his Spanish soldiers' journey in their quest to conquer the Aztec Empire.

As cited earlier, Cortés acquires Malinche after defeating the Tabascans near the area of present day Veracruz. The defeated Tabascans offered various gifts to the victorious Spaniards. Bernal Díaz del Castillo in his sixteenth-century chronicle *The True History of the Conquest of Mexico* recounts this most significant event:

> On the ensuing day [March, 15, 1519] we were visited by many chiefs of the neighbouring districts, who brought with them presents of gold wrought into various forms, some resembling the human face, others of animals, birds, and beasts, such as lizards, dogs, and ducks. Also three diadems, and two pieces in form like the sole of a sandal, with some other articles of little value, nor do I recollect the amount of the whole. They also brought some mantles of very large size, but that part of the present which we held in the highest estimation was twenty women, among whom was the excellent donna Marina, for so she was called after her baptism [which took place on March 20, 1519]. (Keatinge 49)

Francisco López de Gómara recounts this most fortunate event for the Spaniards:

> les dieron hasta veinte mujeres de sus esclavas para que les cociesen pan, y guisaran de comer al ejército, con las cuales pensaban hacerles un gran servicio, como los veían sin mujeres, y porque cada día es menester cocer y moler pan de maíz, en que ocupan mucho tiempo las mugeres. (qtd. in Somonte 11–12)

The seventeenth-century Franciscan friar Diego Cogolludo López, narrates yet another version of the Tabascan gift-giving event:

> Presentaron a Cortés cuatro diademas . . . y unas indias, entre las cuales fue la que mediante Dios, dio la vida a todos los españoles después en la Nueva España. Era hija de grandes caciques y señora de vasallos: de ordinario la nobleza de la sangre, en cualquier estado que se halle quien lo tiene, hace proceder de suerte que manifieste su dueño. (qtd. in Somonte 178–179)

The Lienzo de Tlaxcala pictures these young Indian maidens given to Cortés. A drawing of the twenty women taken from the Lienzo appears in

María del Consuelo García Calderón's book *La intervención de la mujer en los bienes de Hernán Cortés*. The drawing depicts a group of young Indian women. In front appears a woman poised in the manner La Malinche is frequently represented: right hand raised with index finger pointing outward, thumb pointing out and the other three fingers curled inward. The woman distinguishes herself by the pose she assumes and the self-confidence she exudes through her body language and not by her face since the four or so visible faces all look exactly alike. A few of the faces of the other women are visible but most of the bodies and faces merge behind the first four women and are invisible.

The Fray Diego Durán Codex provides us with a portrait of Malinche with Cortés. Plate 55 of the Codex depicts Malinche with the label of Marina, her Christian name, translating for Cortés upon his arrival at Chalchiucueyehcan.

The painting is divided into two parts; on the left side are three sailing ships, with soldiers plainly visible standing on one of the ships. The ships are on the water and two curved lines, denoting the coast, separate land from water. On land is the image of Marina dressed in a long skirted frock with puffy sleeves; it is a Spanish-style dress. Her long hair falls loosely on her shoulders and her arms are crossed with her left arm crossing her chest and hand falling below her waist. Her right arm is lifted across her chest and her hand points a finger upward at the level of her chin. Cortés is depicted sitting on a Spanish chair with an Aztec messenger standing behind him. Malinche, therefore, is represented in her function as translator, a function reiterated in many of the codices.

With respect to Malinche's dress, it does not resemble the usual *huipil* (a long tunic-like garment) she wears. Patricia Rieff Anawalt's study "Atuendos del México antiguo" has a section on "Atuendos femeninos" where she describes the six main types of women's apparel in pre-Hispanic Mesoamerica. The six categories of clothing worn by Indian women were the *huipil* (long embroidered blouse-like garment, tunic-like, worn over a long skirt), the *capa* (cape), the *enredo* (wrapped skirt), *enredo de cuerpo entero* (whole body wrap), *faldilla* (skirt) and the *quechquemitl* (a blouse made from a square and a hole on top) (6-16). Pictorial representations frequently have Malinche wearing a *huipil*, i.e. mostly wearing a skirt with a long, loose top or tunic over it. Sometimes, Malinche wears a cape over her *huipil*, possibly due to the chilly weather of the *altiplano* (highlands) in the surrounding Mexico City area during winter nights in particular.

One of the first scenes presented in the Lienzo de Tlaxcala is the arrival of Cortés and his soldiers in Uliyocan, a town pertaining to the Otomí people (figure 1).

A fierce battle ensued in Uliyocan in which the Spaniards were victorious. After the battle, the surrounding people made peace offerings in the form of food. Malinche is depicted between the Otomí delegation and Cortés and his

Figure 1. Arrival of Cortés and Malinche at Uliyocan. Reproduction authorized by Instituto Nacional de Antropología e Historia.

Spanish soldiers who are all on horseback. The Uliyocan *lámina* (plate) offers an excellent painting of La Malinche; she is standing elegantly attired, her head slightly turned toward Cortés signifying her allegiance. Bearing a pleasant facial demeanor, her arms and hands are outstretched toward the Indians, the palm of her right hand is opened, thus symbolically linking Spaniards to the Indians. She is at the center of the composition and her height is the same as the Indians. However, she commands attention due to her position in the painting (i.e. strategically placed at the center) and due to her bright and flowing huipil. Malinche is featured even taller than Cortés' horse as she stands beside it. Cortés, as usual, is represented as a small figure of a man by comparison. Malinche seems to be pleading a case for the Indians.

After traveling from the coast toward the interior of Mexico on his way to Tenochtitlan, Cortés stops in the town of Atlivetzian, an area belonging to the Tlaxcalans. A section of the Lienzo de Tlaxcala (Plate 2) bearing the heading "Atlivetzian" portrays Malinche, Cortés and his soldiers, upon entering the village (figure 2). The painting is similar to the one above and depicts Malinche standing between the Indians and the Spaniards who are on horseback. She stands between the Spanish soldiers and the Indian *caciques,* or leaders, in the middle of the drawing. The chiefs are depicted bringing flowers and food to the Spaniards as is evident by the basket of tortillas and the three turkeys pictured at the lower left-hand corner. Malinche's long black hair is slightly pulled back exposing her pleasant, smiling face and although barefoot, is dressed in a beau-

Figure 2. Malinche and Cortés enter Village of Alihuetzyan (also spelled Atlivet-zian). Reproduction authorized by Instituto Nacional de Antropología e Historia.

tiful huipil. Through the large, loose sleeves of the huipil her hands peek out. Her figure, although slightly below the Indian males and the Spaniards, makes a commanding figure between the two opposing cultures. She is again at the center of attention in the drawing since she is a substantial figure at the middle of the composition and draws the viewer's eyes toward her.

The next section of the Lienzo de Tlaxcala (Plate 3) bearing the heading, "Tecoatzinco," presents the meeting of Cortés with the Indian dignitaries at the town of Tecoatzinco. The Lienzo's C-section depicts Cortés sitting on a raised platform on a Spanish chair with Malinche at his right-hand side and the Indian dignitaries bringing presents to Cortés. Both Cortés and Malinche are elegantly dressed. Two soldiers are behind Cortés's chair guarding him, holding their lances upward. Malinche functions as an intermediary between Cortés and the Indians and is slightly off-center between the two cultures.

Part of this particular section of the Lienzo was used as a drawing for the book cover by María Elena Landa Abrego titled *Marina en la conquista*. The section used for the book cover was the part detailing Malinche's role as translator between the gift-bearing Indian(s) (a necklace, in this case) and Cortés sitting on his platform. Malinche looms larger than Cortés who is sitting but is wearing a hat and the Indian dignitary who is standing at the same level as Malinche but who appears to be a head shorter than she is. Malinche seems to

be gesturing with her hands—the index finger points towards the Indian figure
and her right hand is raised palm up.

Plate 5 of the Lienzo de Tlaxcala portrays Cortés with a huge cross presenting it to the Tlaxcala leaders. The inscription "yemonavatecque Tlaxcalla"
has been translated as: "They have been baptized in Tlaxcala" (Mariano
Somonte, 49). Malinche's face barely peaks from the large Spanish banner
behind Cortés. However, her face represents her role in the process of converting the Indians to Christianity, which was very significant. According to
Fray Cristóbal de Aldama, she was highly instrumental in the conversion of the
Indians to Catholicism.

> Esta india de hermosura nada vulgar, era dotada de una viveza rara de espíritu,
> y assi pudo en breve imponerse en las verdades de nuestra religión, sus Sagra-
> dos Misterios y en la lengua castellana; sirviendo de intérprete fidelísimo; no
> sólo para facilitar la conquista; sino también, el cathequismo de aquellas
> gentes. (qtd in Somonte 179)

Fernando de Alba Ixtlixóchitl in his *Relación de la venida de los
españoles y principios de la ley evangélica* is equally effusive about Malinche's role in the conquest. He states:

> La lengua Marina fue la encargada de predicar la fe de Cristo, hablándoles a
> la vez del Rey de España. En breves días aprendió la lengua castellana, con
> que excusó mucho trabajo a Cortés, que había sido casi milagroso y muy
> importante para la conversión de los naturales y fundación de nuestra santa fe
> católica. (qtd. in Somonte 181)

Another outstanding depiction of Malinche is in the Lienzo de Tlaxcala
Plate 6 (figure 3). The scene portrays Cortés and Malinche's arrival at the
palace of Xicoténcatl. Malinche is again an imposing figure standing slightly to
the right of the center of the painting while Cortés is sitting to the right of Malinche conversing with Xicoténcatl who is sitting at Cortés's right-hand side.
The inscription "Quitlaquamacaque" translates as: "They gave him food" and
we can see this food at the lower part of the painting: ducks, baskets of tortillas,
birds (in their cages) and other foods (Somonte 39).

Malinche appears in another section of the Lienzo de Tlaxcala within the
context of a Catholic ceremony when the Tlaxcaltecan leaders were being baptized. Plate 8 of the Lienzo records this important event. The imprinted words
at the upper left-hand side "Yemoquayatequique tlatoque" read: "The chiefs
have been baptized." The painting portrays a Catholic priest imparting baptism
to the four leaders of the Tlaxcaltecan Alliance as Cortés and Malinche look on
at the right side of the painting from the viewer's perspective. Cortés is sitting
on a chair holding a crucifix up high. Malinche is behind him slightly to his left.
The four Tlaxcalan leaders are kneeling down receiving the holy sacrament.

Figure 3. Cortés and Malinche at the palace of Xicoténcatl. Reproduction authorized by Instituto Nacional de Antropología e Historia.

Malinche is frequently portrayed during or after a battle confirming what written records narrate regarding her role in the conquest. The Lienzo de Tlaxcala bearing the inscription "Quauhxunalpan" on the upper left-hand side has Malinche beside Cortés. The painting depicts the battle between Aztec and Tapanec indigenous peoples and the Spaniards. The soldiers surround Cortés in a protective circle and at their feet lie two dead warriors. A Tlaxcalteca chief speaks to Cortés and Malinche, who as usual, is between Cortés and the Tlaxcalteca leader.

One of the bloodiest episodes of the Conquest is the massacre at Cholula. After the Tlaxcalan leaders warned Cortés not to take the Cholula route to Tenochtlitan (Mexico City) to see the Mexica Empire, he ignores their advice and initiates his journey to Cholula together with six or seven thousand Tlaxcalcan warriors. In Cholula an old Indian woman informs Malinche that the Cholulan warriors plan to massacre the Spaniards. Malinche rapidly conveys this information to Cortés, who turns the tables on the Cholulan people and massacres thousands of them as punishment. The Lienzo de Tlaxcala (Plate 9) titled "Massacre of Cholula" depicts the horrendous violence (figure 4). Malinche is again prominent in the painting as she stands behind Cortés and his horse. The painting displays a small pyramid where Spanish soldiers and Tlax-

Figure 4. Massacre of Cholula. Reproduction authorized by Instituto Nacional de Antropología e Historia.

calans murder and dismember Cholulan soldiers lying on the ground. Cortés is riding a horse, lance in hand ready to strike; he is viewing the fierce battle taking place. Malinche, dressed in her usual *huipil* is an imposing figure and stands behind him straight as a reed with hands and arms across her chest; oddly enough, she seems to be smiling! Although Cortés is on his horse and she is standing on the ground, she nevertheless, is drawn as a huge figure reaching Cortés's neck and, indeed, looms larger than Cortés even though the Spanish leader and his horse are the central figures in the composition.

From Cholula, Cortés continues his march toward the Aztec capital, Tenochtitlan. The Lienzo de Tlaxcala (Plate 45) titled "The Beginning of the Siege of Tenochtitlan" and bearing the inscription "teciquauhtitlá," again portrays Malinche in the thick of battle. The Lienzo has Malinche participating in the attack at the Xolotl Fort in Tenochtitlan. There are three parts to the Lienzo but Malinche only appears on the top and middle parts. On the top part there is a Spanish sailboat floating on Lake Texcoco and sailing on it appear the head and shoulders of Cortés and Malinche with Spanish soldiers and Indian allies. Malinche serves almost as a masthead at the very front of the boat.

The middle section of the painting features Malinche with a highly decorated shield in one hand and a raised hand with pointed index finger in the other. She is presented right in the middle of the battle. Before her is the temple of the Goddess Toci and Tlaxcalan warriors poised for battle against the Mexica warriors crouched down beside it. Behind Malinche are Cortés and a Spanish soldier; both have their swords drawn in the air above their heads and Malinche seems to be cheering them on. The Spanish soldiers were victorious at this battle.

After the Spaniards defeat the Aztecs (Mexica) Cortés meets with Moctezuma. The Lienzo de Tlaxcala bearing the inscription "Tenochtilan" captures this most significant event and Malinche, as always, is an important part of the meeting. In the above painting labeled "Tenochtlan," Malinche appears as a large, imposing figure behind Cortés's chair. This Lienzo de Tlaxcala *lámina* has the Mexica leader and his advisors on one side with Moctezuma facing Cortés. Cortés sits on a raised deck, his hand extended toward Moctezuma. Malinche has one hand on one side and her right hand is uplifted toward her heart, index finger pointing. Her importance, directly is denoted by her large size. She is painted as an imposing figure, much larger than Cortés. Cortés appears as a small man, almost tiny in stature and even the Indians facing him appear much larger than he does.

Plate 48 of the Lienzo de Tlaxcala shows one of the final scenes where Malinche is depicted. In this scene the Lienzo portrays the imprisonment of Cuauhtémoc, the last Aztec ruler and Moctezuma's successor. Cortés sits in his chair speaking to Mexica warriors who appear angry and defiant. Their jaws are hard set and their fingers point accusingly. Cortés, situated on the left side of the painting, has one arm outstretched and another lifted palms up, as if trying to stop the warriors or as if defending himself from the verbal attacks. Malinche stands behind Cortés; her arms are both open and lifted up at the level of her chest.

The Lienzo de Tlaxcala provides an excellent itinerary of the activities of Cortés and Malinche on their way to conquer the Mexica empire. The Lienzo depicts the importance of Malinche in this historic endeavor displaying her prominently in many of the *láminas*.

Other codices such as the Codex of Azcatitlan, housed in the National Library of Paris, also demonstrate Malinche's importance in the war effort. In this rendition, Malinche walks at the head of the conquistadores together with Cortés and one of his soldiers. Malinche's drawing of her body yields a representation equal to or even larger in size to Cortés's drawn figure. Malinche is handsomely painted with an elegant hairdo and a wide *huipil*.

An excellent rendition of Malinche and Cortés is taken from the Map of San Pedro Tlacotepec (Somonte 145). Malinche, resplendent in a blue and white *huipil* with her hair braided and pinned around her head appears to be walking slightly behind Cortés. She is fully clothed wearing brown shoes and looking very, very elegant. She appears taller than Cortés as is generally the case in other drawings where they appear together.

A similar portrait of the powerful couple appears in a mural at the Church of San Andrés, Ahuahuaztepec in Tlaxcala. The painting featuring the couple on the mural of the Church of San Andrés serves as the cover for the book *Itinerario de Hernán Cortés/Itinerary of Hernán Cortés* written by Jorge Gurría Lacroix. Malinche, identified by her Spanish name, Marina, is resplendent in an elegant *huipil*. She is expertly coifed and is wearing jewelry in her ears and her neck. Her right hand holds a white handkerchief and her left hand appears to be holding onto Cortés's cape. Cortés is likewise very elegantly dressed, walking ahead of Marina. Oddly enough, she appears to be carrying behind her back a basket full of arrows, perhaps signifying her indigenous ethnic identity. An Indian identified as Xicotencal walks behind them, arrow in hand as a sign of his Indian identity also. The painting underscores Malinche's close relationship to Cortés. The inscription states: "De los Señores Conquistadores, pueblo de San Andrés guaguatepeque año . . ." (year not visible in photograph). That Malinche is featured under the inscription of "conquistadores" together with Cortés and the Tlaxcalteca chief, Xicotencal, demonstrates the perception of power this woman had.

An interesting early painting of Cortés and Malinche dating from the 1580–1585 is included in Diego Muñoz Camargo's book *La descripción de la ciudad y de la provincia de Tlaxcala de las Indias y Mar Océano para el buen gobierno y ennoblecimiento dellas*. The artist rendering the portrait of Malinche and Cortés is unknown. The drawing measures 29 x 21 centimeters and is done by pen in black in. It is presently housed at the Dr. William Hunter Museum in the University Library of Glasgow, Scotland. The painting has the "power couple," Malinche and Cortés, kneeling. Malinche looks stunning in her beautiful *huipil*—although she is portrayed barefoot as in many previous paintings or drawings. She has her arms raised and eyes toward the heavens. Most chronicles and historical books that mention Malinche describe her as a committed Christian—a Catholic devoted to the Christian God. The couple, according to the narrative inscribed in the painting itself states: "Cortés ofrece la Nueva España" (Cortés offers New Spain). Cortés has his arm, hat in hand, draped around Malinche. He holds a crucifix in his hand. Between Cortés and Malinche is a staff depicting a castle indicative of the Crown of Castile (Spain). Another couple, Francisco Pizarro and an Indian servant, are beside Cortés and Malinche and offer Perú to the Crown also.

Another source of La Malinche iconography is fray Bernardino de Sahagún's illustrated Book 12 of the *Códice Florentino* (General History of the Things of New Spain). The great ethnographer of the colonial period illustrated his books with drawings on the side of the texts. In several of these drawings, Malinche appears as an attractive woman, elegantly dressed and hair well-coifed. She is depicted for the most part as an interpreter standing between Cortés and Indian emissaries. The pictographic sign for speaking emanates from the mouths of Cortés, Malinche, and the Indian messenger. In these drawings, Malinche is once again a very imposing figure. She is drawn bigger and taller than Cortés and the indigenous messengers.

More contemporary paintings, likewise, depict Malinche in a prominent, powerful role. In the 1974 book *Historia de México Tomo 4* there is a painting representing Moctezuma. In the above work Malinche appears in her usual pose standing on the right side of Cortés serving as translator. Her physical appearance is that of a hefty woman with strong arms and legs and a powerful build. She is shown to be the same height as Cortés. Both the Spanish conquistador and Malinche have their right arms touching their heart, as if moved by what they are seeing.

Miguel González executed the following painting depicting Cortés entering the Mexica Empire (figure 5) found in *Historia de México Tomo 4*. Again

Figure 5. Cuauhtémoc, taken prisoner, is presented to Hernán Cortés. Courtesy of Editorial Salvat, S.L.

Malinche is depicted as a beautiful, tall woman, even slightly taller than Cortés who is standing by her side fully dressed in Spanish regal military clothing. He looks stern and unyielding. Cortés and Malinche are on the steps of a Teocali or pyramid (place of worship) while Moctezuma is painted one step lower denoting the power relations between the participants. Malinche is poised between Cortés and Moctezuma, arms opened, palms up and hands stretched toward Moctezuma. In this manner she is portrayed as serving as a link between the two cultures. Although Malinche is wearing her *huipil*, her features have been somewhat Europeanized. Prominent around her neck is a crucifix denoting her Catholicism and conversion to Christianity. Her face bears a soft pleading expression. A Spanish soldier in full armor stands between Malinche and Moctezuma. The Aztec ruler's hand is outstretched and pointing toward Cortés; he stands between two Spanish soldiers who are in full military regalia as if ready for battle. In fact, the soldier on Moctezuma's left holds a large shield and a lance. Cortés too has both hands on his weapons, i.e. his knife and his sword.

The painting (figure 6) depicts Cortés taking Moctezuma prisoner and is housed in the Museo de América, Madrid, Spain. This time a pudgy Rubue-

Figure 6. Cortés takes Moctezuma prisoner. Courtesy of Editorial Salvat, S.L.

nesque-looking Malinche, in her usual pose, has one outstretched arm with the palm of her hand up and with index finger pointing toward the Spaniards. The other arm sits across her chest with index finger also pointing towards herself or her heart. She is standing behind Moctezuma and has a smile on her face while the Aztec dignitaries show faces of dismay and consternation, deep furrows lining their brows at the terrible scene that is taking place. Two of the Aztec dignitaries are wringing their hands in obvious psychological pain. The Spanish soldiers looking on show impassive faces. Malinche looking downward at Cortés who is placing chains around Moctezuma's ankles is the only person smiling.

José Guadalupe Posada has two book covers from the series Biblioteca del Niño Mexicano, one is titled *Historia de la bella Malintzin o Doña Marina* (1899) and the other is *El incendio de un alma ante los escombros del Anahuac* (1899). Both books are 12.10 x 33 cm and are housed at the University of Hawaii at Manoa in the Thomas Hale Hamilton Library (Jean Charlot collection), Honolulu, Hawaii. Both depict a beautiful Malinche. The former has Malinche alone standing on a hill, while the latter has her sitting while Cortés and a page look on at the burning city of Tenochtitlan. Malinche is portrayed as a voluptuous figure in *El incendio* while looking more like an innocent maiden in the *Historia de la bella Malintzin*. In both drawings she is wearing Indian garments.

Four centuries later, during the Mexican Revolution, José Clemente Orozco and Diego Rivera painted portraits of Malinche and Cortés. In Orozco's mural, featured on the walls of the old Colegio de San Ildefonso (inside in the Grand Patio of the Preparatory School), are the images of Cortés and Malinche. Cortés is portrayed as a virile, strong, powerful conqueror while Malinche is painted as a strong muscular Indian according to Orozco's heavy social realism style of painting. He painted Indians in a "realistic" style instead of idealized noble savages or Europeanized Indians. Malinche's face projects the image of the faithful Indian woman, both serene and enigmatic. Of particular interest is the overall composition of the painting since the seated Cortés steps definitely on a fallen Indian while Malinche seems to be trying to avoid stepping on the fallen body. They are an Adam and Eve, the forebears of a new *mestizo* race, the vanquished one defeated at their feet (Messinger Cypess 93).

Karttunen views this painting with a different perspective, caustically stating: "After the revolution, at the height of the Mexican mural movement in 1926, José Clemente Orozco painted Cortés and Malinche naked together, the corpses of Indians beneath their feet, he reaching across her in a gesture of negation, she voluptuous, low of brow and dull of eye, a veritable Neanderthal" (297).

Diego Rivera's Malinche is a biting satirical criticism of Cortés. It portrays Cortés in armor and Malinche in a trampy-looking modern outfit. This is an ugly caricature of Malinche, the painting projects Rivera's view of her as a sell-out, a whore to the Spanish soldiers. Both figures are small and are surrounded by old colonial and new contemporary conservative Spaniards on one side and Indian revolutionaries on the other. The painting projects the contempt and disrespect many contemporary Mexicans have for the couple. Cortés and Malinche no longer occupy center stage in Rivera's composition. They are to the right of the central figure who is an Indian dressed only in a loincloth (*taparrabos*). The Indian is a commanding, imposing figure, taller and more powerful looking than any of the other characters in the drama. Symbolic of the colonial period and the demise of the "conquistadores" (in all forms) is the snake which is above their heads and who is being devoured by the eagle. The eagle, in turn, protectively covers the oppressed indigenous peoples and progressive Catholic priests such as Miguel Hidalgo y Costilla, beneath its wingspan.

Not surprisingly, the Tlaxcaltecan paintings do not depict Malinche in a negative light. A large contemporary mural in Tlaxcala features Malinche in an active, positive role during the early years of the Spaniard's arrival in Tlaxcala. The huge mural covers the interior walls of the Palacio Municipal located on the city's main plaza. The mural runs from the wall at the entrance on the first floor, throughout the staircase, and on to the walls of the second floor of the colonial building. A part of the mural is featured on a poster (figure 7). Malinche is prominently situated between Cortés and Xicotencal, the elder. She is brightly dressed and her beautiful brown face looks upon the scene she is witnessing, i.e. the encounter of the two cultures, quite satisfied. She is wearing an elegant red and white *huipil*, with her shiny, full hair streaming down her shoulders. Both Cortés and Xicotencal with their respective entourages on each side seem to be at the precise moment they are about to embrace. Malinche stands in the middle, the powerful mediator between the two cultures and looks on approvingly.

The Tlaxcalteca people today are sensitive about Malinche and her role in the conquest. They do not wish to see her portrayed as a traitor. When we were filming for the documentary *Indigenous Always,* directed and produced by Dan Banda, we were informed by a high ranking official that we could not film if the documentary was going to depict Malinche as a traitor. We assured him that was not our purpose and we were granted permission to film.

The Tabascan people have also drawn Malinche in a positive light as can be seen by the coat of arms done for that state in 1598. This is purportedly one of the oldest portraits of Malinche and may bear a resemblance to her (Somonte 59).

Contrary to Karttunen's view regarding the negative perception of Malinche in Mexico since 1821, there are actually numerous books on Malinche that present a positive view of Cortés's interpreter. A 1985 biography by Otilia Meza attempts to rescue the tarnished image of La Malinche. Meza wrote *Mali-*

Figure 7. Meeting between Cortés and Moctezuma. Courtesy of Editorial
Salvat, S.L.

nalli Tenepal: La gran Calumniada, Biografía de La Malinche as an attempt to
"clear" Malinche's name of the negativity surrounding it.

The cover of the book displays a head and shoulders portrait of Malinche.
She is depicted as an attractive, mestizo looking young woman with large eyes,
fine nose and full lips with straight, shoulder-length hair. Behind her are a
group of Spanish soldiers in full armor with their lances and shields at the
ready. Malinche is wearing a white *huipil* and her demeanor is pensive, her
eyes look at a point in the distance—perhaps the future—away from the viewer. It is an attractive portrait of the woman who, according to Meza, has been
besmirched in history.

At the Museo Amparo in Puebla, Mexico there is a fascinating mural on the cafeteria wall titled "Encuentro de Dos Culturas" (The Meeting of Two Cultures) painted by Víctor Mohedano. The 1.50x5 meter acrylic mural, encapsulates the drama of the conquest. On the left side of Malinche is the Mesoamerican Indian culture, an Indian dignitary is carried by two servants. The rich jewels and colorful pageantry of the pre-Hispanic civilizations is on display. On Malinche's right side is a Spaniard on horseback fully dressed for battle—in full armor, with lance and shield on hand. The horse is prancing forward, and behind the horse a friar or missionary priest carries a Catholic banner on a pole unfurled. Malinche stands on a cross, which has been melded from the two great religions, the Aztec and the Spanish, for embedded within the cross, is the image of the Great Mother Earth Goddess Coatlicue. Malinche, standing in front of the cross, holds two broken cords connoting she is the cause of the breach between the two cultures, or the opposite meaning: that she brings together the two cultures. The design on her red dress points toward the latter since it has a small cord (symbolic of an umbilical cord connoting the birth of a new people who will link the two cultures) that unites the thicker, broken cord. The notes to the painting state:

> La obra intenta sintetizar, plásticamente, el encuentro y fusión de dos culturas: la mesoamericana y la española, es decir la indígena y la europea.
>
> El mural se compone, básicamente, de tres partes, por lo que puede ser apreciado o leído como un tríptico:
>
> La cultura española está representada por dos personajes: el principal, a caballo, viste una armadura propia de sus atributos europeos y acorde con su cultura hispánica. Es un conquistador. El segundo personaje es un fraile franciscano, de pie, que representa la evangelización.
>
> La escena que recrea la cultura prehispánica contiene tres personajes: el principal, ricamente ataviado, sostiene en la mano izquierda un par de flechas y con la derecha señala a Quetzacóatl, la Serpiente Emplumada. Los otros dos personajes, de menor rango social, son quienes lo transportan en una litera.
>
> Ambos personajes principales —el español y el indígena— sostienen un diálogo.
>
> En el centro del mural ha sido pintada una mujer. Ella representa la fusión de ambas culturas: la hispana y la indígena. Puede ser vista como una imagen del mestizaje —La Malinche, la patria, etcétera— y sostiene en sus manos una cuerda que representa la unión o la ruptura de las dos culturas que se encuentran. Es un lazo que une o que separa.
>
> Atrás de este personaje femenino el sincretismo religioso es representado por Coatlicue en forma de cruz o viceversa.

Chicana writers, scholars and painters, fascinated by the figure of La Malinche, have written extensively about this important woman in the history of Mexico. Chicana scholars such as Adelaida del Castillo, Tey Diana Rebolledo, and Norma Alarcón have taken a revisionist view of Malinche's role in the conquest and in Mexican history. They take the position that Malinche was not a traitor but a woman who was victimized by a patriarchal culture. A strong, intelligent woman, Malinche took charge of her own destiny. Chicana scholars believe Malinche acted for the good of her people and tried to cushion the traumatic blows of an impending conquest. She was a convert to Catholicism who truly believed in converting her family and her people.

Chicana poets, playwrights, and novelists almost unanimously have sided with Malinche and through their fiction—both prose and poetry—have created positive images of Malinche. Such writers as Erlinda Gonzales-Berry, Lucha Corpi, Pat Mora, Angela de Hoyos, Carmen Tafolla, Cherríe Moraga, Alicia Gaspar de Alba, Gloria Anzaldúa and many others write positively about Malinche and her role in the conquest.

Painters such as Santa Barraza also portray Malinche in a positive light. Her painting titled "La Malinche" is a tender, lovely conceptualization of Malinche that depicts her as the mother of the new *mestizo* race (Herrera-Sobek).

Barraza's Malinche, painted in brilliant colors, bears the face of a beautiful *mestiza*-looking woman. Her turban-topped head signifies her ethnic indigenous ancestry. She is central to the painting, her face and shoulders protruding from behind a maguey plant. She is tenderly looking at an unusual fruit emanating from the maguey plant, a newborn child. Malinche is identified with the fertility of the environment, with the ecology of her surroundings. She is conceptualized as a fertility goddess who, together with the flora of the earth gives life to a new being, symbolic of the new *mestizo* race. Behind her, marginalized, is Cortés. He is a secondary figure in the drama of the birth of a new race. The forlorn, shriveled corpse, hanging from a tree in the background, shows the destruction of the Native American peoples. Center stage, however, is Malinche and her newborn child, born from the entrails of the maguey plant. The conflation of Malinche with another fertility goddess such as, Mayaguel, and the earth goddess, Coatlicue, is obvious. The earth bears the fruit of life and women are principal characters in this miraculous, infinitely unfolding and repeating drama.

Malinche has been accused of treachery, of being a sell-out; but as Karttunen argues in a recent article and as Chicanas have been arguing for the past three decades ever since Adelaida del Castillo published her landmark 1977 article "Malintzin Tenépal: A Preliminary Look into a New Perspective," this hostile conceptualization does not take into consideration the social and historical context of the conquest and women's position within the two societies involved. Karttunen explains:

> It does not appear to me that a question of ethnic loyalty can legitimately be raised here. At this time in Mesoamerica the indigenous peoples had no sense of themselves as "Indians" united in a common cause against Europeans. They identified themselves as Mexihcah; Tlaxcaltecah, Chololtecah, and so on. As

she was none of these, how could Malintzin be a traitor to all or any of them? By all reports, she saw her best hope of survival in Cortés and served him unwaveringly. Rather than the embodiment of treachery, her consistency could be viewed as an exercise in total loyalty. The problem for Mexican national identity after Independence was that the object of her loyalty had been a conquistador. (304)

Furthermore, Karttunen and Chicana scholars stress Malinche's status as a victim of rape and sexual abuse. Malinche was a slave in Maya Chontal society, and she and nineteen other young women were given as objects from one patriarchal society to another. As a slave woman Malinche did not have anything to say about this fateful exchange—she obeyed her masters. Karttunen stresses:

> To reiterate, doña Marina's inevitable fate was rape, not the making of tortillas. She had absolutely no choice about whether she would be sexually used, and very little control over by whom. When she was given to Cortés she had no one to turn to, nowhere to flee, no one to betray. She was not Aztec, not Maya, not "Indian." For some time already she had been nobody's woman and had nothing to lose. That made her dangerous, but it says nothing about her morality. (310-311)

The conclusion by many scholars is that Malinche was a survivor. She survived all the indignities of being a slave as a young child traded from one master to another. Later she survived as best as she could the many years she served the Spaniards.

Malinche is indeed a survivor. Her story is one that is told and retold. Each telling of the story provides new nuances, new facets of a life marked by fate, by good and bad fortune. She, together with the infinite number of other indigenous women and men, create a new group of people—the *mestizos* that through the powerful combination of European and Native American genes survived the holocaust that was the Spanish conquest and its aftermath.

Notes

I owe a debt of gratitude to several people and institutions in writing the above paper. I wish to thank Dan Banda for the opportunity to do research on La Malinche during our filming of the *Indigenous Always* documentary in the Veracruz, Puebla, and Mexico City areas. I thank Stephanie Fetta, a doctoral student from the University of California, Irvine, for her research assistance; the library and film development department at the Museo Amparo in Puebla for their aid in finding books on La Malinche and for doing many of the slides in a short period of three hours. The librarians at the Museo Amparo were superb in finding La Malinche material. The Director of the Museo was most gracious and accommodating in opening up the museum for our research activities. I thank Rolando Romero, for the wonderful conference he hosted on "U.S. Latina/Latino Perspectives on La Malinche" (August 26–28, 1999) at the University of Illinois at Urbana-Champaign, and the work he is doing as editor of the volume. My thanks to Amanda Nolacea Harris for all the work she did for the Malinche conference and for the editing of the present volume.

Funding came from the Luis Leal Endowed Chair, the Center for Chicano Studies, at the University of California, Santa Barbara, SCR-43 funds. I thank Francisco Lomelí, former Chair of the Chicano Studies Department, for the moral support given during the undertaking of this project. Lastly, I thank Melissa Byrne for her help in scanning the graphics.

Works Consulted

Alarcón, Norma. "Traddutora, Traditora: A Paradigmatic Figure of Chicana Feminism." In *Changing Our Power: An Introduction to Women Studies.* Jo Whitehorse Cochran, Dorna Langston, and Carolyn Woodward, eds. Dubuque, IA.: Kendall-Hunt Publishing Co., 1988.

Arqueología Mexicana. Fray Bernardino de Sahagún (Special Issue). VI. 36 (marzo–abril 1999).

Banda, Dan. *Indigenous Always: The Legend of La Malinche and the Conquest of Mexico.* Milwaukee, Wisconsin: Bandana Productions, 2000.

Biografía de Doña Marina. Anales del Museo de Arqueología. México: Ediciones Botas, 1938.

Castillo, Adelaida del. "Malintzin Tenépal: A Preliminary Look into a New Perspective." In *Essays on la Mujer.* Rosaura Sánchez and Rosa Martínez Cruz, eds. Chicano Studies Center Publications, University of California, Los Angeles, 1977. 124–149.

Durán, Fray Diego. *Historia de las indias de Nueva España.* 1867. Tomos I y II. México: Consejo Nacional para la Cultura y las Artes, 1995.

Díaz del Castillo, Bernal. *The True History of the Conquest of Mexico.* Trans. Maurice Bageral St. Leger Keating. La Jolla: Renaissance P, 1979.

_____. *Verdadera historia de la conquista de la Nueva España.* México: Editorial Porrúa, 1967.

Fernández de Castillejo, Federico. *El amor en la conquista: Malintzin.* Buenos Aires: EMECE Editores. (n.d.)

García Calderón, María del Consuelo. *La intervención de la mujer en los bienes de Hernán Cortés.* Puebla: Gobierno del Estado de Puebla, Collección V Centenario, 1992.

García Icazbalceta, J. *Doña Marina. Biografía.* Tomo IV. México: n.d.

Glantz, Margo. *La Malinche, sus padres y sus hijos.* México: Taurus, 2001.

Gómez de Orozco, Federico: *Doña Marina.* México: Ediciones Xochitl, 1942.

Gurría Lacroix, Jorge. *Hernán Cortés y Diego Rivera.* México: INAH, UNAM, 1971.

_____. *Itinerario de Hernán Cortés/Itinerary of Hernan Cortés.* México: Ediciones Euroamericanas, Klaus Thiele, 1973.

Herrera-Sobek, María, ed. *Santa Barraza: Artist of the Borderlands.* College Station: Texas A&M P, 2001. Plate #30.

Karttunen, Frances. "La Malinche (Doña Marina) and 'Malinchismo.'" In *Encyclopedia of Mexico: History, Society and Culture.* Michael Werner, ed. Chicago: Fitzroy Dearborn Publishers, 2001.

_____. "Rethinking Malinche." In *Indian Women of Early Mexico.* Susan Schroeder, Stephanie Wood, and Robert Haskett, eds. Norman: U of Oklahoma P, 1977. 291–312.

Kruger, Hilda. *Malinche o el adiós a los mitos.* México: Edición Cultura, 1944.

Landa de Pérez Cano, Concepción. *La mujer antes, durante y después de la conquista.* Puebla: Gobierno del Estado de Puebla, Colección V Centenario, 1992.

Landa Abrego, María Elena. *Doña Marina.* Madrid: Editorial Egeria, Dirección General de la Mujer, Comunidad de Madrid, 1993.

_____. *Marina en la conquista.* Puebla: Gobierno del Estado de Puebla, Comisión Puebla V Centenario, 1992.

Lanyon, Anna. *La Conquista de La Malinche.* Mexico: Editorial Diana, 2001.

Lienzo de Tlaxcala. (Anonymous). Manuscript housed in the Biblioteca Nacional de Antropología e Historia. Mexico City.

Long, Hanich. *Malinche.* Santa Fe: Venitens Eds., 1929.

Marroquí, José María. *La Llorona. Cuento histórico.* México: Imprenta de I. Cumplido, 1837.

Meade de Angulo, Mercedes. *Doña Luisa Teohquilhuastzin.* Puebla: Gobierno del Estado de Puebla, Colección V Centenario, 1992.

Méndez A. Miguel. *Malintzin.* México: Editora de Periódicos "La Prensa", S.C.L., 1964.

Mesa, Otilia. *Malinalli Tenepal. "La Malinche" La Gran Calumniada! Biografía Novelada.* Mexico City: EDAMEX, S.A., 1985; 1998.

Messinger Cypess, Sandra. *La Malinche in Mexican Literature: From History to Myth.* Austin: U of TX Press, 1991.

México en el mundo de las colecciones de arte. México: México Moderno, 1994.

Mignolo, Walter D. *The Darker Side of the Renaissance: Literacy, Territoriality, and Colonization.* Ann Arbor: U of Michigan P, 1998.

Mohedano, Víctor. "Encuentro de Dos Culturas." Poster and mural. Puebla, Mexico: Museo Amparo. ND.

Muñoz Camargo, Diego. *La Descripción de la ciudad y de la provincial de Tlaxcala de las Indias y Mar Océano para el buen gobierno y ennoblecimiento dellas.* Mexico City: Universidad Autónoma de México, 1981.

Musacchio, Humberto, ed. *Diccionario enciclopédico de México Ilustrado (M-Q).* México: Andrés León Editor, 1990.

Núñez Becerra, Fernanda. *La Malinche: De la historia al mito.* México: INAH, 1996.

Ochoa, Lorenzo, ed. *Conquista, transculturación y mestizaje: Raíz y origen de México.* México: UNAM, Instituto de Investigaciones Antropológicas, 1995.

Orozco, José Clemente. *Cortés and Malinche.* In Sandra Messinger Cypess. *La Malinche in Mexican Literature: From History to Myth.* Austin: U of TX Press, 1991. 93.

Paz, Irineo. *Doña Marina. Novela histórica.* México, 1883.

Posada, José Guadalupe. (illustrator of book cover) *El incendio de una alma ante los escombros del Anahuac.* Mexico: A. Vanegas Arroyo, 1899.

_____. (illustrator of book cover) *Historia de la bella Malintzin o Doña Marina.* Written by Heriberto Frías. Mexico City: Maucci Hermanos, 1900.

Probanza de los buenos servicios y fidelidad con que sirvió en la conquista de Nueva España la famosa Doña Marina. Patronato 56, No. 3, Ramo 4, Archivo General de las Indias, Sevilla, España.

Rebolledo, Tey Diana. *Infinite Divisions: An Anthology of Chicana Literature.* Tucson: University of Arizona Press, 1993.

Rieff Anawalt, Patricia. "Atuendos del México antiguo." *Arqueología Mexicana.* 3. 17 (enero-febrero, 1996): 6–16.

Rivera, Diego. Mural at the Palacio de Cortés in Cuernavaca. In *Historia de México.* Tomo 4. Mexico City: Salvat Editores de México, 1974.

Rodríguez, Gustavo. *Doña Marina. Biografía.* México: Imprenta Secretaría de Relaciones Exteriores, 1935.

Ruiz, Felipe Gonzalo. *Doña Marina. (La india que amó a Cortés).* Madrid: Col. LYKE, 1944.

Sahagún, Fray Bernardino de. *General History of the Things of New Spain* Florentine Codex. Book 12. Charles E. Dibble and Arthur J.O. Anderson, trans. Santa Fe, New Mexico, 1957.

Schroeder, Susan, Stephanie Wood, and Robert Haskett, eds. *Indian Women of Early Mexico.* Norman: U of Oklahoma P, 1997.

Seco, Carlos. *Doña Marina a través de los cronistas.* Estudios Cortesianos del Instituto Fernández de Oviedo. Madrid: Consejo Superior de Investigaciones Científicas, Enero a Junio, 1948. Tomo 31–32.

Smith, Bradley. *Mexico: A History in Art.* New York: Gemini Smith Inc., Doubleday, 1968.

Somonte, Mariano G. *Doña Marina: "La Malinche."* México: Imprenta Edimex, 1969.

Thomas, Hugh. "Cortés y los tlaxcaltecas." *Arqueología Mexicana* 3, 13 (mayo–junio 1995): 42–47.

Williams, Jerry M. and Robert E. Lewis, eds. *Early Images of the Americas: Transfer and Invention:* U of Arizona P, 1993.

The Malinche-Llorona Dichotomy: The Evolution of a Myth
Luis Leal

The archetypal women, La Llorona and La Malinche, are two of the old-est in Mexican oral tradition, the legend of La Malinche dating from the mid-dle of the sixteenth century, and the myth of La Llorona from pre-Hispanic times. However, it was not until much later that they were seen as intimately related. In this paper I want to argue that La Llorona is a mythical figure of pre-Conquest origin and not modeled after La Malinche, a historical character that does not appear until after the landing of Hernán Cortés on the shores of Mexico. La Malinche was a person of flesh and blood, while La Llorona is a mythical figure derived from ancient Mexican goddesses. Some of her charac-teristics, however, have been attributed to Doña Marina, a process common in the creation of mythical characters from historical prototypes.

In their brief study, "Doña Marina and the Legend of La Llorona," George A. Agogino, Dominique E. Stevens, and Lynda Carlotta observed in 1973 that the basis of the woman who weeps might be found in Doña Marina. "The rea-sons for her remorse were the destruction of her people or their subjugation to the pale-faced invader. Her 'children' in this instance are the countless millions of Indians who fell under the rule of the Spanish" (qtd. in Messinger Cypess 175 n 20). Shirleen A. Soto, in her article of 1986, followed that interpretation. Sandra Messinger Cypess in her 1991 book dedicated to La Malinche sum-marizes that relationship between the two figures with these words:

> In the same way that the lexical term *malinchista* was derived from her [Ma-linche's] experiences, so have the figures of La Chingada and La Llorona become involved with her paradigm [...]. The image of La Llorona, or weep-ing woman, at one point became conflated with the image of La Malinche because they share a sadness relating to lost children. (7)

This interpretation appears in some oral versions of the legend of La Llorona and in the 1984 novelette *The Legend of La Llorona* by Rudolfo Anaya.

As we shall try to demonstrate, the myth of La Llorona existed much earlier than the year of the Conquest or even the arrival of the Spanish in Mexico. Malinche makes her appearance in history in 1519, and therefore could not have been the model for La Llorona. The model of La Llorona is to be found, rather, in pre-Conquest mythology, in the form of several old goddesses, among them the woman serpent, Cihuacóatl, who dates back to the time of the Toltecs; Xtabay among the Mayas; Quilaztli (a manifestation of Cihuacóatl); and Coatlicue among the Aztecs. These goddesses, in turn, are derived from the Earth Mother, who appears in a cosmogonic myth transcribed in 1550 from oral tradition:

> Others say that the earth was created in the following way:
> two gods, Calcóatl [Quetzalcóatl?] and Tezcatlipoca brought
> the Goddess of the Earth, Atlalteutli, down from Heaven [. . .]
> And this goddess sometimes wept at night, wanting to eat the hearts
> of men. She would not be silent until they had been given to her.
> (Horcasitas and Butterworth 206)[1]

In the *Monarquía Indiana,* a book dating from 1610, Juan de Torquemada states that "Cihuacóatl [. . .] was the first woman in the world. . . . She always gave birth to twins—a boy and a girl. They say that this goddess used to appear many times with a little cradle on her back; this cradle was called *cozolli.* [. . .] At night they would hear her crying and weeping" (qtd. in Horcasitas and Butterworth 206).[2] In 1910 Thomas A. Janvier, in his book, *Legends of the City of Mexico,* attributed these same motifs to the goddess Quilaztli, the one who gave birth to twins, wore a white dress, and carried a small cradle. Her crying and sobbing were often heard at night.

The goddess Xtabay, who dwelt in the woods, had the power to entrap men, a motif often found in modern variants of the La Llorona legend, and perhaps derived from the primitive Earth Goddess. She also wore a white tunic. There were some goddesses, according to Francisco Hernández's *Antigüedades de la Nueva España* (1580), who became goddesses because they died giving birth to their first child. "They used to say that these goddesses would come down to earth on certain days and inflict countless plagues and misfortunes upon the mortals that they happened to meet" (qtd. in Horcasitas and Butterworth 207).[3]

Of the goddesses derived from the archetype, the Earth Goddess, the most important is Cihuacóatl, the serpent goddess of the Toltecs, Aztecs, and other nations. The process of her transformation from a brave, noble woman into an evil one was described by Fray Bernardino de Sahagún in his *Historia de las cosas de la Nueva España,* a work divided in twelve "books" completed in 1569. In Book VI, dedicated to rhetoric and moral philosophy, Cihuacóatl is presented as a goddess held in high regard, especially by women. Before birth, women were told by the midwife to imitate the brave woman Cihuacóatl (Book VI, ch. 28). The midwife also referred to Cihuacóatl as a "noblewoman" (Book VI, ch. 33). In the book dedicated by Sahagún to the gods, however,

Cihuacóatl is demonized. In a very short chapter about her it is stated that she
was called "a savage beast and an evil omen." Much more important to our
argument is the description of her appearance and her activities, which are like
those attributed to La Llorona today. The following reference is also found in
Sahagún:

> And as she appeared before men, she was covered with chalk, like a court lady.
> She wore earplugs, obsidian earplugs. She appeared in white, garbed in white,
> standing white, pure white. Her womanly hairdress rose up. By night she
> walked weeping, wailing; also was she an omen of war. (Book I, ch. 6, 11)[4]

In the Appendix to Book I, where the idolatry of the Indians is confuted,
Sahagún considers Cihuacóatl an incarnation of the devil. He admonishes the
Indians with these words: "Behold another confusion of your forefathers. They
worshipped a devil in the guise of a woman, named Cihuacóatl. [. . .] She terrified men; she frightened. [. . .] And because of this they celebrated her feast
day. They laid offerings before her, they slew victims before her, that her
anger, her fury, might not fall upon [them]" (Book I, 69–70).

The appropriation of the language and culture of the Toltecs, especially
their mythology, is a well-documented subject. That explains why the goddess
Cihuacóatl is found among the Aztecs during the reign of Moctezuma II. However, we find out in Sahagún that her image had evolved. Here she is not a terrifying demon but a woman saying good-bye to her people. "In the days of this
same [ruler] it happened that [the demon] Cihuacóatl went about weeping, at
night. Everyone heard it wailing and saying: 'My beloved sons, now I am
about to leave you'" (Book VIII, ch.1, 3).

The evolution of the myth, that is, the transformation of the goddess
Cihuacóatl into La Llorona, the frightener of little children, apparently took
place soon after the Conquest of Tenochtitlan. According to Sahagún, during
the time when don Martín Ecatl, the second person to govern Tlatelolco under
the Spaniards, "it came to pass that Cihuacóatl ate a small boy [as] he lay in
his cradle there in Azcapotzalco" (Book VIII, ch.2, p.8). The nature of the
motif of the cradle which, as we have seen, is mentioned in the earliest texts,
was explained by Fray Diego Durán in his *Historia de las Indias de Nueva
España,* a work completed in 1579. Strange as it may seem, it was not con-
textualized as a component of the myth of Cihuacóatl, but demythified. In
chapter 92, dedicated to her, Durán says, among other things:

> The principal goddess was called Cihuacóatl, goddess of the Xochimilca and,
> although she was the particular deity of the Xochimilca, she was venerated in
> Mexico and in Texcoco. The goddess Cihuacóatl was made of stone. She [. . .]
> was dressed [. . .] all in white—skirt, blouse, and mantle. If [her priests] saw
> that eight days had passed and no one had been sacrificed, they took a baby's
> cradle and put in it a sacrificial flint knife, called "The Child of Cihuacóatl"

[. . .]. They wrapped it up in cloth. They would give the cradle to a woman so that she might take it on her back to the market place. They would instruct her to go to the most important merchant woman. She would carry the cradle to the market [. . .] asking her to look after it until she came back. [. . .] Surprised that, not having nursed all day, the baby had not cried [. . .], [the merchant woman] would then open the cradle and find in it the sacrificial knife, the "child" of Cihuacóatl. The people, on seeing this, cried out that the goddess had come and had appeared in the market place. They would say that she had brought along her child to show her hunger and to reproach the lords for their neglect in feeding her. (In Horcasitas and Butterworth 207–208)

In this way, the people would be reminded that it was time to offer a sacrificial victim. The hunger of Cihuacóatl for sacrificial victims is the same as that of the Mother Earth, the archetype of all these goddesses.

Most versions of the modern legend of La Llorona state that children are afraid of her. This motif can also be traced back to the sixteenth century, for Durán tells us that during his time boys were afraid to go inside Cihuacóatl's old temple, which they called the devil's house. "They called it the house of the devil because many idols and stone figures were found there, which the boys went to see but did not dare to go in as they were scared of them" (Historia II 177; my trans.).

In today's versions of La Llorona one of the principal preoccupations is to explain why and how La Malinche became La Llorona. In a version collected in the City of Chihuahua and published in 1950 we find that Doña Marina kills her son rather than letting Cortés take him to Spain. "In despair, Malinche killed her son with a knife. She buried him, with herself besides him. When her spirit left her body, she cried '¡Aaayyy!' Since then her spirit wanders all over calling the attention of the people to her anguished cry. The people call her La Llorona" (Horcasitas and Butterworth 209).[5] "When was Doña Marina first called La Llorona?" is a question we cannot answer.

The significance of the evolution of the La Llorona/La Malinche myth, however, is to be found in the fact that the myth, as old as that of the Fifth Sun, has been preserved in contemporary Mexican and Chicano popular cultures, associating it to the trauma of the Conquest and the creation of the mestizo race. The best-known interpretation of the legend is perhaps that of Octavio Paz, who in 1950, in the chapter "The Sons of La Malinche," included in his book *The Labyrinth of Solitude*, speaks of La Llorona as one of the Mexican representations of maternity. The translator, Lysander Kemp, adds a footnote to explain that La Llorona mentioned by Paz is "The 'Weeping Woman,' who wanders through the streets late at night, weeping and crying out. This belief, still current in some parts of Mexico, derives from pre-Conquest times, when 'La Llorona' was the earth-goddess Cihuacóatl" (75).

What is not understood is that, according to Durán's text, a deeper meaning is to be found in the relation of the legend to the need of the ancient priests to obtain sacrificial victims. When the contemporary mothers warn their children about La Llorona, they are unaware of the fact that they are ritualizing an old pre-Hispanic religious ceremony. And when La Malinche was identified with La Llorona, and therefore with Cihuacóatl and sacrifices, it was easy to present a negative image of her in history and literature, a fact well documented by Doña Marina scholars.

Notes

[1] Taken from the anonymous document, "Histoire du Mechique" [ca. 1550] *Journal de la Société des Américanistes* vol. II (1905): 8–41.

[2] From Fray Juan de Torquemada, *Monarquía Indiana.* [ca. 1610]. Vol. II (México: Editorial Chávez Hayhoe, 1941) 61.

[3] From Francisco Hernández, *Antigüedades de la Nueva España.* [ca. 1580]. (México: Editorial Pedro Robredo, 1945) 139.

[4] All quotations and references to Sahagún are from the English translation of the *Florentine Codex* by Anderson and Dibble. The spelling of Ciuacoatl has been changed to Cihuacóatl.

[5] Original source: *Mesoamerican Notes I* (Mexico: Mexico City College, 1950).

Works Cited

Agogino, George A., Dominique E. Stevens and Lynda Carlotta. "Doña Marina and the Legend of La Llorona." *Anthropological Journal of Canada* 2.1 (1973): 27–29.

Anaya, Rudolfo. *The Legend of La Llorona. A Short Novel.* Berkeley: Tonatiuh-Quinto Sol International, 1984.

Durán, Fray Diego. *Historia de las Indias de Nueva España y islas de tierra firme.* 2 vols. México: Editora Nacional, 1951.

———. *The Aztecs: The History of the Indies of New Spain.* Translated with Notes by Doris Heyden and Fernando Horcasitas. New York: Orion P, 1964.

González Obregón, Luis. "La Llorona." *Las calles de México.* 1922. 2 tomos en uno. México. 4ª. ed. México: Ediciones Botas, 1941. 17–20.

Horcasitas, Fernando, and Douglas Butterworth. "La Llorona." *Tlalocan* 4 (1962–1964): 204–224.

Janvier, Thomas A. *Legends of the City of Mexico.* New York: Harper and Brothers, 1910.

Messinger Cypess, Sandra. *La Malinche in Mexican Literature: From History to Myth.* Austin: U of Texas P, 1991.

Paz, Octavio. *The Labyrinth of Solitude: Life and Thought in Mexico.* Trans. Lysander Kemp. New York: Grove P, 1961.

Sahagún, Fray Bernardino. *Florentine Codex: General History of the Things of New Spain.* In Thirteen Parts. Trans. Aztec to English, with notes and illustration, Arthur J. O. Anderson and Charles Dibble. 2nd. ed. rev.: Salt Lake City: U of Utah/Museum of New Mexico, Santa Fe, NM: The School of American Research, 1953–1982.

Soto, Shirlene A. "Tres modelos culturales: La Virgen de Guadalupe, La Malinche y La Llorona." *Fem* 10.48 (1986): 13–16.

La Malinche as Metaphor
Tere Romo

The worst kind of betrayal lies in making us believe that the Indian woman is the betrayer.

—Gloria Anzaldúa, *Borderlands/La Frontera*

1999 marked an important anniversary for Mexicans on both sides of the border. In 1519, Cortés arrived on the coast of present-day Tabasco and takes Malinalli Tenepal as his translator. Four hundred and eighty years later, *La Malinche* (as she becomes known) is still a very important historical figure who has evolved into a significant icon and cultural metaphor in Mexico and the United States. Key to the discourse on La Malinche are issues of identity, gender and class politics, and racism—all very relevant and timely subjects tackled by contemporary multicultural artists, including Chicanos/as.

As a transplanted Mexican, I grew up with La Malinche in my home. A framed Mexican calendar with Helguera's rendition of *La Noche Triste* still hangs in a prominent place in my parent's living room. Though I will talk specifically about the image later, I bring it up now in order to clarify my attraction to La Malinche. Because of that artwork, I grew up with a positive notion of her. In fact, that portrait of her and Cortés helped to explain why we had all the different hues and gradation of eye, skin, and hair colors in my family. For me, she was also part of a glorious Mexican past that my parents proudly displayed. Ironically, it was not until the Chicano Movement when I read the now infamous Octavio Paz essay, "Los Hijos de Malinche" did I discover the more prevalent and deeply seated negative interpretation of La Malinche. I think it was at this point that the seed was planted in me to delve further into these conflicting histories, an exploration that I am now pursuing as curator of The Mexican Museum in San Francisco.

Planned as a multi-media and interdisciplinary exhibition, *La Malinche as Metaphor* traces the visual constructions of La Malinche from her earliest representations to contemporary representations, in Mexico and the United States. As an art historian, I intend to chart the development of these images as reflections of the predominant art practices of each period. As a Chicana curator, it is equally important to examine the role these images serve within their sociopolitical environment. In this essay I focus on the latter.

Though La Malinche is a historical person, she has come to "stand in," to become "code" for many negative attributes. She is the common metaphor for the female traitor: the native woman who betrayed her race by not only assisting (i.e., translating for) the conquerors, but also by informing them of native plots. As a result, so the story goes, she caused the death of many of her people, allowing the Spanish to succeed in their conquest. La Malinche has also become "code" for the person who sells out to foreign interest and values; one who welcomes the victimizers in and willingly becomes the victim. A good example of this metaphor is the Gabino Palomares song, *La Maldición de Malinche.*

Consequently, over the almost 500 hundred years since she unwittingly became part of the historical drama that was the conquest of Mexico, La Malinche has been used (and abused) to signify that which is negative in regards to race (i.e., Indian), gender (i.e., female), and class (i.e., conquered people). Over the last twenty-five years, Chicana artists and scholars have revisited this very male and Eurocentric picture of La Malinche and are revising her place in Mexican history. What is emerging is a recontextualized Malinche as a Chicana: a strong, very independent woman who stepped outside the prescribed female role of her time. However, this interpretation of La Malinche, inconceivable to previous historians and artists, continues to pose a dilemma. In the words of Christine Brooke-Rose, "Traditionally, men belong to groups, to society. Women belong to men" (Brooke-Rose 57).

My article focuses on five metaphors and their representation in the visual arts. They are: "La Malinche as *Lengua* / Interpreter," "La Malinche as Indianness," "La Malinche as Seductive Traitor," "La Malinche as *Mestizaje*" and finally, "La Malinche as Chicana."

La Malinche as Lengua/Interpreter

Not much is known about the young woman who began her life as Malinali Tenepal. We do know that she was the daughter of a cacique from the Nahualt-speaking Totonac region of eastern Mexico. When her father died, her mother remarried and gave birth to a son. Soon after, Malinalli was sold to slave-traders who took her to the Tabasco coast area. There she learned the Maya language, which in addition to her native Nahuatl made her indispensable to Cortés during his campaign to conquer Mexico for the Spanish crown.

In her article entitled, "Lengua o Diosa? The Early Imaging of Malinche," Jeanette Favrot Peterson describes their first meeting as recorded by Cortés' personal secretary, López de Gómara in which Cortés "took La Malinche aside and promised her, somewhat darkly, 'more than liberty' if she would establish friendship between him and the men of her country." By consenting to become

Cortés's translator, La Malinche's role in the conquest was to grow or diminish according to the motives of the scribe. In some cases, she was simply referred to as *la lengua,* devoid of any name and relegated to the role of mouthpiece. In other accounts, she is elevated to a pivotal role whereby "her linguistic skills and knowledge of Indian mores were most essential" to the military campaign (Favrot Peterson 3).

This characterization can be seen clearly in the numerous codex depictions of La Malinche in the company of Cortés. The earliest visual representation of the couple is a painting on fig bark by Moctezuma's artists sent to document the arrival of the foreign visitors (Karttunen 1). This painting was made less than a month after she was given to Cortés along with 19 other women, and it already shows them side by side. La Malinche's image is found prominently throughout the Florentine Codex and within the colonial era paintings con-imissioned by the city of Tlaxcala.

The "Manuscrito del aperramiento" is representative of these various images, but it is also an interesting native-produced legal document of colonial Mexico. Illustrated are six plaintiffs who have brought judicial action against Cortés and Malinche. As described in Toltec writing, Cortés had "summoned the six native leaders under the pretext of offering Christian instruction," as represented by the rosary La Malinche holds in her hand. Instead, Cortés had enslaved them (Brotherston 38). As in many of these early documents, La Malinche is portrayed at Cortés's side.

The Codex Durán offers another colonial example, but is unique in its illustration of La Malinche. She is placed in the center of the picture frame— clearly the focus of the image. Though La Malinche is pictured in her customary standing pose, looking sideways with lifted hand signifying speech, this Malinche is not wearing the indigenous *huipil,* but a European-style dress. Her long flowing hair is blond and skin is fair. This is not a portrait of an indigenous woman, but of a young woman of the European court.

Part of a series, the Codex Durán image illustrates Cortés's landing on Mexican soil in 1519 and does contain some historical accuracy, such as Cortés's black clothing appropriate to Good Friday. However, the governing *cacique* standing next to him, Teuhtlile, did not actually come to meet Cortés until Easter Sunday. More telling is the lively conversation between La Malinche and Cortés as indicated by their open mouths and pointed fingers. Just as highly unlikely is the way they speak directly at each other and without the aid of Aguilar, the rescued Spanish soldier who spoke Maya and Spanish. It is apparent that the artist sought to elevate La Malinche in recognition of her role in the conquest by making her the central figure and bestowing upon her the reigning standards of beauty—light skin, blond hair, and the civilized dress of a court lady.

In 1942, Miguel Covarrubias painted an illustration of La Malinche for the translation of Bernal Díaz del Castillo's book *The Discovery and Conquest of*

Mexico. The same image was used by William H. Prescott for his book entitled, *The Conquest of Mexico* in 1949. Obviously, Covarrubias referenced the codex representations for Malinche's pose, dress, and the ubiquitous speech scrolls. Though Covarrubias has identified Malinche by her Christian name, Doña Marina, she has Mayan-like features and black hair. He has clearly emphasized her role as the indigenous interpreter. Situated in the middle, both visually and figuratively, Doña Marina mediates between the Aztecs and the Spaniards. With the Spaniards to her back, she addresses the Aztecs as their representative. Her pose is full of dynamism and, more significantly, she is without Cortés at her side. No longer the mouthpiece, this Doña Marina is in charge. Ironically, aside from presenting an initial positive assessment, Prescott leaves Malinche out of the remainder of the book. Instead, he concentrates on Cortés's exploits, crediting his character and military prowess for the successful conquest of Mexico (Prescott 114–115).

Chicana artist, Patricia Ruiz-Bayon takes this designation of interpreter to a conceptual level with her piece entitled, *La Serpiente* (1995). The title derives from the serpent-like form she creates with photographs arranged on parallel circular grid patterns. The interior circle is composed of images of a woman carrying a heavy load that bends her down. The outer band has pictures of a woman with folded hands. The central image shows an eye peering through hands that form a triangle. This multi-layered piece draws from Western and indigenous symbolism, including the snake that eats itself and Quetzalcóatl.

However, Ruiz Bayon's incorporation of hands provides important conceptual clues. Within the central image, the hands are in the foreground, forming the triangle shape that encloses her eye and at the same time, provides a means to see through. Within Mesoamerican society, the placement of hands in the pictorial documents known as codices was crucial to the understanding of the role, class, and therefore, importance of the speaker. Though Malinche's role as interpreter was carried out by means of linking three different languages, we have seen that the use of her hands was pivotal in portraying her important status. Thus, her hands came to symbolize her ability to address persons outside of her status as a woman and slave. Her hands formed/framed her public identity, yet they also allowed her to step beyond her sociopolitical limitations. But then only to an extent, as exemplified by Ruiz Bayon's grid created out of clasped hands along the serpent's body. There is recognition that with conversion to Christianity, La Malinche's hands were silenced in a position of prayer and her status reverted to the servitude of an indigenous woman.

La Malinche as Indianness

In his second letter to the Spanish King, Cortés refers to Marina for the first time as *"la lengua que yo tengo, que es una india de desta tierra"* [my interpreter, who is an Indian woman from (Putunchan Tabasco)] (qtd. in

Messinger Cypess 26, 179). Though he later refers to her as "Marina," the important racial attribute of "Indian" has formed and re-formed her myth. That she was a native is a historical fact, yet the pictorialization of this ethnic distinction becomes a significant indicator. As an important representative of the conquered race, La Malinche/Marina also becomes a metaphor for "Indianness," "glorious Aztec past," and even a gauge for the current (often) racist notions of beauty.

In the codices, depictions of La Malinche/Marina were primarily within the context of her role as interpreter. She was illustrated within events crucial to the conquest and even depicted as a heroine in Tlaxcala. However, in the 19th century after the independence of Mexico from Spain, she took on another role. In *La Marina/La Malinche* from 1852, she is Manuel Vilar's personification of a noble savage sculpted in the style of classic Greco-Roman statues. Much in keeping with the prevalent artistic canon of that period, it conforms to the classical aesthetics of the European art academy. This Malinche has the classic features and pose of a Greek or Roman goddess. Though ironic, it is no surprise that it was Vilar, a Spaniard, who is "considered to have introduced the 'theme of the indigenous' to academic sculptural practice" (Widdifield 81). With this piece (and two others depicting Moctezuma and Tlahuicole), Vilar expressed the conservative values of the time; note the crucifix around Marina/La Malinche's neck. Taken together, the three statues "embodied the ideals of a Catholic, imperial state"—to which the newly independent Mexico aspired. However, these notable figures and others from Mexico's ancient and powerful heritage only helped to solidify the position of those in power, specifically the criollos (Spaniards born in Mexico) who could claim a cultural right vis à vis their "ancestors." Of course, these illustrious ancestors could not be related to their blood descendants—the disenfranchised indigenous population—so their representation reached across the ocean to European antiquity.

In stark contrast to Vilar's statue is the portrait painted by Alfredo Ramos Martínez in the late 1930s-early 40s. Here La Malinche's indigenous face is featured prominently, her head almost bursting out of the picture frame. Her black hair, braided and bound in the traditional manner of native women of central Mexico, sets off a face rendered in earth colors. Even the small sections of what appear to be a wall in the background have an earthen quality. Whereas previous illustrations showed her looking sideways, this Malinche's compelling eyes gaze directly at the viewer. Without the title of *La Malinche*, it would be difficult for most viewers to discern her identity. In fact, Ramos Martínez painted many portraits of indigenous woman along with scenes of rural Mexican life. Ramos Martínez was an *indigenista* in that he believed that forging a true national art was based on "the ancestry of the people themselves." Unlike the artists of the previous century, he and other artists associated with the Mexican Renaissance included the contemporary natives in this project. They believed in the "value of race, insofar as its purity was considered to enclose, intrinsically, [a] creative potential which, when stimulated, produced an authentic art rooted in its own being" (Moyssen 31). In this portrait, Ramos Martínez places the historical Malinche within the contemporary world of other indigenous women and re-establishes her native origins as a source of dignity, pride, and beauty.

During this same period, Antonio Ruiz painted one of the most well known images of La Malinche. Entitled, *The Dream of La Malinche,* the dream-like imagery has led many to label it "surrealist." However, it is still in the vein of the social realist style of that period and owes more to the same pre-conquest and folk culture sources that informed much of Ramos Martínez's later art, as well as that of Miguel Covarrubias, Frida Kahlo, and Diego Rivera. Rich in symbolism, *The Dream of La Malinche* shows a dark-skinned La Malinche asleep and her body forming valleys and a large mountain at the center of the picture. On her, Ruiz has recreated a series of rural scenes, complete with houses, orchards, and even a bullfighting ring. At the top of the mountain is a colonial church reminiscent of Cholula, which had been an important sacred site before the Spanish had destroyed the temple, covered the pyramid, and constructed a Catholic church on top. As a symbol of the indigenous past, La Malinche provides the very foundation for Mexico. Even though she has been "converted/conquered," her true indigenous nature remains, awaiting the end of her slumber. Just as Ramos Martínez had created a Malinche from earth tones, Ruiz literally transforms her into the earth. Ramos Martínez and other artists repeated this linkage between "india and earth" in an effort to reformulate a nationalist art based on *indigenismo.*

Thirty-five years later, Alberto Gironella paints his own *The Dream of Doña Marina 2.* Aside from addressing her by her Christian name, Gironella's *Dream* has little to do with the earlier Ruiz painting. In fact, Gironella's piece references a Spanish painting by Antonio de Pereda called *The Dream of the Nobleman.* "In Pereda's painting, a Spanish nobleman dozes off before a table laden with the bric-a-brac of worldly possessions while an angel appears above with a message: 'Eternity troubles [him] soon it flies away and he dies'" (Day 140). In Gironella's rendition, the angel wearing a feathered headdress is Doña Marina, hovering over a sleeping Spaniard who sits at a table full of the spoils of conquest, as evidenced by a jewelry box. However, there are also skulls and what appears to be either a mask or the brown face of a native in the lower right-hand corner. Though doña Marina is very much a key figure in the painting's title, the fragmentation and almost abstract quality of the painting have rendered her incidental to the Spaniard and his table. Her wings and light skin have more to do with her role as the "stand-in" angel in someone else's dream than with the drama of the fall of Tenochtitlan.

Jorge González Camarena painted his own portrait of *Malinali* in 1979. Aside from calling her by her indigenous name, González Camarena has all but removed the ethnic attributes of an indigenous Malinche. Her pale, almost ghostlike face is framed by hair in a stylized pageboy cut. Red splotches—blood?—provide the only color. Though she faces the viewer, this Malinche's gaze has reverted to the sideways glance. Her sad, tearful eyes and down-turned mouth compose a painful expression. This repentant, sorrowful woman is lost in the very thoughts that have caused this pain. However, in removing many of the traces of her ethnicity, González Camarena has brought her into the realm of La Llorona and an "everywoman," at the same time. In the half-closed eyes and the wisp of hair that brushes on her check, there is a sexual-ization not found in prior examples. This piece personifies the modern con-flicting male views of La Malinche.

Cecilia Alvarez's painting entitled *La Malinche Tenía su Razones* (1995), provides a contemporary Chicana interpretation. Utilizing a quasi-codex style of painting, Alvarez foregrounds La Malinche's dark face against her black hair. The reasons for her tears, and ultimately for her actions, are depicted in the background. Painted cells (the last one partially blocked) repeat the times that she was "given" to others—first to the Mayan slave-traders, then the Spaniards. Martha Cotera in her book *Diosa y Hembra,* cites other significant factors: ". . . she was taken by Cortés as a lover, mothered his child, and was later discarded by him when he brought a wife from Spain. Symbolically, she has represented the thousands of Indian women who through similar circum-stances suffered the same fate" (Cotera 33). Malinche's tears in Alvarez's painting are based on the injustices inflicted upon her and not on any guilt for being a traitor. In addition, Alvarez's title further confers vindication for any so-called "treason."

La Malinche as Mestizaje

As stated before, the historical fact that Malinche did *not* have the first mixed-race child has been lost. In fact, one of the principal ways she has been represented in the twentieth century has been within the context of what I call the "national couple." The 1926 mural by José Clemente Orozco painted at the Escuela Nacional Preparatoria in Mexico City is a good example. In the style of a married couple portrait, Malinche and Cortés sit side by side with hands interlocked. However, both are naked and Cortés's stark, almost white skin contrasts with Malinche's dark brown skin.

Orozco's use of this couple as "text" for his mural points to its function within the Mexican mural movement of this period. As one of the *Tres Grandes,* he along with Rivera and Siqueiros painted many government-sponsored murals that sought to educate the public regarding their Mexican history. The story of the foundation of the Mexican nation itself was a very important source for all three muralists. Though the least politically motivated of the three, Orozco subtly addresses the inherent power relations of the conquest. While Cortés holds one of her hands, Malinche casts her eyes downward towards the native figure on the ground. Cortés's restraining gesture (with his other hand) clearly indicates that she, too, is under the control of his will (Herren 6).

Jorge González Camarena's *La Pareja* of 1964, follows up on this same theme. In this almost cubist rendition, Cortés and La Malinche are called "The Couple," implying union and equality. In fact, they almost seem to be one, merging seamlessly as they stride side by side. However, the power relations are very apparent. While Cortés is portrayed very powerful in his complete set of armor, La Malinche's nakedness accentuates her sexuality and vulnerability. While he has a military purpose, she is solely for sex and procreation. Symbols of their different backgrounds are incorporated: a large steel sword, Greek column and lion's head for Cortés and the semblance of an Aztec eagle warrior's headdress for her. Clearly, he is shown to have the advantage in this relationship, and more importantly, their mestizo children—los *Mexicanos*—have received more valuable assets from *him*.

In Dulce María Nuñez's treatment of Malinche, there is a juxtaposition of the ancient with the modern. Her painting, *Filiación,* of 1987 draws from these multiple sources for this particular "Lineage," or as Núñez describes it: "personal data, including place of birth, address, and occupation, etc." A band of *nopales* frames the top portion, while the Cortés and La Malinche of Orozco's mural form the significant left quadrant. Though each occupies its own sphere, a third figure mirrors and connects them. To the right is a portrait of the Mexican boxer, Guadalupe Pintor, with the national colors behind him. "El boxeador está allá como un representate del pueblo y Cortés y La Malinche están allí como sus padres históricos" (The boxer represents the people and Cortés and La Malinche are there as his historical antecedents) (Kirkingard Sullivan 17). Strategically, Núñez has placed the Mexican national seal below Cortés, and the famous volcano, Ixtacihuatl under La Malinche—Núñez's personal metaphor for the power of the Mexican woman. Though she references the mestizaje icon of the Orozco mural, Núñez also re-connects La Malinche to a source of natural power and by extension, to the power of all women.

A portrait of *Cortés y La Malinche* by Alejandro Arango provides a contemporary contrast to Núñez. In Arango's painting, the power and gender relations become central again. A very light-skinned Cortés cradles a dark, almost doll-like version of Malinche. Though their eyes are locked on each other and they appear to be in conversation, their nude bodies denote the encounter as sexual. Both bodies are flat and cartoon-like, however, Cortés's body is rendered more realistically, while La Malinche's figure is flatter on the picture frame and decorated with dots. Very telling is the size difference, with Malinche less than half the size of Cortés. Here Cortés is entertaining himself with a live doll, nothing more. The power relations are so great in this depiction of the "national couple" that mestizo offspring from this union are not feasible, and certainly not a consideration.

Along with the serious nation-building agenda, the Cortés/Malinche couple has also been recreated in popular culture, especially Mexican calendars. These were reproduced in great numbers during the twentieth century, in versions I call "the greatest story ever told," or the national couple as "star-crossed lovers." Some of the images draw from stories of La Malinche casting a spell of love over Cortés as soon as he set eyes on her. Other versions explain (and excuse) La Malinche's so-called treacherous behavior by blaming it on *her* great love for Cortés. In all cases, the imagery, much of it created by Jesús de la Helguera, is very romantic and sensual. These Malinche/Cortés stories of mestizaje emphasize the human element of their sexual relationship, elevating mestizos to "love children," products of two equally consenting adults who were destined to come together and produce "la raza cósmica," the Mexican race.

Contemporary Chicano artist, David Ávalos's art centers on deeper analytical deconstruction of the mestizo concept. On the entrance to his installation entitled "Café Mestizo," (1989) Ávalos incorporated an image of Malinche and Cortés from the Lienzo de Tlaxcala. Inside are three separate, but related mini-installations very much like altars. One of them is the *Hubcap Milagro #5 Straight Razor Taco (Homage to Malinche)*. It consists of a hubcap with a heart mounted on top that also functions as a vagina with a razor, an ax, *penca de nopal,* and a copy of Cooper's *Last of the Mohicans*. The central sculpture of the heart is a bicultural symbol of love for the European and of sacrifice for the Mesoamerican. Ávalos's heart also has a *vagina dentata,* a threatening symbol of castration and pain. However, as homage to Malinche, Ávalos has subverted the implied threat of loss of manhood. Instead, it is an indictment against the value system implicit in Cooper's novel, which Ávalos explains as: "it is better that the Mohican nation perish than that Uncas and Cora live to produce mestizos" (Ávalos 3). However, he also believes that in denying herself a relationship with a native man (i.e., the razor), Malinche also contributed to the Spaniard's genocide of the indigenous race. "The view that Malinche was a betrayer is an odd one. After all these centuries the circumstances of our birth are still a source of both terror and fascination" (Brookman 12). Here again, another example of the modern conflicting male beliefs and feelings towards La Malinche.

La Malinche as Seductive Traitor

> Here I am
> in the judgment seat you call me traitor
> who have I betrayed?
> —Claribel Alegría. *Malinche*

Since this is Malinche's most common identification, I will not spend a great amount of time on this metaphor. My intent is to utilize this section as an introduction for the final "La Malinche as Chicana" metaphor. However, it is very telling that males created all the images representing aspects of this metaphor.

In the late 1920s, J. Nieto Hernández was commissioned to create a painting for the Mexico City branch office of an American bank. The artist was asked to pictorialize the meeting between the Western and Mesoamerican cultures. In her placement, clothing and demeanor, Malinche is very much a central figure in this painting. While Moctezuma and Cortés seem to melt into the people around them, Malinche with her white huipil and long black braids clearly stands out. Yet it is her sly, coy glance at Cortés that situate her as the "seductress." Her only role here is to position herself as Cortés's beautiful woman.

Chicano painter, César Martínez offers another version of Spain meets Mesoamerica in *La Malinche as Carmen* (1988). Yet, this is not the sedate and staged version by Nieto Hernández. This one is full of the all the color, tension, and drama of a bullfight along with the passion of the referenced opera. Partly cartoon and very surreal, this historic meeting is played out in a bullring, while members of the Catholic Church (representing Spain) and a jaguar (symbol of pre-conquest Mexico) watch. Though not the central figure, Malinche as Carmen is prominent. Dressed in Spanish flamenco attire, she sports a tattoo of a jaguar on her arm and a picture of Cortés, his horse and Catholic cross on her fan. Full of symbolism which crosses cultures and historical time, it marks Malinche as the ill-fated woman who could not (like her namesake) overcome the events she set in motion with her sexual power and treachery.

In Teddy Sandoval's *La Traición de Malinche,* her disembodied head is shown actively seducing Cortés's head in a jungle garden. (Of special note is her position on top.) Directly across from this we see the direct results of her actions: the death of a young Aztec warrior. This warrior symbolizes the Mexican people as evidenced by the corn he holds in his hand. Malinche's actions based on her lust for Cortés drove her to not only betray her own people, but to destroy them (as depicted by the dagger through the warrior's heart). The floating brown eyes in the piece convey a sense of accountabiity—Malinche's treason has been "seen" by her people and it will be remembered.

The earliest Chicano image of La Malinche that I have found is in a 1974 issue of *Revista Chicano-Riqueña.* Most likely an ink drawing, it personifies for me the "Malinche=traitor=monster" interpretation. Barely discernible beneath the bouffant hairstyle, she is composed of an exposed huge breast, deformed arms, and massive thighs that end with feet pointing to one side. The hair style, breast, and naked body not only express Malinche's sexuality, but also personify how this notorious traitor to her people *should* look like, a seductress *a la grotesque.*

Not as gruesome is *Malintzin Through Malinchista Eyes* (1995) by César

Martínez. Devoid of very few human features, this Malinche is abstracted into raw sexuality. She is stripped down to clouds of hair and red lips—basic sexual symbols. Barely noticeable in the center of her chest and site of her heart, is an outline of Cortés on his horse. This is conceived as a portrait of how someone who acts like Malinche sees/interprets her. Yet, rather than presenting a favorable image of her, (which would justify their actions), this Malinchista sees Malintzin as not quite human and entirely sexual—much as *machos* see all women. Thus, in this painting "machos" and "malinchistas" become one in the same.

La Malinche as Chicana

Much like other periods before in Mexico whereby its artists and scholars had reached back in history for a glorious past on which to build a future nationalism, Chicanos, too, embarked on a reclamation process to recoup a heritage that had been denigrated for too long. We looked to immediate Mexican heroes, such as Emiliano Zapata, and also delved into Mexico's pre-conquest past for our rightful claim to this continent. *Chicanismo,* itself embodied the concepts of nationalism and *indigenismo,* much like prior cultural movements of Mexico. However, the Chicano nationalist project strove to build nationhood as a site of resistance. For Chicanos, there is recognition that we are mestizos not only by virtue of our mixed-race Mexican heritage, but also as a consequence of our marginalized condition in the United States. In fact, *pochismo* becomes another layer of mestizaje.

It would be Chicanas, however, within and outside the Movement that would question and critique many of the long-standing male versions of Mexican history and their manifestation in Chicano cultural studies and art. The Chicana artist's re-evaluation of such icons as the Virgen de Guadalupe, La Llorona, and La Malinche are part of this on-going discourse. The section on "La Malinche as Chicana" positions visual representations of Malinche within Chicana issues of self-determination, self-representation and, especially, female spirituality. "*Somos hijas de Malinche*" writes Delia Islas, "*Su soledad fue muy grande y ahora hijas de ella, vámonos a sacarla de allí y traerla aquí*" (We are daughters of Malinche. Her loneliness was great and now as her daughters, let us rescue her and bring her here) (Islas 18).

Santa Barraza's *La Malinche* (1991) is a small painting on tin meant to function as a *retablo*. According to Barraza, she chose this medium because it is a "mestizo visual interpretation of Christian testimony" (Barraza 14). As such, she believes it be an example of the merger of cultural symbols and appropriation of techniques that is the mestizo experience. Within this piece, Barraza utilizes La Malinche as the central image, the source of mestizaje, as represented by the fetus growing inside her. Hovering to one side is a red-headed Cortés. Wearing the traditional headdress of indigenous women, this Malinche casts her gaze downward, very much in the tradition of the Virgen de Guadalupe. Swirling around her are the defining events that not only shaped Malinche's life, but indigenous peoples in general: Christianity and violence. Yet, by incorporating the maguey, Barraza re-establishes a site of resistance and survival. The maguey serves as a symbol of rejuvenation and life; its leaves, needles, and core provide various forms of sustenance. There is also a direct reference to *Maya yuel,* the ancient goddess of sustenance who was represented by the Aztecs with nipples located at the end of her maguey leaves. In this painting, Barraza has merged the mestizo child with this indigenous plant; the maguey and mestizo become survival itself.

Another example of this multivalent Chicana interpretation of Malinche is Cristina Cárdenas, *Malinche, Coatlicue, y La Virgen de Remedios* (1992). As the name states, three female deities are represented in this piece: a large Malinche stands in front of Coatlicue, small standards of the *Virgen de Remedios* encircle her. Cárdenas used amate paper to create the large piece and cloth for the small pieces. Within this piece, Cárdenas has joined "three symbols to follow or to condemn," by virtue of their power (Cárdenas 58). For her, Malinche represents one woman's reaction to the evidence of cruelty by the Spanish. Coatlicue symbolizes the duality of contemporary Mexico—a powerful earth mother who has also been personified as a monster. La Virgen de los Remedios was the image on the Spaniard's banners and thus represents Christianity coming to Mexico.

In Cárdenas's placement of the three figures, Malinche forms a matrix for the conflicting cosmologies represented by her indigenous heritage and the foreign conquest. As she stands before us, Coatlicue who stands behind her protects her. However, as Cárdenas explains, she "is also caught by the imposing religion of a new goddess around her" (Cárdenas 58). Note, too, the crucifix she holds in her hands. Aside from its depiction of elements of Chicana spirituality, Cárdenas's piece also positions Malinche within the general Chicano context of religious and spiritual mestizaje.

Carmen Lomas Garza created an ofrenda to Malinche as part of a larger installation for Día de los Muertos entitled, *Homenaje a Tenochtitlan* in 1992. Created as a "redemptive memorial" for Malinche, it also includes pictures of her grandmother and two close friends. Lomas Garza pays tribute to all four persons whom she credits with influencing her personally and artistically. For Lomas Garza, Malinche's role is not only as an interpreter (as designated by her codex image), but also as an educated leader and cultural diplomat. "We are all Malinches, those of us who are educated," Lomas Garza states. "In explaining our culture to others, we also run the risk of being seen by our community as collaborating with the enemy" (Mesa-Bains).

The final piece, a triptych by Annie López symbolizes the "Malinche as Chicana" metaphor the best. Entitled: *Sold as Slave, Interpreter and Companion, and Survivor,* (1995) López describes it as follows. "Upon first glance, you see nothing but their outward seductive appearance, but they are actually intelligent, emotional, and loving human beings" (López). Besides being a loving tribute to female members of her family, this piece calls into question the power of labels. Especially those that are placed on us by others, and specifically those labels that are indicators of roles that then define us as women. In not so subtle a play on words, López subverts the negative connotation of these same labels applied to La Malinche over the last four centuries. Implicit is a demand that we think about these concepts not only as historical revisions, but within a contemporary discourse of gender politics.

I want to close with a stanza from Claribel Alegría's poem entitled "Malinche" in which she asks,

> To whom must I render accounts?
> To whom?
> Tell me.
> To Whom?

Our answer should be, "only to yourself."

Works Cited

Ávalos, David. "Welcome to Cafe Mestizo." *Cafe Mestizo.* New York: Intar Gallery, 1989.

Barraza, Santa, "Mestizaje." *Encuentro: Invasion of the Americas and the Making of the Mestizo.* Venice, CA: SPARC, 1991.

Brookman, Philip. "Conversations at Cafe Mestizo: The Public Art of David Avalos," *Cafe Mestizo.* New York: Intar Gallery, 1989.

Brooke-Rose, Christine. "Illiterations." *Breaking the Sequence: Women's Experimental Fiction* eds. Ellen G. Friedmen and Miriam Fuchs. Princeton: Princeton UP, 1989. 55–71.

Brotherston, Gordon. *Image of the New World: The American Continent Portrayed in Native Texts.* London: Thames and Hudson, 1979.

Cárdenas, Cristina. "Artist Statement." *Counter Colón-ialismo.* San Diego: Centro Cultural de la Raza, Phoenix: MARS Artspace, and Austin: MEXIC-ARTE Museum, 1992.

Cotera, Martha. *Diosa y Hembra: The History and Heritage of Chicanas in the United States.* Austin: Information Systems Development, 1976.

Day, Holiday T. "Alberto Gironella, 1929–." *The Art of the Fantastic: Latin America, 1920–1987.* Indianapolis: Indianapolis Museum of Art, 1987.

Favrot Peterson, Jeanette. "Lengua o Diosa? The Early Imaging of Malinche." Unpublished essay.

Herren, Angela. "Representing and Reinventing La Malinche in the 20th Century." Unpublished essay, 1999.

Islas, Delia. "Hijas de La Malinche." *Imágenes de la Chicana.* Stanford: Chicano P, 1974.

Kirking, Clayton C. and Edward J. Sullivan, "Pintando una vida." *Dulce María Núñez.* Monterrey: MARCO, 1993.

Karttunen, Frances. *Between Worlds: Interpreters, Guides, and Survivors.* New Brunswick: Rutgers UP, 1994.

López, Annie. "Artist Statement," *Rethinking La Malinche* exhibition at Austin: MEXIC-ARTE Museum, 1995.

Mesa-Bains, Amalia. "Redeeming Our Dead: Homenaje a Tenochtitlan." Exhibition brochure for *Carmen Lomas Garza: Homenaje a Tenochtitlan.* Northampton: Smith College Museum of Art, 1992.

Messinger Cypess, Sandra. *La Malinche in Mexican Literature* (Austin: U of TX P, 1991.

Moyssen L., Xavier. "Alfredo Ramos Martínez: Change and Fidelity." *Un homenaje a Alfredo Ramos Martínez.* Monterrey: MARCO, 1997.

Prescott, William H. *The Conquest of Mexico.* New York: The Heritage P, 1949.

Widdifield, Stacie G. *The Embodiment of the National in Late Nineteenth-Century Mexican Painting.* Tucson: U of Arizona P, 1996.

Conclusion
Malinche, c'est moi!

Malinche Makeover: One Gay Latino's Perspective

Franco Mondini-Ruiz

Monsters are the most interesting people and do the most interesting Thangs
. . . I wuz just telling my girlfriend Sylvia . . . bobby pin please . . . that
monsters are so interesting.

—Bugs Bunny (posing as a chatty hairdresser while applying
dynamite curlers to placated and bewildered monster, ca *1955*).

I.

Monster Cut	$5.00
Donkey Lady Perms	$10.00
La Frida	$12.00

La Malinche is a kind of monster; at least according to the myth that has
been passed down to me. A whorish traitoress, betrayer of the Aztecs, a sleeper
with the enemy. I'm kind of a monster too; at least according to the myth that has
been passed down to me. Most of my life, however, I got to be a secret monster.

II. Introductory Offer

Allow me to introduce myself. Here's my card. My name is Franco Mondini HYPHEN Ruiz. I am an assimilated, or rather, *acculturated* 38-year-old,
light-skinned, gay Latino; offspring of an upper-class European father and a
working class San Antonio mestiza mother. In Spanish-Colonial Mexico there
was a specific name for my caste, but, at the moment, I don't recall it—it was
one of the *less* offensive nomenclatures. In Spanish-Colonial Mexico, there
were also specific names for my sexual orientation, and today there are many,
many more; most are of a *more* offensive nature.

Oh yeah, and I used to be a rich, young lawyer and today I'm a less young
struggling artist.

III. Cry Me a River

Back to monsters. Growing up in South Texas in the '60s and '70s one did not hear or learn much about Mexico, Mexicans and especially Mexican women. The little I did know indicated that Mexican women of renown were either venerated virgins or monstrous creatures.

Let's see; venerated virgins. There's La Virgen de Guadalupe, Sor Juana Inez de la Cruz (if you ignore the lesbian thing) and, of course, our mothers.

The monsters? There's La Malinche, very bad; then there's that Aztec filth goddess with serpent limbs and unspeakable appetites. There's also the donkey Lady as we shall hereinafter describe and also the "other" Donkey Lady in Nuevo Laredo's Zona that has sex with a live donkey on stage. And what about the mustachioed, uni-browed Frida Kahlo, butchered body, life as a bloody (albeit picturesque) ritual of sadness and pain.

Growing up in the '60s and '70s one did not learn much about gay people either, except that they were freakish, evil and going to hell at the end of their lonely tormented lives. I grew up in a small hill country town near San Antonio. The landowners and local professionals were of German stock, mostly Catholic and Lutheran, fiercely conservative, wealthy and tidy. I hung around with their Adidas-clad, golden sons. I, after all, as a secret monster, was not detectably gay nor was I detectably Mexican.

About 20% of the town's population was of Mexican descent. Half of that 20% were from older Mexican families and lived in the flood-prone land near the river. The Flats.

They were active members of the Church; they worked as stonemasons, owned beauty shops, Mexican food restaurants, and auto repair shops.

Sometimes, but not often, their sons played on the football team and an occasional daughter might be a cheerleader or a straight-A student. They pretty much kept to themselves socially and were unspokenly viewed as my hometown's second-class citizens. The undocumented ranch workers from Mexico, the "wetbacks" comprised the other half of the 20%. They were the lowest rung of ranching-based society. The children of the "wetbacks" kept almost exclusively to themselves. I recall in elementary school they were mostly girls. "Where were the boys?" I never wondered.

The girls were usually in the separate portable building that was for the Special-Ed students. The girls were often two or three years older than the rest of us. Their Indian features, out-of-style clothing and hair, developed bodies and foreign stiff mannerisms, laugh, and speech shockingly contrasted with the rest of us Brady Bunch wannabes. They were social outcasts and scary misfits that by sixth grade would have long disappeared from most memories.

It was one of these girls, Carolina Rodríguez, that told us about the donkey lady. Carolina spoke the best English of the group although it reached us through a spitty lisp. She was not pretty, her clothes smelled sour, she was fat and her nose was tragically shaped like a pig's snout. She used to amaze and terrify us by folding her eyelids back making her eyes look like bloody sockets. She would laugh as everyone ran squealing away from her.

I felt sorry for her. When I was within spitting range, I was scared of her and of myself. I froze in her presence for I was a secret member of her order. I too was a Mexican, only one generation away from her oily-haired, ugly, "No Mexicans Allowed" poverty. I too was an outcast; one unutterable secret away from scorn, ridicule and hell.

Carolina taught us in the third grade that the donkey lady lived in the Flats and that she had actually seen her near the creek; half-woman (presumed Mexican, for who else lived in the Flats?) and half-donkey. Apparently her huge donkey head would sway back as she cried and brayed, lamenting the babies she had drowned there.

IV. Thirty Years Later

The donkey lady is still reputed to live in the Flats. The whereabouts of Carolina and her commiserates: Dolores, Rosa, and Esperanza, became of no import decades ago except that the 250-pound Rosa was spotted in the '70s working a back room of a low-budget strip-club on Hildebrande Street in San Antonio.

The whereabouts of Franco Mondini is also not generally known. But, I know. When he was about 25 he was devoured by an ugly monster; part Carolina Rodriguez, part donkey lady, part Malinche, part "dick-suckin' faggot."

For all my talk of monsters, I actually don't believe in them. A monster is simply a title bestowed by people who fear and (here's the lawyer side of me coming out) what people fear is the unknown. And, what is unknown is the unlearned, the untaught. I learned ever so slowly that I was not ugly, not evil, not a bad person, not a traitor, not the cause of civilization's downfall.

I hope that Carolina Rodríguez eventually learned or was taught that she was not an ugly freak either. I hope Esperanza, Dolores, and Rosa eventually learned that they grew up in an environment immensely ignorant of their heritage, their history, their worth, and their beauty.

V. It's Show Time

So what I did was give myself a makeover. I had a "hyphen-implant." Franco Mondini became Franco Mondini-Ruiz. Connected again, at least visually, with my mother's cosmic race past, connected with La Malinche, connected with living the truth.

My makeover was not the Jenny Jones Show type. "My Mother Dresses Like a Slut." A tattooed 45-year old mother of four in "slutty" clothes triumphantly emerges to the hoots and hollers of the studio audience as a tastefully dressed woman in a conservative navy-blue pant suit with a new hairdo and bounce in her step. Her teenaged daughter, teary-eyed, is finally proud of her mother that now looks normal.

No, no, no, no, no, no, no. No, my makeover did the opposite. My makeover exposed the trashy tattoos, the slutty clothes, the mixed-race blood and the mixed-sex impulses of the non-hyphenated Franco Mondini. My makeover was one of the intellect and of the soul and of personal and cultural history.

So even though I can make you girls a good deal, let's pass on the obvious. I won't wax Frida's "'stache" and won't pluck one single eyebrow. We won't even think about bleaching much less capping the donkey lady's long teeth. We shall resist retrofitting the Nuevo Laredo donkey lady in a new Donna Karan, and I refuse to touch La Malinche. Marina's been subject to the same bullshit we queers have always been; monsterized and vilified for sleeping with the enemy. In my case, other queers.

I like her; cheap slave-girl sandals and all. No, I don't think her eyes look treacherous and I love the red nail polish that matches her teeth. Would you call that Tabasco red? I'm proud of her and she's bilingual too. And her legacy? "You're soaking in it!"

Living in Tongues

Amanda Nolacea Harris

Claimed to be Mexico
more than they
among unbelievers.

the one
whose mother's gone,
leaving child
abandoned

the one
who speaks other tongues
mother washed hands
crossing oceans,
crossing sands,
living in tongues
so foreign.

claims even more to be Mexico
more than they know
cast aside
left alone
to survive

another mother,
cradling child,
dries layers of tears
in sweet Mexican tongue,
teaching
not to be a stranger.

learned to speak
as mother
oblivious to her quest.

makes liberty and security
in sayer's ability
voice across oceans,
cadence over sands,
things mother couldn't,
speaks as father can

claims to be Mexico
reads books and dug-up paintings
sings songs and sways the rhythms
sits in grass and finds,
mother speaking tongues
could not explain

why

Contributors

Alfred Arteaga, Associate Professor at the University of California-Berkeley, is considered a cutting-edge poet, critic, author, editor, and educator. His publications include *Chicano Poetics: Heterotexts and Hybridities*, *An Other Tongue: Nation and Ethnicity in the Linguistic Borderlands*, *Chiasmus of the Woman Writer: Sor Juana Ines de la Cruz*, *Tricks of Gender Xing*, "The Chicano-Mexican Corrido," *Cantos*, and *House with the Blue Bed*.

Antonia I. Castañeda is Associate Professor of History at St. Mary's University, San Antonio, Tejas. Her research and teaching focus on gender, sexuality and women of color in California and the Borderlands from the 16th century to the present. Her historiographical article, "Women of Color and the Rewriting of Western History: The Discourse, Politics, and Decolonization of History," received the Joan Jensen/Darlis Miller Award from the Coalition for Western Women's History (1993), and the Louis Knott Kootz Award for best article published in the Pacific Historical Review (1993). She is currently working on a cultural history of native women in colonial Alta California and a cultural history of Tejana farm workers. Castañeda is co-editor, with Dr. Deena J. González, of *Chicana Identity Matters*, a book series with the University of Texas Press.

Debra A. Castillo is Stephen H. Weiss Presidential Fellow and Emerson-Hinchliff Professor of Romance Studies and Comparative Literature at Cornell University. She specializes in contemporary narrative from the Spanish-speaking world, women's studies, and cultural theory. She is author of several books, including *The Translated World: A Postmodern Tour of Libraries in Literature* (1984), *Talking Back: Strategies for a Latin American Feminist Literary Criticism* (1992), *Easy Women: Sex and Gender in Modern Mexican Fiction* (1998) and (cowrote with María Socorro Tabuenca Córdoba) *Border Women: Writing from La Frontera* (Minnesota 2002). She is also translator of Federico Campbell's *Tijuana: Stories on the Border* (1994), and co-editor of various volumes of essays. Her most recent book is *Redreaming America! Toward a Bilingual American Culture* (SUNY, 2005).

Sandra Messinger Cypess is currently Professor of Latin American Literature and Chair of the Department of Spanish and Portuguese at the University of Maryland, whose faculty she joined in 1994 after having been at SUNY Binghamton University since 1976. Prof. Cypess received her BA at Brooklyn College, majoring in Spanish and French. Her MA was awarded from Cornell and her PhD from the University of Illinois. Author of numerous essays, her research deals primarily with women writers, the representation of Women in Latin American Literature, and Latin American theatre. Her theoretical focus centers on feminist theory and semiotics. Her interest in Mexican literature in particular was inspired in part by Luis Leal at the University of Illinois. She has published extensively on writers from Mexico (Villaurrutia, Carballido, Garro, Castellanos, Berman). Her book, *La Malinche in Mexican Literature: from History to Myth* (U Texas Press, 1991), was completed after being in Mexico under the auspices of an NEH summer fellowship, and is considered one of the major pieces of scholarship on that figure. Co-editor of three additional books, she is also co-editor with Mario Rojas of the Drama section of the Handbook of Latin American Studies. She is also the author of the chapter on Twentieth Century Latin American theatre for the Cambridge History of Latin American Literature.

Alicia Gaspar de Alba is the editor of a popular culture collection, *Velvet Barrios: Popular Culture & Chicana/o Sexualities* (2003), and the author of a historical novel, *Sor Juana's Second Dream* (UNM Press, 1999) released recently by Grijalbo in Spain and México in 2001, as well as a translation in German in 2002. Gaspar de Alba is also the author of *Chicano Art Inside/Outside the Master's House: Cultural Politics and the Cara Exhibition* (1998), a collection of short fiction, *The Mystery of Survival and Other Stories* (1994), and a book of poems, *Beggar on the Córdoba Bridge, Three Times a Woman: Chicana Poetry* (Palgrave, 1993). Among her many recognitions she has received a Rockefeller Fellowship for Latino/a Cultural Study at the Smithsonian, a Minority Scholar-in-Residence Fellowship at Pomona College, a Ford Foundation Dissertation Fellowship, and a a Massachusetts Artists Foundation Fellowship in Poetry. Her writing has received numerous awards, including the Premio Aztlán in 1994, sponsored by Rudolfo and Patricia Anaya and the University of New Mexico for the best work of fiction in English by an emerging Chicana or Chicano writer, the Border-Ford/Pellicer-Frost Award in Poetry, and Best Historical Novel in the Latino Literary Hall of Fame. She teaches at UCLA in the César Chávez Department for Chicana & Chicano Studies. Gaspar de Alba's new novel on the maquiladora murders in the El Paso/Júarez area, *Desert Blood: The Juárez Murders* was published by Arte Público Press in 2005.

Deena J. González chairs the Department of Chicana/o Studies at Loyola Marymount University in Los Angeles. She is author of *Refusing The Favor: The Spanish-Mexican Women Of Santa Fe, 1820–1880* (Oxford Univ. Press, 1999); with Suzanne Oboler, she is editing the first major encyclopedia of Latino/as in the U.S. (Oxford Univ. Press, forthcoming, 2005). Deena J. González was the first Chicana Ph.D. in UC Berkeley's History Department (1985).

Amanda Nolacea Harris is a doctoral candidate in US Latina/o Literature in the Department of Spanish, Italian & Portuguese at the University of Illinois. Harris Fonseca, the Managing Editor for *Discourse: Journal for Theoretical Studies in Media and Culture*, has served as research assistant in the development and teaching of Latina/Latino Studies Program courses in US Latina feminism, 19th-Century US Latina/o Literature, and 20th-Century US Latina/o literature at the University of Illinois. Harris Fonseca coordinated research and translation for Dan Banda's (of Bandana Production) *Indigenous Always, the Legend of La Malinche and the Conquest of Mexico*, which received five EMMY nominations and aired internationally.

María Herrera Sobek is Associate Vice Chancellor for Diversity, Equity and Academic Policy at UC Santa Barbara. She is the first to hold the unique Luis Leal Endowed Chair which was established in1989 in honor of UC Santa Barbara Professor Luis Leal. She is considered to be one of the most distinguished and productive scholars in the field, a researcher skilled in literary analysis, archival work, ethno-feminist poetics, and folklore. Herrera-Sobek earned her doctorate at UCLA in 1975 and has taught at UC Irvine. Among her many awards and recognitions Herrera Sobek has received a Ford Foundation Grant, Orange County Book of the Year, Teacher of the Year, Hispanic Woman of the Year, and Modern Language Association Distinguished Scholar awards. She also has been an honoree of the Harvard Foundation of Intercultural and Race Relations, and active in many international Chicana/o, feminist, and cultural studies organizations. The author of three books and editor of twelve others, she has taught as a visiting professor at Harvard and Stanford universities.

Guisela Latorre is currently an assistant professor in the Chicano Studies Department at the University of California, Santa Barbara, where she teaches Chicana/o and U.S. Latina/o Art. Her work has focused primarily on Chicana artistic production and on the gendered artistic practices and iconographies of U.S. Latina/o art. She has published articles in the journals *Discourse: Journal for Theoretical Studies in Media and Culture* (1999) and *Art Words* (1995) as well as in the exhibition catalogue *Lipchitz and the Avant-Garde: From Paris to New York* (2001). In addition, Professor Latorre has forthcoming essays in the anthologies *Geographies of Latinidad* (Duke University Press, 2003) and *Disciplines on the Line: Feminist Research on Spanish, Latin American, and Latina Women* (Juan de la Cuesta, 2003)

Luis Leal, Professor Emeritus of the University of Illinois, now teaches in the Department of Chicano Studies at the University of California in Santa Barbara. Leal is internationally renowned for his research concerning Mexico, Latin America, and the experiences of Chicanos. His 55-year career has included teaching posts at the University of Chicago, the University of Mississippi, Emory University, and the University of Illinois. A prolific researcher and writer, Leal is the author of 16 books and the recipient of numerous honors. In 1988, he received the Distinguished Scholarly Award from the National Association for Chicano Studies in recognition of his lifetime achievement, and in 1997 he was awarded the Mexican Order of the Aztec Eagle, the highest honor granted to foreign citizens by the Mexican government. More recently Leal was honored for his scholarly contributions in the areas of Mexican literature and culture during the fifth annual Colloquium on Mexican Literature at UCSB in October. In 1998 President Bill Clinton honored Dr. Leal with the National Humanities Medal for his outstanding lifelong contribution to the study and promotion of the literature of Mexico and Latin America, as well as to the writing of Chicana/Chicano authors in the United States.

Franco Mondini-Ruiz, an independent artist, received his BA from St. Mary's University and his JD from St. Mary's University Law School. A native of San Antonio, Mondini-Ruiz is part of a generation of acculturated Latinos whose backgrounds belong both to San Antonio's inner-city barrio and its Anglo-centric suburban sprawl. Mondini-Ruiz abandoned a successful law practice in 1994 and devotes his time fully to a brand of gender and culture-based art and political activism which addresses San Antonio's fragmented and unjust "caste" systems. His most recent art projects include *Infinite Botánica,* a traditional botánica, avant-garde gallery, and cultural salon which, through its lavish and surreal parties and events, socially integrates San Antonio's marginalized outsiders such as ethnics, gays, "radicals," and the poor with the city's art world, political, and social elite insiders. He has recently installed an interpretation of *Infinite Botánica* at Bard College, New York. A recipient of a New Forms Regional Initiative Grant and an Art Pace International Residency, Mondini-Ruiz currently lives and works in New York and San Antonio.

Rolando J. Romero, an associate professor in the Department of Spanish, Italian, and Portuguese at the University of Illinois, Urbana-Champaign, teaches U.S. Latina/Latino and Mexican literatures. He is the founding director of the Latina/Latino Studies Program at the University of Illinos, Urbana-Champaign. He is the General Editor of *Discourse: Journal of Theoretical Studies in Media and Culture.* He has published essays in *Revista de Estudios Hispánicos, Confluencia*, and *Revista Iberoamericana*, among others. His essay on *Blade Runner* "The Post-Modern Hybrid: Do Aliens Dream of Alien

Sheep?" was published in *The Effects of the Nation: Mexican Art in an Age of Globalization* (Eds. Carl Good and John V. Waldron. Temple UP, 2001.) His "The Alamo, Slavery, and the Politics of Memory" was published in *Decolonial Voices: Chicana and Chicano Cultural Studies in the 21ˢᵗ Century* (Eds. Arturo Aldama and Naomi H. Quiñones. Indiana UP, 2001). He served as Chief Academic Consultant for Dan Banda's "Indigenous Always: The Legend of La Malinche and the Conquest of Mexico," a PBS documentary that explores the life of Doña Marina.

Terezita Romo, the Curator at The Mexican Museum in San Francisco, has also served as the Arts Director at the Mexican Fine Arts Center Museum in Chicago and Administrative/Artistic Director of La Raza/Galería Posada in Sacramento. Romo is a member of the internationally renowned artist group, RCAF/Royal Chicano Air Force, a key collective that helped to define the Chicano art movement. As curator and cultural critic, Romo has written and presented papers on Chicano art history; the formulation/construction of mestizaje in Mexican and Chicano art, especially with regards to transcultural influences; the deconstruction and transformation of Mexican icons and images by Chicano artists; and the documentation of Chicana artists within an art historical context. She is currently organizing an exhibition on La Malinche. In 1999, Romo was one of three senior scholars chosen for a Rockefeller Humanities Fellowship in Latino Cultural Resources, sponsored by the Smithsonian Institution and the Inter-University Program for Latino Research. She was in residence at the National Museum of American Art conducting research on Chicano art iconography.